Intentionality and Transcendence

Contemporary Phenomenological Thought

Burt C. Hopkins and Steven Galt Crowell, editors

Intentionality and Transcendence
Closure and Openness in Husserl's Phenomenology

Damian Byers

THE UNIVERSITY OF WISCONSIN PRESS / NOESIS PRESS, LTD.

The University of Wisconsin Press
1930 Monroe Street
Madison, Wisconsin 53711

www.wisc.edu/wisconsinpress/

3 Henrietta Street
London WC2E 8LU, England

Noesis Press, Ltd.
P.O. Box 60102
Shoreline, Washington 98160

www.noesispress.com
info@noesispress.com

Copyright © 2002
Noesis Press, Ltd.
All rights reserved

1   3   5   4   2

No part of this book may be used or reproduced in any manner whatsoever without written permission. No part of this book may be stored in a retrieval system or transmitted in any form or by any means including electronic, electrostatic, magnetic tape, mechanical, photocopying, or otherwise without the prior permission in writing of the publisher.

Production by Marcus Brainard

A Cataloging-in-Publication record for this book is available
from the Library of Congress
ISBN 0-299-18850-7 (cloth)
ISBN 0-299-18854-X (paper)

*For Philippa,
and for my parents,
Gwen and Bruce*

Contents

Preface   xi

Part One
Search for Method

Chapter One: Husserl's Problem   3
     § 1. The Phenomenon of Knowing: Transcendence and Intentionality   3
     § 2. The Conflict within Knowing   5
     § 3. The Problem   6

Chapter Two: Beginnings of Phenomenological Method:
The Epistemological Reduction   7
     § 1. "Presuppositionlessness" as the Ideal Guiding the Development of Method   7
     § 2. The Meaning of Epistemological Reduction   7
     § 3. Reduction as Abstractive Exclusion   16
     § 4. The Domain of Pure Immanence: Husserl's First Proposal   17
     § 5. Conclusion   18

Chapter Three: Abstractive Exclusion as a Procedure of Enclosure   21
     § 1. The "Narrow Phenomenological Sphere": The "Lived-through"
     as the Domain of Immanence   21
     § 2. Two Kinds of Really Inherent Content   23
     § 3. The Meaning of the Region of the Really Inherent: Intentional Act?   26
     § 4. The Expansion of the "Narrow Phenomenological Sphere"   27
     § 5. Proto-Epoché: The Emergence of the Intentional Object   30
     § 6. Refocused Presuppositionlessness   32
     § 7. The Phenomenological Sense of the Intentional Object   34
     § 8. Phenomenological Reduction as Enclosure   39
     § 9. Methodological Premonitions of Openness: The Dialectic of
     Intention and Fulfillment   42

Chapter Four: Examination and Critique of the Reduction
as a Procedure of Abstractive Exclusion   49
     § 1. Presuppositions Underlying the Procedure of Abstractive Exclusion   49
     § 2. The Actual Practice of Abstraction in Mundane Phenomenology:
     The Attempt to Establish "Purity" within the General Thesis
     of the Natural Attitude   52
     § 3. Exclusion   53

viii   CONTENTS

§ 4. The General Thesis of the Natural Attitude   54
§ 5. Conclusion   55

Chapter Five: The Transcendental Reduction   57

§ 1. Restatement of the Epistemological Problem in Light of the Ontology of the Natural Attitude   57
§ 2. The Dual-Directedness of the Horizon of Prefamiliarity   59
§ 3. Worldliness as the Presupposition of the Natural Attitude   60
§ 4. Transcendental Reduction   62
§ 5. Thematization of Transcendence and Intentionality through the Transcendental Reduction: Transcendence as Transcendental Acceptance; Intentionality as Transcendental Acceptor   72
§ 6. Conclusion   76

Part Two
Analysis and Discoveries

Chapter Six: Reorienting the Problem   81

Chapter Seven: Husserl's Preliminary Determination of the Domains of Immanence and Transcendence   85

§ 1. The Principle of Indubitability   85
§ 2. Application of the Principle   87

Chapter Eight: The Constitution and Status of the Real Object   93

§ 1. The Constitution of the Real Object: Transcendence as Identity   94
§ 2. The Being of the Object   99
§ 3. The Presumptiveness of the Object   107
§ 4. Real Object as Transcendence-in-Immanence   108
§ 5. The First Aspect of Openness: "Facticity"   110
§ 6. The Law of the Synthesis   111
§ 7. The Principle of Synthesis: No Intrusion of Alterity   118
§ 8. Facticity and Openness   119

Chapter Nine: The Immanent Object: Primal Constitution of Identity   131

§ 1. From Static to Genetic Phenomenology   131
§ 2. The Constitution of the Immanent Object: Temporal Syntheses   142
§ 3. The Constitution of the Immanent Object: Kinaesthetic and Associative Syntheses   153
§ 4. The Status of the Immanent Object   165

Chapter Ten: Derrida and Non-Phenomenologically Reducible Transcendence   171

§ 1. Context for Discussion of Derrida   171
§ 2. Derrida's Position and its Implications for the Husserlian Enterprise   172
§ 3. The Dynamic of Recollection and Expectation   174

§ 4. Critique of Derrida	175
§ 5. Conclusion	178
Chapter Eleven: Immanence as Absolute Subjectivity	181
Conclusion	189
§ 1. Object as Infinite Idea	190
§ 2. The Development of Transcendental Constitutional Abilities and Powers	192
§ 3. Protention and Actualization	194
§ 4. The Incompleteness of the Identity of the "Ego"	195
§ 5. Beyond Metaphysics	196
Bibliography	199
Index of Names	203
Index of Subjects	204

Preface

Husserl's phenomenology can be understood as an attempt to resolve the problem of knowledge. If so read, his philosophical thinking can be seen to display a deep unity, a profound development, that contains a seemingly irresistible internal logic. This book is about the form Husserl struggles to give that problem, the way this form influences the development of the phenomenological method, and the results of its application. In seeking to explicate these three, our aim is to clarify the meaning of Husserl's solution.

In the beginning, he regards the problem of knowledge as the problem of the "objectivity" of what is known: a "separateness" of the known from the knower is required if a self-refuting psychologism is to be avoided. But the possibility of this separateness initially remains an enigma.

Later, with the transcendental turn, the problem of knowledge assumes its properly phenomenological form and is reformulated as the problem of intentionality and transcendence. This reformulation enables Husserl to propose his solution: transcendental idealism. But this "metaphysics" carries with it the specter of closure, of resolving the problem of the "inside" and the "outside" resolutely in favor of the "inside." In the end, it seems that the philosophy dedicated to the preservation of alterity, and of intentionality, may be forced into a self-renunciation. For does not idealism's resolution of these problems only proceed by refusing an In-itself, an outside, an alterity, in short, any genuinely problematic domain of otherness? Is not transcendental phenomenology, then, a philosophy of closure and control? This book attempts to demonstrate the senses in which it is; but it also attempts to show the ways in which Husserl's phenomenology is ultimately and most truly a philosophy of openness and vulnerability.

Part One investigates the path Husserl takes in attempting to find an appropriate formulation of his problem and shows how the sense of the problem and the method developed for its resolution are intricately and necessarily interrelated.

Chapter One presents the issue of knowledge by outlining its structure as a phenomenon, to show how knowledge emerges as a *phenomenological* problem. The reason for this is that philosophy does not *invent* the problem of knowledge, but rather fixes upon the fact that the "fact" of cognition does not explain its own possibility and that, upon reflection, the possibility of a subject's attaining an object without subjectivizing and thereby denaturing that object is deeply problematic. It is this enigma, essential to the very meaning of the *experience* of knowing, that generates the particular Husserlian form of the problem of knowledge: that of *cognition*, in its possibility and meaning. However, if cognition is a problem, then philosophy seems deprived of a starting point from which to begin to resolve this most fundamental quandary. Can a method be found that yields a starting point for a scientific epistemology, a starting point that does not compromise the investigation by presupposing, implicitly or explicitly, a solution to the problem that has been raised?

Chapter Two outlines Husserl's first attempts to articulate the sense of this difficulty, because certain essential characteristics of this formulation provide powerful methodological motivations that set phenomenology on its decisive and characteristic course. If what is at stake is the *possibility* of cognition's reaching its object, then the fundamental methodological requirement of any scientific epistemology will be that it not presuppose the possession or attainment of any object, nor the acceptance of any sense of what it may be for an object to be cognized. On the contrary, the determination of this sense is to emerge from the investigation itself. Thus the guiding principle of the first form of phenomenological-epistemological investigation is that of *presuppositionlessness*—specifically, regarding the meaning of cognition.

Chapter Three investigates Husserl's development of this principle into methodological practice. If a scientific epistemology is to be possible, it must find for itself a domain of investigation; yet this domain must be "uncontaminated" by any objectivity, the problematic term. The first articulation of this domain is as the "intending" facet of the cognitive act, a domain established through abstraction from all object-terms. Husserl calls this procedure of abstraction 'epistemological reduction'. It is the first form of the properly phenomenological reduction, which is to satisfy the demand for presuppositionlessness and yield a "pure" domain for investigation by abstractively excluding all objectivity from "knowing." This is meant to give access to a domain of purely immanent intentional acts as the subject matter for scientific epistemology. On reflection, it emerges that the first form of phenomenological procedure operates as a *de facto* delimitation and restriction, producing a domain for investigation that is effectively closed in upon itself vis-à-vis any objective externality.

But such a methodological proposal cannot be carried out, as Chapter Four shows. Once Husserl actually begins his investigation, he discovers that it is impossible to describe the "purely" immanent components of the intentional act without making reference to the object—which the methodological abstraction is meant to exclude—in which that act terminates. Does this mean that presuppositionlessness cannot be attained and that the ideal of a scientific epistemology ought to be abandoned? In response to this problem, Husserl offers a refinement of method, thanks to which "objectivity" can now be recognized within the domain demarcated by the epistemological reduction, thus preserving the possibility of a scientific epistemology. "Presuppositionlessness," the hallmark of the claim to scientificity, is now maintained by drawing a distinction between intentional and real objectivity, whereby all real objectivity—all being "in itself"—remains excluded. Intentional objectivity is included, but only because intentional objects are not genuine transcendencies: such objects exist merely for an act and only insofar as an act "intends" them. This broadening of the narrow sphere of investigation to include the intentional object is justified in terms of a scientific epistemology because intentional objectivity is considered as *constituted* by the act. However, real or genuine objectivity remains abstractively excluded, and the domain for investigation still retains the character of self-enclosure.

Chapter Five undertakes an examination and a critique of reduction as abstractive exclusion and goes on to discuss and justify the consequent introduction of the properly transcendental reduction. The critique centers on two major problems that emerge if reduction is considered as an abstractive exclusion. First, presuppositionlessness is not really attained because such a procedure necessarily conceives the demarcated and enclosed domain as a *part* of a larger and preexistent whole; as such the method involves a precommitment to a domain of being extrinsic to that of the domain to be investigated, a precommitment to transcendence. In fact this very precommitment is drawn upon and informs the whole distinction between intentional and non-intentional objectivity. This precommitment is further intimated in Husserl's notorious characterization of such an investigation as a phenomenological *psychology*, a determination that refers implicitly to an extra-psychical domain of being in which the psychological is grounded. Clearly, "presuppositionlessness" must be reconceived. Second, because "real" transcendence has been excluded from the enclosed domain of investigation, acts that attain genuine transcendence are ultimately excluded from any phenomenological interrogation. The original problem—that of the possibility of the openness of knowing subjectivity to a region other than or outside of it under the heading of 'objectivity'—therefore defies resolution if access to it is posed in terms of a procedure of abstractive exclusion.

Husserl's re-conception of the problem is evident in the development of the *transcendental* reduction. No longer a procedure of abstractive exclusion, transcendental reduction now becomes a *defamiliarization* of a deep and all-pervasive ontic ordering—including an ontic determination of the subject and the object—to which Husserl refers as the 'natural attitude'. This ontic ordering orders not only *objectivity* but (necessarily) *subjectivity* as well. The ordering is done by the orderer—that is, the cognitive agent operating within the natural attitude. "Presuppositionlessness" will now require both the naturalizing cognitive agent to disengage this (metaphysically) ordering framework and to reject its complicity in the ongoing affirmation of that framework. "Transcendence" is thereby formally and explicitly incorporated in the domain of phenomenological investigation and becomes a theme precisely in its appearing. With this radical recasting of method, reduction is no longer exclusion, and it appears that the domain that is thereby established for phenomenological investigation is no longer closed in upon itself. With this hard-won final clarification of phenomenology as properly transcendental, the way is now open to begin the concrete investigation of the phenomenon of knowing and to establish once and for all the genuine meaning and possibility of knowing subjectivity attaining its other, objectivity.

Part Two turns to an analysis of the application of the mature phenomenological method and outlines the main discoveries that flow from it.

Chapter Six begins the examination of the transcendental phenomenological investigation of knowing by reestablishing the phenomenological task in light of the previously discussed refinements of method: transcendental phenomenology becomes the investigation of what is in its appearing.

To center phenomenological investigation around the notion of appearing, however, is to accept a primordial bifurcation within the pregiven domain of investigation: there is that which appears and that to which the appearing appears. What sense can these two "regions" now have in light of phenomenological method as transcendental reduction? Chapter Seven outlines Husserl's preliminary determination of the domains of immanence and transcendence, his early mapping of the disputed territory, which provides the groundwork for his subsequent investigations. Here the "object" is the transcendent, which is to be clarified by bringing to light its constitution by the transcendental functionary, and "consciousness" is understood as immanence, intentionality pure and simple. Consciousness is thereby understood as activity, and in this Husserl sees the possibility of a solution to his problem: objectivity, as transcendence, will be *constituted* in and through this activity. Consciousness will be presented as a being that conceals no excess, as adequately given, and hence as providing a "foundation" from which to observe the progressive constitution of transcendence. However, this Cartesian predilection becomes progressively confounded as the investigation proceeds. The status of the "alterity" of the object, as well as of the meaning of the openness of subjectivity, at this point becomes somewhat unclear: although objectivity has not been excluded, what are the implications for the openness of subjectivity to otherness if otherness is considered as "objectivity" and objectivity is present only as constituted in the activity of the knowing subject?

Chapter Eight pursues this issue by examining in detail the constitution of the real object so as to determine the meaning and status of the "intentional openness" that knowing seems to be. As Husserl's investigation progresses, the most crucial sense of the problem named by the term 'object' comes to be identity because, though being "one," the object always only emerges out of a flux of appearing. This chapter then moves on to consider the issue of alterity and the real object from two points of view. First, it poses the question of the status of the object that appears and concludes that, as the product of a synthesis of identification, all such entities are "transcendencies in immanence" and nothing "in themselves." These entities are further determined: on the one hand, as "rules" or "indices" for the harmonious gathering of the flux of appearings and, on the other, as an "empty X" or principle of unification. The meaning of what it is to be an object for a knowing subject thereby receives a decisive clarification—but only insofar as the very sense of transcendence emerges as constituted. Alterity, as embodied in identical objects, begins to appear to be conditioned by the synthetic activity of the knowing subject, and the openness of the knowing subject is likewise circumscribed and "enclosed." Second, the chapter goes on to investigate what it is that governs the synthesis in its gathering function; it does so by posing the following question: although the object as constituted product may be no genuine alterity, could it not be that the synthesis that yields that identity is itself governed by an external demand? The meaning of the synthesis of identification is then investigated: the synthesis effects a gathering together of flux moments such that they exhibit the character of "belonging together." But how is this character achieved? By satisfying expectations that are expressed in the conditional 'if–then', a condition that can be exercised as a function of the 'I can'. So understood, the synthesis is governed solely by the experiential capabilities of the intentional functionary. No alterity—as the alterity of identity—is encountered. But by considering the dynamic of intention and fulfillment and the issue of "facticity," Husserl's investigation takes an unexpected turn: in identifying a radical contingency at the heart of the absolute streaming flux of experience that founds both world and ego, both these "pregiven" domains emerge as co-constituted modes of being. Almost behind Husserl's back, a new way of approaching the openness of both the world and the transcendental subject begins to emerge.

Up to this point the phenomenological analyses of concern in the present study have been "static," as Husserl terms them. That is to say, objects have been clarified in terms of their constitution, but identity as such is still not posed as a fundamental problem. Static phenomenology describes the constitutional achievements of a synthesis—but that synthesis gathers up elements that are seemingly just "there" for it. However, if phenomenology seeks to bring all hidden assumptions and prejudgments to clarity through constitutional analysis, then new and fundamental questions must be posed: What is the status of the elements gathered in the synthesis? What is the status of the "immanent" object, the hyletic data? Chapter Nine turns to genetic phenomenology in order to investigate the status of such "proto-objects." This it does by explicating the originarily constituting syntheses of time consciousness, the kinaesthetic syntheses, and the syntheses of association. The conclusion reached here is that all objects are to be resolved ultimately into the terms of their constitution as identities and that, conversely, all identity is constituted in syntheses of identification. All are constituted results; no alterity is indicated by the hyle, and closure seems to be unavoidable.

Chapter Ten turns from Husserl to Derrida's critique of phenomenology as a metaphysics of presence that essentially asserts the irreducibility of transcendence, affirming the discovery of an alterity always already within the dynamic of originary temporalization. By maintaining that transcendence ultimately cannot be approached by means of constitutional analysis, Derrida's critique purports to redeem alterity, though at the cost of dismantling the basic architecture of Husserl's procedure. However, it becomes clear upon closer inspection that Derrida draws an invalid conclusion from his misleading and inappropriate identification of the dynamic of recollection and expectation with that of retention and protention. Whatever alterity is encountered in the dynamic of originary temporalization, it is not that of an identity, and the temporal displacement in question is unable to motivate the loss of "metaphysical assurance" as Derrida asserts. Since flux moments are not identities, Husserl's position proves to remain intact, but with one alarming consequence: it seems that alterity has been denied and closure affirmed once again.

No discussion of transcendence would be complete without a focused discussion of Husserl's characterization of immanence. This is undertaken in Chapter Eleven, where it is shown that any "consciousness" or "ego" conceived of as an identity is itself a constituted result, which indicates a more primal synthesis or gathering. But what might this be? Nothing other than the ultimately flowing, primally streaming "living present," the originary site of all synthesis, including the synthesis that results in the gathering of the ego itself.

The Conclusion draws attention to the various ways in which, despite the forms of closure outlined, Husserl's transcendental phenomenology is ultimately and eminently a philosophy of openness. Four discoveries, more or less latent within the entire previous discussions, are elaborated.

First, though the object is only constituted in the synthetic gathering of the intentional functionary, the conceptual determination of an object is always infinitely open—and, given the interdependence between the object's actuality and its (originary) conceptualization, so is the object in its being.

Second, the constitutional capacities of the intentional functionary themselves undergo constant development—a development whose trajectory can never be preempted.

Third, the identity of the intentional functionary is always incomplete, always becoming.

And fourth, protention—the way in which the intentional functionary projects itself into the future and by which it assimilates the "to come"—has no command over what actually comes to pass. The "ground" of what comes to pass and of the mode of development of the intentional functionary—though in no sense an identity—is "other" than the intentional functionary.

These final discoveries have significance regarding the assessment of whether or not Husserl's phenomenology is still situated within the horizon of philosophical culture summarily referred to as 'metaphysics'. The book concludes with a brief discussion of this point, and outlines several ways—some more explicit, some less—in which Husserl's phenomenology is at its heart, and in the articulation of its deepest revelations, non-metaphysical, at least if the term 'metaphysics' is taken to indicate a system of thought that, governed by the will to totalization and domination, reduces being to being-present.

Many people deserve recognition for helping me complete this book, but particular thanks is due to Professor James R. Mensch of St. Francis Xavier University, Professor Burt Hopkins of Seattle University, and the anonymous readers from Noesis Press, who saw what I was trying to say more clearly than I myself did. Professor Eduard Marbach of the University of Bern encouraged me in my project, as did Drs. Marion Tapper, Chris Cordner, and Barry Taylor, all of the University of Melbourne. Marcus Brainard helped me correct many infelicities of expression. I owe a vast and special debt, though, to Professor Marc Richir of the University of Paris VII. At great expense he gave of himself in an extraordinary way; he first enabled me to believe that maybe I could say something in philosophy and to see what that might be.

Part One

Search for Method

Chapter One
Husserl's Problem

§ 1. The Phenomenon of Knowing: Transcendence and Intentionality

Straightforwardly and prior to any theory, knowing is the phenomenon of a self's *attaining* something that is not self, something that is *other* than it. Provisionally, we can call that which attains 'subject' and that which is attained 'object'. The most original sense of knowing thus affirms a *difference* within the domain of being. However, this difference is not such as to preclude a unification. In fact, it is only by virtue of being brought together that their characterization as 'different' derives meaning.

§ 1.1. The Object Known

This difference is one of being. Most fundamentally and generally, it is that of the object's independence vis-à-vis the being that knows the object in its independence. Although, as known, the object is found "within" the knowing, its being is a "being more than" the being of the knowing; object-being is being in excess of the subjectivity that attains it and thus a being other than subjectivity. It is precisely this sense of otherness as excess beyond the knowing that is referred to when object-being is spoken of as 'being in itself'. This character of excess shows itself in at least two ways. First, not only may the knower (in principle) return again in different knowings to the one identical object; the one identical object is (in principle) also available for other actual and possible knowers. But such availability is only possible if the object maintains itself in itself: if the being of the object exceeds—is not identical with—the being of the knowing that attains it. Were this not the case, the vanishing of the knowing would also be the vanishing of the object known, and it would be impossible (in principle) for the very same object to be attained in some other attaining.[1]

---

1. See, e.g., *LI*, 11–13/253–54. (For clarification of the conventions and the abbreviations used in citing throughout this study, see the Bibliography, 199–203 below.) Among other things, the psychologism that Husserl attacks in the *Prolegomena* is forced to deny this purely "phenomenological," pretheoretical aspect of the phenomenon of knowing (in the specific case of objectivity considered as ideal and knowing considered as a psychological function) because of a prior commitment to a naturalistic theory of being. Husserl employs two arguments against psychologism. On the one hand, he advances a purely negative critique based on the skeptical-relativistic consequences that such a theory of being cannot avoid. On the other hand—and this is more significant for the themes of this introduction—

Second, this excess is revealed by the fallibility of knowing. An object may show itself to be other than it is taken to be at any time. But such error is only possible if some moment of the being of the object escapes attainment, escapes possession, in the knowing. Thus, far from being a denial of or threat to knowing, the possibility of error is an essential factor in maintaining the very sense of the phenomenon. For were it not possible for the object to be in excess of what it is taken to be in its showing, the possibility of error would vanish. Were the otherness, the excess, of the object an illusion and an impossibility, then error would be as well.[2]

The "object" is thus given as a being that, beyond the moment of it appropriated by the "subject" in knowing the object, holds something in reserve. As being that sustains such an excess, as "being in itself," object-being always bears within itself an unfamiliarity that threatens knowing's grasp: knowing is putative rather than certain. Were the object in its being-known to lose this character of excess, knowing would no longer affirm a difference within being; knowing would thereby reveal itself to be utter appropriation. The object would no longer be "over against" the knowing, no longer sustained as "other."

The term 'transcendence' names this being in excess of the knowing and being known to be so. To be transcendent is to be other than, to be independent of, the knowing of such transcendence, however the being of the knowing may come to be understood.

§ 1.2. The Knowing of the Object

As the affirmation of a difference within being, the phenomenon of knowing speaks not only of the known but also of the knowing, with respect to which the known is determined as "other." As the attaining of what is "other than," knowing is necessarily a tending toward an alien "outside," a tending, in Emmanuel Levinas's words, "towards a yonder."[3] As a tending toward being that is other and as the "bringing home" of this otherness as it is in itself in the form of 'consciousness of', knowing is self-transcending. Thus, the phenomenon entails that knowing does not remain within itself. Were it to do so, then no otherness, no "in itself" could ever present itself and knowing could only effect a relation of self to self. Before it can be the attaining of the object, knowing must first be an openness to the unfamiliar, to otherness.

---

he charges psychologism with simply falsifying the phenomenon of knowing in the very first instance—due to its monistic ontology: it commits an inadmissible *metabasis*.

2. See Descartes's Third Meditation. The possibility of the self's being in error regarding itself is generated through the finding of "another" in the self. Freud's metaphysics of the psyche is a paradigmatic example of this. And, for all his criticisms of Descartes, Sartre shows himself to be fundamentally Cartesian on this score, for his abolition of "opaqueness"—and otherness—within consciousness is what allows his account of bad faith, as well as a degree of "therapeutic treatment" in the form of his existential analysis.

3. Emmanuel Levinas, *Totality and Infinity*, trans. Alphonso Lingis (Pittsburgh: Duquesne University, 1969), 33.

What we are calling 'knowing' is therefore a "being directed beyond itself." The most original sense of this phenomenon is *intentionality*. Thanks to a mysterious self-transcending, a mysterious being directed "beyond," a relatedness to some alterity is achieved.

§ 2. The Conflict within Knowing

The phenomenon of knowing does not establish how knowing is possible. This is of particular concern because, upon reflection, a substantial conflict can be found within the phenomenon.

Knowing renders the known familiar. In fact, knowing renders the known familiar even as being "in itself." But how can this be possible? Must not knowing—in some sense—*become* its object in the familiarization that knowing is? Does knowing not appropriate, assimilate the known? If not, would not the known remain *unknown*? But objectivity is transcendence, is being in excess of appropriation. What, then, in its being known becomes of the meaning of the "in itselfness" of the object? To know the object as "object" is to know it as being such that something of it remains in excess; its *objectness*, its separation from knowing, is thereby preserved. But is knowing not precisely the *overcoming* of any such excess? Knowing thus sustains a conflict within its own sense; it is a phenomenon that both sustains and obliterates a radical distance between knowing and what is known.

Husserl wonders about this problem as he ponders the meaning of an In-itself that is actually assimilated. In-itselfness is only known *insofar as it is amenable to being known*. Thus, if it is possible that knowing itself may limit what can be known of transcendence, the very meaning of the difference, the alterity, of the known becomes problematic. The question becomes: "What does it mean to say that the object has 'intrinsic being'. . . ?" (*LI*, 13/254).

Being an object—that is, being an In-itself—has, upon reflection, become problematic. Does not its being-known put an In-itself into relation with a knower and thereby alter its status precisely as an In-itself? Is not the knowing of the object as in itself the overcoming of any concealment and thereby of any ontological separation? How is it not the case that *known* in-itselfness is not merely a character generated by the knowing itself? After all, the ontological character of being "in itself" is established within knowing itself:

> Whatever exists for a man like me and is accepted by him, exists for him and is accepted in his own conscious life, which, in all consciousness of a world and in all scientific doing, keeps to itself. All my distinguishing between genuine and deceptive experience and between being and illusion in experience goes on within the sphere itself of my consciousness. . . . Evidently actual, intellectually necessary, inconsistent, thinkable, probable, and the like—all these are characteristics that occur within the realm itself of my consciousness. . . . Every grounding, every showing of the truth and being, goes on wholly within myself. . . . (*CM*, 115)

This realization raises the possibility of an intentionality that attains an In-itself as a content within itself. Husserl wonders whether these conflicting demands are not such as to threaten the self-transcending that intentionality is held to be. He immediately asks: "But how can this business, going on wholly within the immanency of conscious life, acquire objective significance? How can evidence claim to be more than a characteristic of consciousness within me?" Thus the obscurity of the meaning of the In-itself that enters into knowing places the "objectivity" of the object in question; it also places the self-transcendence of the intentionality of knowing in question. Husserl sees the non-intentionality of knowing as the corollary of the non-objectivity of the known, as the closure of knowing in upon itself:

> How do I, the cognizing subject, know if I can ever really know, that there exist *not only my own* lived experiences, these acts of cognition, *but also* what they cognize? How can I ever know that there is anything at all that could be set over against cognition *as its object*?
> Shall I say: only phenomena are truly given to the cognizing subject, he never does and never can break out of the circle of his own lived experiences, so that in truth he could only say: I exist, and all that is not-I is mere phenomenon dissolving into concatenations of phenomena? (*Hua* II, 20/15–16)

In the final analysis, it seems that the conflict within the phenomenon of intentionality and knowing amounts to a denial of its own straightforward sense.

§ 3. The Problem

What is in question here is the very possibility of the phenomenon of intentionality. Knowing has been revealed by reflection to be an "enigma." To begin with, the authenticity of the epistemological relation is in question. In wondering how it is even possible that knowing transcend itself, the "objectivity" of knowledge becomes open to doubt: "What is in question is what cognition can accomplish, the meaning of its claim to validity and correctness, the meaning of the distinction between genuine and merely apparent cognition" (25/20). Underlying this question is a more fundamental ontological problem: What is the *being* of the transcendent and what is the *being* of the functioning intentionality, such that the epistemological relation is even possible? As Husserl puts it:

> What is in question is . . . also the meaning of being an object that exists and exists as what it is whether it is cognized or not and that as object is an object of possible cognition, in principle cognizable, even if in fact it has never been and never will be cognized, but is in principle perceptible, imaginable, determinable by predicates in a possible judging, etc.

The problem, then, is transcendence. It is unclear just what object-being really is. Likewise, it is unclear just what intentionality, as self-transcendence, really is. And this suggests that the genuine meaning of each of the notions of 'object' and 'subject', 'intentionality' and 'transcendence' is unclear. Their clarification must therefore become the theme of the investigation.

Chapter Two
Beginnings of Phenomenological Method: The Epistemological Reduction

§ 1. "Presuppositionlessness" as the Ideal Guiding the Development of Method

"Presuppositionlessness" as a methodological ideal in phenomenology refers neither to the attempt to establish a *tabula rasa* from which philosophical investigation might begin nor to a belief that such an aspiration is even desirable. It is rather the methodological corollary of an investigation motivated by a question or an uncertainty: the attempt to achieve "presuppositionlessness" is the attempt to keep open the question at the heart of the investigation, to avoid having the answer prefigured by a continually presupposed, though never questioned, horizon of preacceptances. It is a precautionary measure taken by the investigator to protect the investigation from compromise. In this case, Husserl must develop a method that frees his investigation from presupposing answers to his problem—that of the meaning and possibility of transcendence—but that at the same time allows his problem to be posed as the object of inquiry. In short, though not presupposing its meaning, the method must provide access to transcendence and the intentionality whose sense it is to attain it.

§ 2. The Meaning of Epistemological Reduction

The first form of the method developed by Husserl to achieve presuppositionlessness is the "epistemological reduction." This becomes the phenomenological reduction, which is not to be confused with the transcendental reduction. Two things determine the meaning of this method: first, the sense of the presupposition from which the investigation must be freed and, second, the meaning of the operation that effects this freeing. We shall discuss these in turn.

§ 2.1. The First Sense of Presupposition

The meaning of 'presupposition' is determined in any given case by an understanding of the question motivating the investigation. What is simply in question here is *knowing and the known*. Husserl writes that knowing's "reaching its object has become enigmatic and dubious as far as its meaning and possibility are concerned" (*Hua* II, 24/20).

As a consequence, an epistemology, a "science of cognition" is required. And it is clear that "an epistemological investigation that can seriously claim to be scientific . . . must satisfy the principle of freedom from presuppositions" (*LI*, 24/263). But what would the vitiating presupposition be here? Not that there is a phenomenon of "cognition" in general. It would make no sense to deny *that*. Rather, the presupposition would involve *presuming* clarity where in fact there was obscurity or enigma. And what is unclear here is not whether there is a phenomenon of cognition, but rather *the meaning of its achievement* and *the meaning of that which is attained* in this achievement. Thus Husserl proposes that the main problem for a scientific epistemology is "the riddle of transcendence" (*Hua* II, 43/33, 36/28).

It is this riddle that must be kept alive by excluding presuppositions regarding the How and the What of transcendence:

> If . . . the riddle connected with the initial establishment of the discipline lies here, it becomes more definitely clear what must not be claimed as presupposed. Nothing transcendent may be used as a presupposition. If I do not understand *how* it is possible that cognition reach something transcendent, then I also do not know *whether* it is possible. (36/29)

If the being-sense (the "objectivity") of transcendence is unclear, then transcendence itself can never be employed in any *explanation* of the achievement of cognition; to do so would be to attempt a clarification by employing something that is itself in need of clarification—and that can itself be clarified only once the original lack of clarity has been resolved. The demand for presuppositionlessness thus means

> that the problem of the How (how cognition of the transcendent is possible and, even more generally, how cognition is at all possible) can never be answered on the basis of a presupposed knowledge of the transcendent, or prior judgments about it, no matter whence the knowledge or judgments are borrowed, not even if they are taken from the exact sciences. (38/30)

Therefore, what cannot be presupposed—or better said: what cannot be employed as an unproblematic given within the investigation itself, as something making up part of the investigation's stock of "tools"—is any determination of the being-sense 'object' or any particular understanding of the meaning of the achievement known as 'cognition'.[1] Husserl thus lays down what could be understood as the principle of scientificity in epistemology:

---

1. For example, causal theories of perception attempt such a clarification in terms of the explanatory power of the *object* cognized. This is an unacceptable procedure, for it requires that a particular being-determination of the object be presupposed and then employed to explain the "achievement" of cognition. Here the *problem* of transcendence (i.e. the lack of clarity about its meaning and the possibility of its being attained) is "clarified" by presupposing that 'object' and 'cognitive relation' be understood in a particular way. Yet this offers no genuine clarification at all. As Husserl says, one cannot go "from the That to the How" of cognition (*Hua* II, 37/29). And further: "the cognitions with which the critique of

we arrive at a sufficient and complete deduction of the epistemological principle that an epistemological reduction has to be accomplished in the case of every epistemological inquiry of whatever sort of cognition. That is to say, every transcendency that is involved must be bracketed, or be assigned the index of indifference, of epistemological nullity, an index that indicates: the existence of all these transcendencies, whether I believe in them or not, is not my concern here; this in not the place to make judgments about them; they are entirely irrelevant. (39/31)

But what sense is given to the expression 'every transcendency' against which the reduction is to be directed? In these early stages, Husserl identifies two forms: the transcendent object and transcendent apperception. A scientific epistemology must be purified of presuppositions under both headings.[2]

§ 2.1.1. First Demarcation of the Transcendent: Reduction to Act-Immanence

The task here is to develop a principle that will allow the identification—and hence exclusion—of transcendent objectivity while allowing immanence (pure act) to emerge as a domain for epistemological investigation. Proposed is that the riddle of transcendence will then be open to resolution by means of an investigation of how, in its immanence, the act achieves its relation to or presentation of the transcendence it attains. Some observations regarding the various meanings of the term 'immanence' and the terms 'act' and 'pure act' are first required here.

§ 2.1.1.1. Immanence

In Husserl's mature—that is, transcendental—phenomenology, the term 'immanence' will come to be used in at least two ways. Most generally, it will be used to refer to the discovery made by transcendental phenomenology that both intentional act and intentional object belong to the same sphere of being. An exemplary expression of this conclusion can be found in § 49 of *Ideas I*, where Husserl says: "consciousness considered in its 'purity' must be held to be a self-contained complex of being... into which nothing can penetrate and out of which nothing can slip" (*Id. I*, 93). Further, that "the whole spatiotemporal world... is by its sense a merely intentional being, thus one that has the merely secondary sense of a being for a consciousness. It is a being posited by consciousness in its experiences that principially can be intuited and determined only as something identical belonging to motivated multiplicities of

---

cognition must begin may contain nothing doubtful or questionable. They may contain none of what precipitates epistemological confusion and gives rise to the critique of cognition" (34/27).

2. See *LI*, 16/256: "Such purity means that we must keep out the falsifying intrusion of all assertions based on the naive acceptance and assessment of objects, whose existence has been posited in the acts now receiving phenomenological treatment."

appearances—beyond that it is nothing." By reference to this usage of 'immanence', transcendence is "transcendence-in-immanence." More specifically, Husserl also uses the term 'immanence' in a particularly technical way to designate the mode of being of phenomena which, though available to phenomenological reflection, do not give themselves in adumbrations or perspectives. On this basis, such immanent phenomena are understood by Husserl to be among the components of the intending act itself—as distinct from the object that that act intends or reaches—and are thus to be distinguished from phenomena that are transcendent to the intending act. Establishing a precedent that will be followed henceforth, Husserl refers in *Ideas I* to such phenomena as "really inherent moments" of the "stream of lived experiences" (*Id. I*, 65).

Prior to the transcendental turn marked by *Ideas I*, neither of these two senses is clearly employed by Husserl. His sense of the domain that will be the legitimate subject matter for transcendental phenomenological investigation—concrete transcendental subjectivity and intersubjectivity—has not yet crystallized, and the domain of the "immanent" sought by the epistemological inquiry of the *Logical Investigations* has a sense taken directly from the rather crude terms of the problem at hand: the riddle of transcendence. At this stage, immanence is understood by Husserl to characterize a region of being that is epistemologically unproblematic. And given that epistemological problematicity concerns the legitimacy of the existence claims of "transcendence," the immanent domain will be that of the intending act as such, precisely in its intending. It will be what Husserl will later come to call the "noetic" dimension of concrete subjectivity, in contradistinction to the essentially correlated "noematic" dimension. Two assertions are made of the domain of immanence at this early stage, both of which Husserl will later reject: first, the explicit assertion that the epistemologically secure domain of immanence must be rid of all "transcendence" (it will be purely "noetic" and thus not in any way include the "noematic"); and, second, the implicit assertion that this immanent act dimension is to be reached via an abstraction from the concrete human cognizing subjectivity and as such remains psychological, even if no assumptions drawn from the ontology of the psyche are allowed to function as assumptions for the procedure of descriptive psychological analysis.

It is noteworthy that a domain of immanence so conceived is particularly Cartesian and that Husserl's criticism of Descartes in the *Cartesian Meditations* focuses on and rejects precisely these two assertions. Husserl is well placed to understand these two shortcomings: he himself held them early in his development.

§ 2.1.1.2. Act

At this point we should also say something more about Husserl's use of the term 'act'. He understands "acts"—or, more fully, "intentional acts"—from the *Logical Investigations* on to be "intentional lived experiences" (*Id. I*, 64). By 'intentional' Husserl means to refer to the defining characteristic of consciousness, which is that of being consciousness of something. Insofar as consciousness is consciousness of something, Husserl says it is "intentionally referred" to that something. The essential import of this claim is that *relation* to an object is an essential characteristic of consciousness as such and is strictly speaking *internal* to consciousness itself. The conscious act, considered in and of itself, necessarily presents the achievement of relation to an object: "In the essence of the lived experience itself lies not only that it is consciousness but also whereof it is consciousness. . . ." This means that acts of consciousness—for the phenomenologist—cannot be considered as mere psychological occurrences taking place in nature, in abstraction from an achieved relation to some transcendency, and that might (somehow) later be brought into (real) relation. On the contrary, "intentional relatedness to an object" is an essential characteristic of any "act," considered in and of itself and without any prior interpretation according to ontological or metaphysical presuppositions. In general, Husserl uses the word *Erlebnis* (lived experience) to refer to the kind of being possessed by acts.

In referring to 'pure act', we are here referring to Husserl's attempt to isolate the domain of consciousness in its intending as such, in abstraction from the object intended. Husserl is still struggling to find a way to secure a domain of investigation that, in being accepted by the phenomenologist as a field of investigation, would be free of the obscurity bound up with the riddle of transcendence. Husserl has yet to distinguish intentional objectivity or "noema" from real objectivity, and so is tempted to try to secure his domain of investigation by excluding all object-terms of intentional acts. At this stage the "pure" act will be the intending component of the intentional act considered in abstraction from the intended term of that act. Here "purity" will be arrived at through a process of abstraction. Later, Husserl will develop a far deeper notion of purity, in accordance with his developed insights into the meaning of the presupposition of the natural attitude, and the concomitant transcendental reduction.

§ 2.1.1.3. Adequation

Returning to our discussion, we can say that Husserl's move at this point is not driven by the phenomenology of the problem—for as yet there is no phenomenology. Rather, it is driven by a purely formal demand, which has the structure: if transcendence is problematic, then *unclarified* transcendence can only enter with a *presupposed* sense. If the investigation is to proceed scientifically, it must exclude the presupposed. Therefore, it must exclude all transcendence, all otherness. It must establish its domain by demarcating a region of pure immanence, from which all transcendence has been excluded.

Husserl thus proposes the principle of adequation as the device for distinguishing between the truly immanent, the "really inherent" content of the act, and its transcendent other, the object.

Formally, we know that the principle of adequation is that of pure immanence. But how does Husserl identify the purely immanent? By identifying being in excess *as* being that can show itself to be other. Husserl first speaks of this phenomenon in terms of doubt and certainty, of dubitability and indubitability. Any being that sustains excess must in principle be able to manifest this excess, this "more than" that is still concealed, still held in reserve. In fact, as noted, being able to manifest what has remained concealed is the very meaning of transcendence. But in the unfolding of this excess, the entity could come to show itself to be other than it appeared to be at any given time. That is, as being that sustains an excess of being, what any such being ever appears to be is always open to doubt. The manifestation of excess may at any time force a cancellation of the sense of the appearing in question.

That Husserl's principle of adequation is founded on the impossibility of an entity's being able to manifest itself as other, and therefore not sustaining any excess of being, can be seen in his account of the distinction between "inner" and "outer" perception, a distinction he employs in an attempt to establish the subject matter of descriptive psychology. By 'outer perception' we understand the perception of physical things, properties, events, etc.; all other perceptions are "inner" perceptions. As such, inner perception yields a restricted domain of "self," from which all "transcendent" objects have been abstracted. Could it be that the principle to which the phenomenological reduction seeks to give expression is satisfied in the distinction between inner and outer perception? Husserl denies this and supports his position by showing that *at least some* objects of inner perception are open to doubt, from which it follows that the domain available to inner perception includes transcendencies.

Husserl makes this clear by noting that many inner perceptions of psychic states "are perceived with a bodily location." As such, the object of that kind of perception is a real transcendency: "That anxiety tightens my throat, that pain bores into my tooth, that grief gnaws at my heart: I perceive these things as I perceive that the wind shakes the trees or that this box is square and brown in color, etc." (*LI*, 761/859). The example of a pain in the tooth illustrates the point at issue; the *objects* of such *inner* perceptions are not indubitably given:

> In the perception of a toothache, for example, an actual lived experience is perceived, and yet our perception often deceives: the pain appears to bore into a healthy tooth. The possibility of error is plain. The perceived object is not the pain as experienced [*erlebt*] but the pain in a transcendent reference as connected with the tooth. (770–71/866)

To say that the objects of inner perception are perceived "as" the objects of outer perception are perceived is to say that the objects of inner perception are (often) the ontological equivalent of the objects of outer perception: they are both (always in the case of outer, often in that of inner perception) transcendencies. This is established in view of "the possibility of error"; is it possible, in other words, for such objects to reveal themselves as other. Because the distinction between outer and inner perception does not coincide with that between the corrigible and the incorrigible, "inner and outer perception . . . are of quite the same epistemological character" (*LI*, 760/859).

Having rejected inner perception as the mode of access to the purely immanent, Husserl then gives an account of why it is that adequate perception is appropriate. An adequate perception is one whose object sustains no concealedness, no excess, and hence no possibility of showing itself as other than it claims to be at any time. An adequate perception is

> one ascribing nothing to its object that is not intuitively presented, and given as a really inherent part of the perceptual lived experience, and one that, conversely, intuitively presents and posits its objects just as they are in fact experienced in and with their perception. Every perception is characterized by the intention of grasping its object as present, and *in propria persona*. To this intention perception corresponds with complete perfection, achieves adequacy, if the object is itself actually present, and in the strictest sense present *in propria persona*, is exhaustively apprehended as that which it is, and is therefore itself a really inherent factor in our perceiving of it. It is accordingly clear, and evident from the mere essence of perception, that adequate perception can only be "inner" perception, that it can only be trained upon lived experiences simultaneously given, and belonging to a single lived experience with itself. . . . One cannot, however, at all concur with the converse opinion and say, in psychological language, that each percept directed at one's own lived experience . . . need be adequate. (365–66/542)

The purely immanent, the really inherent, is that which is "exhaustively apprehended." That is, that which is so apprehended sustains no concealedness whatsoever. For this reason, and for it alone, the purely immanent resists all doubtfulness. As "exhaustively apprehended," it cannot show itself to be other, for there is no more of it to allow further apprehension. Husserl then reaffirms this by speaking of the non-transcendent in terms of its being one with its apprehension; that is, the immanent is strictly speaking *nothing other than* the intentional functioning itself. Husserl attempts to define this certainty in terms of *ontological* possibilities: he uses the metaphor of 'dwelling within' (*Einwohnen*) the knowing and of having no being that does not so dwell in order to account for the fundamental meaning of dubitability. To "dwell within" the knowing itself is to sustain no excess beyond the knowing. Hence it is impossible for such an entity to show itself in another way. As dwelling within, nothing of its being is concealed or hidden, nothing is yet to be revealed:

> I can doubt the truth of an inadequate, merely adumbrating perception: the intended or, if one likes, intentional object is not immanent in the act of appearing. The intention is there, but the object itself . . . is not one with it. How could its existence be evident to me? But I cannot doubt an adequate,

> purely immanent perception precisely because there are no residual intentions in it that must yet achieve fulfillment. The whole intention, or the intention in all its respects, is fulfilled. Or as we also expressed it: the object is in our perception as merely believed to exist, but is also itself actually given, and as what it is believed to be. It is of the essence of adequate perception that the intuited object itself truly and actually dwells in it. . . . (770/866)

In the case of adequate perception, "the experienced content is also the object of perception" (769-70/865); in the case of inadequate perception, "content and object fall asunder." In this latter case, Husserl specifically points to the *difference* that exists between object and act: "The content represents *what does not lie within it itself*" (770/866).

The content of the "narrow phenomenological sphere" Husserl calls 'the really inherent content of the intentional function'. Purified of all transcendence, it is the domain of the "genuinely immanent." This really inherent content, "adequately" given, is "beyond question" (*Hua* II, 5/3–4).

§ 2.1.2. Transcendent Apperception

We have seen that Husserl interprets the demand for presuppositionlessness as the inhibition of all transcendent affirmations. Clearly this means that any particular transcendency that an intentional function claims to have attained must undergo exclusion. But the question remains whether the exclusion of the non-really inherent content of the act is all that is required to achieve phenomenological purity. Does the exclusion of the "object" of the act actually effect the inhibition of "all transcendent affirmations"?

In the second edition of the *Logical Investigations* it becomes clear that phenomenological purity demands more than the exclusion of the object-correlate of the act. In the *Prolegomena* Husserl observes that, as a consequence of its presuppositionlessness, epistemology "precedes metaphysics, as it precedes psychology and all other disciplines" (*Proleg*, 226/221). Therefore "no metaphysical, scientific and, above all, no psychological assertions can . . . function as premises" (*LI*, 27–28/265).

It follows from this that the desired "purification" requires more than just the exclusion of the particular object of the act in question. It requires that the *apperception* according to which this really inherent stratum of experience is determinately placed within the order of objective nature as a *de facto* lived experience taking place in a real human being, and thus is understood as a component part of the real world, also be put out of action because such an apperception affirms the existence of a domain of being that is transcendent to the "kernel" isolated by the reduction. Furthermore, in knowing this to be so, it affirms that this transcendent domain has been attained in an act of knowing.[3]

---

3. This is the enduring insight to be gained here. It is not prominent at this stage, but it is a definite premonition of the "general thesis" proper to the natural attitude.

Just as the transcendent object of the intentional act is not a really inherent feature of the act, neither can the metaphysical-ontological determination of the intentional function be read off it as a really inherent feature. Therefore, all such metaphysical determinations of the region of the phenomenologically pure, really inherent act-immanence must also undergo exclusion. Reductive purification, beyond the exclusion of the object, also "prohibits . . . any application . . . of naturalistic interpretations and assertions. It forbids us, i.e., to set [the intentional functionings] up as psychological realities (even in an indefinitely general or exemplary fashion) as the states of 'mind-endowed beings' of any sort whatsoever" (*LI*, 16/256). The reason for this is that if the act-intentionality—the phenomenologically pure "kernel" of the empirical ego—is given to the phenomenologist as naturally apperceived, then the pure "kernel" is not properly pure. For such an apperception effects an ontological determination of that region, which, far from inhibiting all transcendent affirmation, actually places this "kernel" within an order of transcendencies—that is, within the order of objective real worldly objects. This is exactly why Husserl says: "Exactly regarded, all psychic phenomena seen in natural or empirical-scientific attitudes are perceived transcendently" (761/860). This means that the intentional function isolated by the reduction cannot be *considered* by the investigation to be a region within nature and hence that, in the development of its method, the predetermination of the being of its subject matter as governed by the rules governing natural being is not available to it. Its intentional functioning cannot be considered as *caused* by a transcendency, nor can its functioning be assumed to have to obey the laws of transcendent nature. Husserl says:

> Pure phenomenology . . . does not build upon the ground given by transcendent apperception, of physical and animal, and so of psycho-physical nature, it makes no empirical assertions, it propounds no judgments that relate to objects transcending consciousness: it establishes no truths concerning natural realities, whether physical or psychic [such as the dependency of the intentional function upon various physiological and bodily functions], therefore, in the historical sense—and borrows no such truths as assumed premises. (765/862)

In other words, the scientific epistemology being developed here is not *psychology*, in spite of several comments to the contrary to be found in the first edition of the *Logical Investigations*.

For psychology, as a particular branch of the more general science of nature, intentional functioning is itself part of nature. Psychology is thus ontologically precommitted, and it is entirely appropriate for this precommitment to show itself in the methodological procedure of the discipline. But it is precisely such precommitments that distinguish psychology from phenomenology. Husserl says:

> When in psychology, as the objective science of animal mentality, we mean by perception of psychic phenomena the perceptions that a man has

of his own lived experiences, which the perceiver apprehends as belonging to himself, this particular person, all inner perceptions are no less cases of transcendent apperception than are outer perceptions. Among these are some that (with some abstraction) count as adequate insofar as they seize man's own (relevant) lived experiences in their very selves. But insofar as even these "adequate" inner perceptions apperceive the lived experiences they apprehend as those of a percipient, psycho-physical, personal ego, and so as belonging to the presented objective world, they are in this respect infected with an essential inadequacy. (772/867–68)[4]

Psychology is thus *necessarily* implicated in the affirmation of transcendence. However, thanks to the phenomenologically reductive exclusion of "all transcendent affirmations," not only does phenomenology not deal with the actually transcendent object of the intentional act; it does not deal with the pure content of the "phenomenologically reduced ego" *as* "states of animal organisms." If it is constitutive of the very essence of psychology that its subject matter be states of animal organisms and if it is then proper of psychology to develop a method by which to study intentionality *as* a state of an animal organism, then it follows that phenomenology must be distinguished from psychology in principle. Its method is different *because* its subject matter is different: its subject matter is not intentionality *as* a state of an animal organism, but intentionality *as such*. Consequently phenomenology is a science that is wholly different from psychology.

§ 3. Reduction as Abstractive Exclusion

The *presupposed* is "that which precipitates epistemological confusion and . . . gives impetus to the critique of cognition" (*Hua* II, 5/3). It is nothing less than "everything transcendent." And the operation directed against all transcendencies is an "epistemological reduction." Because of the need to distinguish this investigation from that of descriptive psychology, he calls this epistemological reduction a 'phenomenological reduction':

> the really inherent immanent, or equivalently, the adequately self-given, is beyond question. I may make use of it. That which is transcendent (not really inherently immanent) I may not use. Therefore, I must perform a phenomenological reduction: I must exclude all transcendent positings. (*Hua* II, 5/3–4)

Such a reduction yields, on the one hand, a discipline and, on the other, a region for investigation that, not being transcendent, seems to offer itself unproblematically. The operation is reduction: assigning an "index of indifference," effecting a bracketing, an exclusion of those transcendencies from the stock of tools on hand. By virtue of this, the reduction achieves what Husserl

---

4. Husserl makes the same point in the introduction to the second volume of the *Investigations* (23/261–62).

calls 'purity'. Such purity requires "the purely phenomenological attitude, which inhibits all transcendent positings" (*LI*, 761/860).

This is neither to *deny* their being nor to take a skeptical stance toward them. Rather, the reductive exclusion is such that, "whether I believe in them or not," I make no judgments about them. Through reduction they become "entirely irrelevant" to me. That is to say, all but the really inherent content of the act undergoes exclusion from the purview of the investigation. Or at least that is Husserl's intention.

Thus the reduction operates by separating off "what is in its [i.e. the intentional function's] 'lived experience,' namely what really inherently composes it, from what 'is in it' in an inauthentic or 'intentional' sense" (361/539). Such a reduction (as the isolation of a particular region through the exclusion, the expulsion, of all transcendencies) effects what is in fact a *narrowing of focus*. As such a restriction, this methodological access construes its subject matter—intentionality—as a particular region, which is isolable, identifiable, and thereby accessible through a process of *abstractive exclusion*. The subject matter for the new scientific epistemology is what is left over when a whole range of items—transcendencies (which, together with the narrow domain of intentional functioning, make up the originally given whole)—are simply excluded from the purview of the investigation on the ground that they are not properly possessed.

§ 4. The Domain of Pure Immanence: Husserl's First Proposal

Husserl gives the first formulation of the procedure of presuppositionlessness in the introduction to the second volume of the *Logical Investigations* and continues to develop it as he proceeds. He later says: "In really inherent phenomenological treatment, objectivity itself counts as nothing: in general it transcends the act" (427/587). Phenomenology is to investigate intentionality in its functioning; the genuine sense of the self-transcendence it effects, as well as the genuine sense of the "in itselfness" of that which such functioning attains, is to be determined through an investigation of functioning intentionality as such rather than of the object of any knowing act. The ideal of presuppositionlessness is respected in that phenomenology is to be an exclusively "subjective" investigation, employing no notion of, nor commitment to, "object-being" or "self-transcendence":

> Instead of becoming lost in the performance of acts built intricately on one another and instead of, as it were, naively positing the existence of the objects intended in their sense and then going on to characterize them, or of assuming such objects hypothetically, of drawing conclusions from all this, etc., we must rather practice "reflection," that is, make these acts themselves, and their meaning-content, our objects. When objects are intuited, thought of, theoretically pondered on, and thereby given to us as actualities in certain ontic modalities, we must direct our theoretical interest away from such objects, not posit them as realities as they appear or hold in

the intentions of our acts. These acts, contrariwise, though hitherto not objective, must now be made objects of apprehension and theoretical positing. (14/254–55)

Here we arrive at the initial determination of the conception and task of the phenomenological enterprise. The demand to be free from presuppositions means that it is no longer the object of the act that must be investigated in order to determine its being, its "objectivity," its "reality." No longer *is that to which the cognitive act is directed* to be studied. Rather, it is *the directing-itself-toward as such* that is to be studied. In the clarification of this being-directed, the being-sense of the object will be clarified because it is through such being-directed that the object is encountered and its being-sense established. And *only* in this way is it encountered and established. As Husserl says:

> such direction to objects, such presentation and meaning of what is not really [*reell*] part of the phenomenological makeup of our lived experiences, is a descriptive feature of the lived experiences in question, whose sense it should be possible to fix and clarify by considering the lived experiences themselves. In no other way would it be possible. (25/264)

In other words, the aim must be to offer a clarification of the very sense of intentionality; the investigation would attempt to establish the possible meaning of 'object-being'—and thereby of 'intentionality'—by investigating how it is that being "in itself" is encountered.[5]

§ 5. Conclusion

Thus the purification of the domain of the really inherent through the exclusion of all transcendence yields—if it is actually possible to execute this operation—a domain of immanence that is utterly "self-saturated." It establishes the intentional as a kind of "autistic" functioning, completely closed up within itself. Since all transcendence has been expelled, the domain manifests no otherness than or from itself. Note, however, that this method still represents only a proposal from Husserl; it is not yet grounded in the phenomenology of the matter. It remains to be seen whether 'presupposition' has been properly conceived and whether the epistemological-phenomenological reduction can really establish freedom from such an intrusion.

A number of questions present themselves here. If the domain so delimited is genuine intentionality, how is it to be understood that pure immanence can come to present to itself something that does not lie within itself? How does this restriction still maintain intentionality in its *openness* to transcen-

---

5. Thus the fundamental principle of phenomenological investigation emerges: the meaning of 'object' and 'intentional functionary' is to be established through their respective showings of themselves, through an examination of the ways in which their respective being-senses are to be achieved. No preacceptance regarding genuine meaning of such being senses may be tolerated by the investigation.

dence? No less important, what kind of "content" shows itself "adequately"? Is there a fact of the *phenomenal givenness* of a domain that can become the object of a "scientific epistemology" in which no otherness is sustained, or is the adequate givenness of immanent entities a myth?

In the next chapter we shall investigate the delimiting function of the epistemological-phenomenological reduction and ask whether it is in fact possible to exclude the object in which the intentional act terminates. Alternatively, we shall also ask whether the reduction as developed to this point effects such an enclosure as to preclude any investigation of precisely those acts that form the heart of the problem, acts that attain genuine transcendence.

Chapter Three
Abstractive Exclusion as a Procedure of Enclosure

§ 1. The "Narrow Phenomenological Sphere": The "Lived-through" as the Domain of Immanence

Prior to and outside of phenomenology, Husserl has proposed a method: the reduction. Phenomenological analysis itself begins with the investigation of the intentional act, from which all transcendence has been excluded. What does Husserl find when he begins the inquiry?

Our analysis of his progress is guided by a particular concern: Is a procedure that establishes its domain of study through an *enclosure* appropriately geared to the revealing of *intentionality*, a mode of being the very meaning of which is as essentially self-transcending, that it is nothing other than a going beyond, an overcoming of enclosure? Would such a procedure not force a denaturing of its target such that, in its essential breaking out of a well defined enclosure (the "self"), intentionality would be unable to show itself? We shall now attempt to show how and why this question must be answered affirmatively.

Having developed a *plan*, an a priori schematization of the problem, Husserl begins to investigate actual acts. The reduction seeks to delimit intentional functioning as a domain for phenomenological investigation. It must therefore yield a field of stable identities that offer themselves for interrogation. As was seen, such identities must satisfy the demand of adequate givenness. But what does the restriction to "adequacy" leave the phenomenologist to work with? What actually are the really inherent contents of the field delimited by the reduction?

Husserl's account of what makes up this sphere varies from the first to the second edition of the *Logical Investigations* in an extremely significant respect. In the first edition, following the reductive exclusion in its strictest form, Husserl attempts to exclude the object-term of all acts, except where such objects are, in his terminology, adequately given—that is, except where such terms are *immanent* objects, thereby qualifying as really inherent components of acts:[1] "By the really inherent phenomenological content of an act

---

1. These objects in turn only become terms of acts through a particular kind of phenomenological *reflection*, a redirection of intentionality back upon itself.

we mean the sum total of its concrete and abstract parts . . . the sum total of the partial lived experiences that really inherently constitute it" (*LI*, 411/576). However, this position changes in the second edition, which includes intentional objects within the domain of phenomenological investigation. We shall follow the argument for this change.

Husserl tries to express the intention to grasp sheer immanence (under the heading of really inherent content) by claiming that there is a domain of givenness that does not present itself as "over against," but instead presents itself as not sustaining any hiddenness or excess. There is, so he claims, a domain of givenness that does not show itself as an "object." Husserl attempts to alert us to this by pointing out that there are two fundamentally different ways in which contents for consciousness can be *originarily* present. Some—which he recognizes as transcendencies—are "perceived"; others—which he recognizes as immanencies—are "lived through [*erlebt*]" (360/538).[2]

The contrast here is between adequate and inadequate perception or intuition, which was touched on above. That which is adequately perceived is now understood as something "lived through." The original phenomenological exclusion of transcendencies can be put as being a limitation to the sphere of lived experiences. Husserl defines the phenomenological sense of the term 'lived experience' (*Erlebnis*) by way of the distinction between really inherent and intentional content of acts.

Husserl's example here is the experience of a war. He says that when someone claims to have "experienced [*erlebt*]" such a war he means that *what* the person can be said to have "experienced" are certain real-worldly events, which are genuine transcendencies; but for the intentional functionary, access to such events can only take place via an "experiencing," which consists in the perceptual and judicative acts *through which* such events are related to the empirical ego. An examination of this phenomenon reveals that the mode of pres-

---

2. Interestingly, *Erleben* (living through) is a temporal notion, and what is so given—the *Erlebnis* (lived experience)—is given temporally. Husserl has not yet thought through the implications of this for his claim regarding the possibility of adequately given objects. In fact, once genetic phenomenology begins to be developed in the investigations of time-consciousness, the notion of such givenness is exposed as a myth. But the employment of the notion of *Erleben* with its essential reference to temporality as the most conducive way of pointing to the being of intentional functioning is a striking premonition of Husserl's at this stage of the investigation. For to "live through"—originarily—is simply to temporalize. Here the ground is already being prepared for the insight into functioning intentionality as originary temporalization.

Note also that the "object" is by no means to be fundamentally understood in terms of *identity*, as comes to be the case for Husserl after the turn to genetic phenomenology. If it were, the domain of the really inherent would also be an object-domain. Rather, the presupposition proper to the natural attitude forms the fundamental orientation here: to be an object is to be *outside the mind, or nonmental*. Transcendence is still understood fundamentally with reference to consciousness as a spatiotemporally located mode of being. Transcendencies are only either other spatial things or ideal entities.

ence of that which comes to be for consciousness *through* the functioning act is different from the mode of presence of those acts themselves. The distinction is this: the domain delimited by the reduction—the phenomenologically reduced ego—as the stream of really inherent immanence that has now become a field for investigation, the "experiencing consciousness in the phenomenologically paradigmatic sense . . . naturally does not have these events in itself as 'psychic lived experiences,' as its really inherent constituents or contents" (361/540). On the contrary: "What it finds in itself, what are really [*reell*] present in it, are the relevant acts of perceiving, judging, etc." (361-62/540).

It could be said that both dimensions are "experienced." But to be present as "experienced" means something different in each case.[3] To experience certain outer events means that consciousness "lives through" certain acts of perceiving, which are directed toward the outer events; the outer events are not present as "lived through" but as "perceived," "judged," etc. They do not have their *being* as something "lived through." What is present as "lived through" is now identified with the phenomenological concept of *lived experience*.

This allows a conception of the phenomenologically reduced ego to emerge. It is that unity that is made up of all that is present as "lived through," as "experienced" in the phenomenological sense. That is, the phenomenologically reduced ego is pure act, considered in abstraction from the objects of those acts. This reduced ego is to make up the field of pure immanence to be investigated by phenomenology.

§ 2. Two Kinds of Really Inherent Content

In speaking of the "content proper" of the phenomenologically reduced ego as what is present as lived through, Husserl further determines the meaning of the region of adequate givenness. Dealing with the paradigmatic intentional act, that of thing-perception, he believes he finds, broadly speaking, two different kinds of such content: sense or hyletic data and the act-character of the act.

§ 2.1. Sense or Hyletic Data

He begins by considering the phenomenon of appearance, seeking an answer to the following question: How is the distinction between really inherent and non-really inherent content to be made, and how is the really inherent content to be understood?

His analysis turns upon an ambiguity he finds in the use of the term 'appearance', which typically conceals the problem of intentionality. On the one hand, the term can have an immanent reference insofar as it presupposes a distinction between a purely subjective "appearance" and the actual "being"

---

3. In *Ideas I* Husserl develops this through the notion of *Abschattung* (adumbration).

of the object and refers to the *experience* in which the object's appearing consists. On the other hand, 'appearance' can have a transcendent reference, indicating that moment of the object in its actual being which shows itself. On the one hand, I have, for instance, a sensation and, on the other, a property or quality of the object itself. But the ambiguity is such that 'appearance' can be used equally of both. For this reason Husserl believes that instead of recognizing two utterly different entities here, it is possible to be misled into believing that one merely encounters two different aspects of one and the same thing:

> These two, the color-sensation and the object's objective coloring, are often confounded. In our time people have favored a form of words according to which both are the same thing, only seen from a different standpoint or with a different interest: psychologically or subjectively speaking, one has a sensation; physically or objectively speaking, one has a property of an external thing. Here it is enough to point to the readily grasped difference between the red of this ball, objectively seen as uniform, and the indubitable and even necessary adumbration in the subjective color-sensations in our perception—a difference repeated in all sorts of objective properties and the sense-complexes that correspond to them. (359/537–38)

But this is to be blind to the fact that the two different ways of being originarily present justify a distinction between two different modes of being. A little later Husserl concludes:

> We cannot too sharply stress the equivocation that allows us to use the word 'appearance' both of the lived experience in which the object's appearing consists (e.g. the concrete perceptual lived experience in which the object itself seems present to us) and of the object that appears as such. The deceptive spell of this equivocation vanishes as soon as one takes phenomenological account as to how little of the object that appears is as such to be found in the lived experience of its appearing. The appearing of the physical thing (the lived experience) is not the thing that appears (that seems to stand before us *in propria persona*). As belonging in a conscious connection, we experience [*erleben*] the appearings [*Erscheinungen*]; as belonging in the phenomenal world, physical things appear before us. The appearings [of the thing] does not itself appear to us, they are lived through [*erlebt*]. (359–60/538)

The sense of Husserl's distinction here is ontological. The being of the object is not to be found "in" the lived experience of its appearing. Yet—and this is precisely the problem—there is something "in" this immanence *through which* what is not in it as an *actual* content comes to be presented *for* it.

The exclusion of the transcendence therefore does not leave the phenomenologist confronting nothing. The "object that appears as such," along with all of its objective properties and qualities, undergoes exclusion, leaving within the domain of immanence only that component of the intentional achieving which corresponds to the objective property—namely, "the experience in which the object's appearing consists," the "sense-complexes that correspond" to such objective moments, though that are given not as perceived but as lived through (see 400/568). While, for example, the color-property of the perceived object is not present as a really inherent component part of the lived experience, there is nonetheless a really inherent part of the lived experience that "corresponds" to it: "Our color-sensation corresponds to it, that qualitatively determinate phenomenological color-aspect" (358/537).

The experienced sensations that, as really inherent contents of consciousness, "correspond" to the intended objective property of the object are also referred to as "representatives" of the object (525/655). They help to present transcendent objects without themselves being transcendencies. Later, Husserl will call these lived-through sensations "hyletic data."

§ 2.2. The Objectifying Function; the "Act-Character" of the Act: Consciousness of Identity

But the "sensations"—or, in the case of non-perceptual acts, whatever content happens to serve as the "basis of interpretation" (399/567; see 186/399)—are not the only really inherent components of the intentional act. For possession of sensations *alone* is not enough to render the phenomenon in question an *intentional* act: "A real being . . . merely having contents inside it such as the lived experiences of sense but unable to interpret these objectively or otherwise use them to make objects present to itself . . . would not be called a psychic being by anyone anymore" (378–79/553). Needless to say, such a being, remaining utterly locked within itself, would not be an intentional being either.[4]

Therefore, by simply identifying the hyletic dimension of the act of perception, that in virtue of which such experience is an *act* that *perceives* an object is not yet apparent. The phenomenologist still needs to discover in the act that extra really inherent component in virtue of which it *exceeds* itself and becomes related through such hyletic data to an object. Husserl locates this "surplus" in what he calls the 'act-character' proper of the act, wherein the act has its essential character of going beyond itself and attaining an object. This act-character is an "objectivating intention" that "animates" the sensations such that they come to function as "representatives" of an object. This act-character, Husserl says, "is also called an interpretation, conception, apperception in relation to the sensations really inherently present in this act" (400/568). He develops this further by drawing attention to the fact that, on the one hand, the one identical object can be intended though the experienced presenting sensations that are continually changing and that, on the other hand, the same experienced presenting sensations can represent completely different intentional

---

4. This is the point at which a correction to the anthropological application of intentional language to non-consciousnesses (such as computers and plants) and microbiological entities (such as genes) must be made and the temptations to misunderstand both intentional and non-intentional entities through the use of such language removed.

objects. For example, in the perceiving of a box, I see the one box, but I do not see my sensations. Throughout the course of such a perception, the *objective* "content" of consciousness (the identical box) remains the same, but the *experienced* sense content (the hyle) undergoes continual change. In this case, "very different contents are therefore experienced, though the same object is perceived" (396/565). In spite of this flux, we perceive one and the same object. The box is not present as lived through, but the consciousness *of* the box—that is, consciousness of the hyletic data as giving of an object from which, thanks to the reduction, the phenomenologist has abstracted—is something given as lived through. Which is to say: what the act-character of the act amounts to is the "*taking* of hyle as giving of something else." Such "taking" is nothing other than the achieving of a consciousness of identity, and this "consciousness of identity" is "itself something that belongs to the sphere of our lived experiences" (397/566). Husserl says:

> we experience a "consciousness of identity," that is, a claim to apprehend identity. I now ask: On what does this consciousness depend? Must we not reply that different sensational contents are given but that we "take" or apperceive them "in the same sense," and that to take them in this sense is an experienced character [*Erlebnischarakter*], which first of all makes up the "existence of the object for me"?

As something that is "found in experience itself" as a really inherent component of the act, this act-character is itself originally present as lived through. As such, their mode of givenness is essentially different from the givenness of the object:

> Sensations, and the acts "interpreting" them, are alike experienced, but they do not appear as objects: they are not seen, heard, or perceived by any sense. Objects, on the other hand, appear and are perceived, but they are not experienced. Naturally we exclude the case of adequate perception. (399/567)[5]

§ 3. The Meaning of the Region of the Really Inherent: Intentional Act

It is Husserl's intention to secure the intentional function as a field of study by applying the epistemological reduction. To do so, he contends, the

---

5. See, e.g., Husserl's observation at *LI*, 397/566: "within this widest sphere of what can be experienced [*Erlebbaren*], we believe we have found an evident difference between intentional lived experiences, in whose case objective intentions arise through immanent characters of the lived experiences in question, and lived experiences in whose case this does not occur, contents that may serve as the building-blocks of acts without being acts themselves." And again: "Apperception is our surplus, which is found in lived experience itself, in its descriptive content as opposed to the raw existence of sense [*Empfindung*]; it is the act-character that, as it were, ensouls sense and is in essence such as to make us perceive this or that object, for example, see this tree, hear this ringing, smell this scent of flowers, etc." (399/567).

reduction must isolate a domain of pure immanence while also capturing that immanence in its self-transcending function. But does this method succeed?

The reduction excludes all transcendence, asking that transcendence be of no account at all—for it is in question and excluded. The problem then becomes how it is possible for intentionality to show itself if the very meaning of the method designed to elicit it is such as to rule out any reference to transcendence—that in virtue of which intentionality shows itself to be such. How does intentionality manifest itself—defined as 'consciousness of . . .'—in the absence of an object? If no transcendence is shown, by what right can a "self-transcendence" still manifest itself?

Thus it seems that the methodological demand of the reduction—that presuppositionlessness be attained—is in direct conflict with the requirement that it isolate self-transcendence as such in its very functioning. To show that the exclusion of transcendence in turn obliterates intentional functioning itself is our next task.

§ 4. The Expansion of the "Narrow Phenomenological Sphere"

Our concern has been that the systematic exclusion of transcendence from the legitimate domain of phenomenology would rob the act of that which essentially defined it as intentional. However, the phenomenology of the act enables the development of a solution. Husserl is not only compelled to locate an Object[6] within his new sphere; he is also justified in doing so, though only by revising the notion of transcendence as presupposition and consequently that of reduction. The question to be investigated is: What is the significance of the *inseparability* of intentional function from the object it purports to attain?

§ 4.1. The *de facto* Presence of "Transcendence" within the Purified Region

We note to begin with that as a matter of phenomenological practice and contrary to Husserl's intentions it is simply not possible to describe intentional functioning without also referring in that very description to the transcendence claimed in that intentional act.

This is because intentional acts are *essentially* referential. Where the act in question refers to a non-adequately given object—as do the overwhelming majority of intentional acts—such an act cannot be studied other than as an act

---

6. I use 'Object' rather than 'object' here to indicate that it is not just a unique kind of object, or a quasi-object of some kind, that is found within the "purified region," but objectivity as such. This holds simply because, insofar as the domain of phenomenological investigation is the universal sphere of intentional acts, every kind of correlated objectivity is now found—legitimately, though in a way not yet fully clarified—undeniably within the purified region.

whose very meaning is that of "referring to a transcendence." Thus it is impossible to describe, for example, an act of perception without at the same time referring to that in virtue of which it is recognized *as* such an act and, furthermore, as just *this* act and not any other—that is, without referring to the object of the perception. Husserl soon recognizes in the second edition of the *Logical Investigations*, and contrary to his earlier intentions, that:

> One has, further, to employ expressions that stand for what is intentional in such acts, for the object to which they are directed. It is in fact impossible to describe referential acts without using expressions that recur to the things to which such acts refer. . . . 'objectivity' . . . is necessarily introduced into almost all phenomenological descriptions. (15–16/256)

In attempting to make the distinction between the really inherent and the non-really inherent contents or components of the intentional act, a reference to the supposedly excluded non-really inherent transcendencies is unavoidable. Husserl then recognizes that "the distinction and description of intentional lived experiences without regard to their intentional objects is impossible" (202/412).

The meaning of the reduction was precisely to establish a discipline that would not presuppose any transcendent objectivity, nor concern itself with any. However, the analysis of the phenomenological field of act-immanence cannot proceed without reference to act-transcendence: analytical practice shows methodological intention to presuppositionlessness so interpreted to be a self-contradictory and impossible requirement.

§ 4.2. The *de jure* Presence of "Transcendence" within the Purified Region: Proto-Constitution

Can there be a *de jure* justification of this widening to include the non-really inherent—and hence "transcendent"—contents of acts such that the ideal of presuppositionlessness remains intact? The stipulation here would have to be that both the "relation" to such transcendencies and their being would not remain an "enigma"; the transcendence would be both epistemologically and ontologically unproblematic. In fact this stipulation is met in terms of a preliminary notion of 'constitution' (see 397/566: *ausmachen*).

To see this, let us put the now problematic demand of the reduction to one side and consider Husserl's discovery of the really inherent act-components—a discovery not compromised by any inability to exclude the term of the act, lying as it does in the distinction between act and object.

There are, we recall, two different kinds of really inherent act-components (in the case of perceptual intentionality): the hyletic/sense data moment and the act-character, which is responsible for the "taking" of the hyletic moment *as* representative.

What does the phenomenologist have if both of these kinds of really inherent act-components are present? Certainly more than the two act-components themselves: for Husserl understands the act-character to be an "interpreting" function (400/568)[7] that "goes to work" upon the non-intentional really inherent act-components; in other places, he speaks of the non-intentional really inherent components as a "raw existence" that is "ensouled" by the "apperceptive surplus" so as to function as a "representative" of a transcendent entity (398/567). Sensations are "contents that receive objectifying 'interpretation' (apperception) in our act of intuition. It is in the 'interpretation' that the appearance of the corresponding objective characters or properties is realized" (198/409).

With this understanding of the function of the act-character, Husserl is already employing a theory of constitution: to "take" the experienced sensations in this way, to take them as "representative" of a transcendency, "is an experienced character through which the 'being of the object' is first constituted" (397/566). On this account, perceptual intentionality is a "constitution" through a "sense bestowal." This sense bestowal is an "objectifying interpretation" through which the act exceeds itself and through which the object appears to us. As Theodore De Boer expresses it:

> The intentional act is active; it does something with the sensation. This immanent sensation-content is its material; it is what is apperceived. Through the act, the immanent content is conceived of as a transcendent property.[8]

The actual manner of operation remains rather mysterious at this stage. Husserl says simply that the objectifying interpretation—and thereby constitution—is the taking of the non-intentional "sense" contents in such a way as to *mean* some particular objectivity that is distinguished from that sense content. But it is thanks to this function that what is meant is not these sense contents but an object meant "through" them. The "taking" of non-intentional contents in this particular way simply *is* perception. Husserl says: "We call the experiencing of sensations in this conscious manner [i.e. the 'apperceptive ensouling' of them] *the perception of the object* in question" (*LI*, 396/565).

Thus any object that is present as a *result* of the mutual operation of the two really inherent act-components no longer poses the epistemological problem to which Husserl responds with the first form of reductive exclusion. The meaning and possibility of its being known is clear: the act itself, in its objectifying function, generates it. Such objects "are first constituted as being what they are for us, and as what they count for us, in varying forms of objective intention" (169/385).

---

7. See also, e.g., *LI*, 397/556, where Husserl speaks of "intentions, united with the sensations they interpret."

8. Theodore De Boer, *The Development of Husserl's Thought*, trans. Alvin Plantinga (The Hague: Nijhoff, 1978), 133.

Therefore, whenever both of the really inherent act-components are present—when, in other words, an intentional act is present—the object *claimed* in that act is *necessarily* present as so claimed; for the interpreting of sensations is itself just as much a really inherent component of the act as the non-intentional sense moment.

Clearly the intentional lived experiences and the object-term that is thereby also present are not the same. Husserl stresses this continually. But given that the act-character itself is an "ensouling" of the sensations, an interpreting, then such an act-character *is nothing other than* an apperception that effects the presence of an object-term. Furthermore—and this is the key to Husserl's willingness to include it within the phenomenological sphere—the object is given indubitably in that its being given is *nothing other than* the "ensouling" of sensations in the way peculiar to the perceptual act-character. The intending of such an object is nothing more than the animation of the sensations in this manner. This accounts—epistemologically—for the *de jure* inclusion of such an "intentional" object within the phenomenologically delimited sphere.

§ 5. Proto-Epoché: The Emergence of the Intentional Object

Where does the *de jure* presence of such an object leave phenomenology's concern for presuppositionlessness? On closer inspection, it proves to emerge intact, without compromise.

In fact the focus of Husserl's concern shifts. Whereas initially the problematic transcendence was simply assumed to be identical with the term of the act *simpliciter*, Husserl now sees such an identification to be simplistic. The integrity of the phenomenological method is preserved insofar as the "object" of the epistemological reduction is no longer the "natural" term of the act but rather a particular ontological determination of such a term. This can be shown as follows.

The question to be asked is: What is the *status* of the act-term that is now legitimately entertained by the phenomenologist? We recall a decisive statement by Husserl from which a "proto-epoché" can be derived: "We call the experiencing of sensations in this conscious manner [i.e. the 'apperceptive ensouling' of them] *the perception of the object in question*" (396/565). That is to say, such an object is the *product* of the act. By accounting for it in this way, the phenomenologist can confront an object that neither needs nor refers to any further entity whose being and presence would not be accounted for in terms of act-constitution. That is, in recognizing the act-term, no ontological independence above and beyond the being of the act is entertained. Husserl simply recognizes what is present as a functional result of the intentional act itself. This means that for the phenomenologist the act-term is in no way in ontological excess of the being of the act itself. Though not identical with the being of the act-function, such an object is not problematically *transcendent* to or outside or independent of it. To say that such an object is present within the strict phenomenological sphere is to say "no more that that certain lived experiences are present" (386/558).

This is not to *deny* transcendence or excess. It is simply to deny transcendence or excess to the act-term in question. And because the act in question is *assumed* by Husserl—as still a prisoner of the yet to be discovered natural attitude—to be ontically determined as the lived experience proper to a human being, a natural entity, then one would expect Husserl to deny that such an act-term could be identified with a *real* object, where 'real' carries with it the ontic predetermination of being independent, and in excess, of the human mind and volitional capacity.[9]

This is in fact what happens. Thanks to this "epoché"—though Husserl does not yet use the term—such "subsidiarily described objectivity . . . has undergone a change of sense, in virtue of which it now belongs to the sphere of phenomenology" (16/256).

Husserl then asserts an ontological equivalence between the being of the intentional act and the being of the object claimed in that act once the reduction has been enacted. This object-term is now called the '*intentional* object', which reveals 'intentional' to be an ontological term, serving to distinguish this object-term from any object-in-itself: "If this lived experience is present, then *eo ipso* and through its own essence . . . the intentional 'relation to the object' is achieved and the object is 'intentionally present'; these two phrases mean exactly the same thing" (386/558). To say that they mean the same thing is to assert an ontological *equivalence*. Considered in this way, the intentionally referred-to object is completely dependent for its existence upon the being and operation of the act; if the act disappears, the object intended also disappears, for the act is that which makes the object appear: "We must note that nothing scientifically or metaphysically transcendent should be substituted for this object; by 'the object' we meant the object as it appears in this intuition, as it counts (so to say) for this intuition" (201/411). Husserl immediately adds: "I may be deceived about the existence of the object of perception but not about the fact that I do perceive it as determined in this or that way, that my perception's target is not some totally different object, a pine-tree, for example, instead of a cockchafer" (201/412). The intentional object is thus a transcendence-in-immanence, whose "phenomenological legitimacy" is bought at the cost of its genuine transcendence. Husserl's distinction between the object

---

9. One could, of course, pose the question of the *cause* of the hyletic or sense data act-component and believe that by asking this question the link with the real, extra-immanent transcendency is established. But this would be an unphenomenological way of proceeding and beyond the means of the descriptive psychology established here. Suffice it to say that, on the basis of two immanent act-components and their mutual interaction, an object of a kind is thereby *also* present *legitimately*: legitimately, because the cognitive relation in this case is no longer problematic.

as given in the act and the object as possibly independent of the act, the object "in itself," establishes the possibility of the proto-epoché.

This allows the operation a particular kind of abstraction, thanks to which an object can be recognized by the phenomenologist—the investigator of acts—without requiring a commitment to any objectivity that transcends the region of lived experience in the particular mode of 'in itself'. Thus a transcendence is admitted within the sphere of phenomenology, but not the transcendence of a "thing in itself": "such subsidiarily described objectivity . . . has undergone a change of sense, in virtue of which it now belongs to the sphere of phenomenology" (16/256).[10] The objects of concern in this particular kind of description are not ontologically determined as *real*; it is considered only as the referred-to of a referring act. Admittedly, this is already to offer a positive ontological determination of the object, for the object is affirmed to have being in the mode of 'referred to'. The important thing here, however, is that being-in-excess of the act is denied to such an object through the operation of this proto-epoché. Objectivity now enters the domain of phenomenology, but only as "merely intentional."

§ 6. Refocused Presuppositionlessness

With the target of the reductive exclusion shifting from act-term pure and simple to transcendence qua being-in-itself, the phenomenological investigation is set to proceed—its commitment to presuppositionlessness intact, though with a far more refined sense of what the vitiating presupposition would be for a scientific epistemology.

To say that the object is an intentional object is to say that the object sustains no being beyond its being as intended by the act in question. To later say that the object is *entertained only as meant* is not to say that the phenomenologist deals only with objects whose mode of being has been determined as the being of a mere meaning (we shall deal with this soon). It is to say that the being of the object is utterly exhausted by the act of meaning, that it is fully contained in and in no way exceeds that act. The essential point here lies in Husserl's pre-

---

10. Consider also Husserl's note to the second edition of the *Investigations*: "In the first edition I wrote 'real [*reell*] or phenomenological' for 'real' [referring to the term *reell*]. The word 'phenomenological' like the word 'descriptive' was used in the first edition only in connection with really inherent elements of lived experience, and in the present edition it has so far been used predominantly in this sense. This corresponds to one's naturally starting with the psychological point of view. It became plainer and plainer, however, as I reviewed the completed investigations and pondered on their themes more deeply . . . that the description of intentional objectivity as such, as we are conscious of it in the concrete act-experience [*Akterlebnis*], represents a distinct descriptive dimension where purely intuitive description may be adequately practiced, a dimension opposed to that of the really inherent act-constituents, but which also deserve to be called 'phenomenological'" (411/576).

scription that the intentional object is to be considered only "as it counts for the act." He could have added: and any moment of it that exceeds its being "contained" by the act, any moment that is not the result of the *activity* of the act—that is, any unknown moment—is excluded. Herein lies the essential distinction between the real and the intentional object. The real object exists "in itself"; the intentional object has being only as, and insofar as it is, aimed-at or referred-to. The intentional object is nothing *beyond* what arises as a result of the operation of the really inherent intentional content. That an act refers to an object is "due to nothing that stays outside of the presentation, but to its own inner peculiarity alone" (451/603). Due to the fact that the intentional object sustains no "otherness" beyond its being meant, it is not possible for the object to show itself to be other than as it is taken to be, for it is nothing beyond what it is taken to be. The object may not *really* be as it is intended to be, but all real being has been excluded by virtue of the determination of the intentional object as an "intentional effect." Clearly, then, this intentional object is in no way a genuine transcendency: the intentional object belongs to the sphere only because Husserl can develop an understanding of it that satisfies the ontological determination of the epistemologically unproblematic sphere of immanence.

Husserl has identified a difference in modes of being present *within* the intentional function (really inherent and intentional) and then goes on to see in this difference an instance of immanence (really inherent content) and transcendence (intentional content). But although the intentional content is not present in the same way as is the really inherent content, the intentional content is still not a transcendence in the genuine sense, for in attaining it intentionality does not attain any "beyond"; rather, it terminates in a product of its own making, in which nothing is hidden or concealed from it.[11] 'Presupposition' no longer means 'object *simpliciter*' but 'object in itself', an object that is or could be more than just that intended by—and hence contained in—the act.

But what is meant by 'real' here? What kind of impoverishment of the field of experience does this proto-epoché effect, given that all objectivity, as it counts intentionally for its act, is now *included* as data for phenomenological investigation? Conversely, what kind of an intentionality is captured here, studied not in its going beyond itself but only in its termination in a product of its own achievement, an intentional object that only has being *as intended*? Does this mean that the intentionality directed toward real—genuine—transcendence is itself also systematically abstracted from and hence unable to be clarified?

---

11. If the intentional object is to be distinguished from the real object, then one would expect Husserl to distinguish the intentional relation from the real relation. And he does so: It is a "misunderstanding" of the intentional relation to believe that with it "we are dealing with a real [*real*] event or a real relationship, taking place between 'consciousness' or 'the ego,' on the one hand, and that of which there is consciousness, on the other" (*LI*, 385/557).

§ 7. The Phenomenological Sense of the Intentional Object

In order to understand the meaning of this reductive exclusion more fully, we need to understand what it is that the reduction is now directed against. It will in fact emerge that it is directed against nothing that could present itself as an object, an identity, but rather against a particular ontic affirmation regarding the being of any object-identity—an affirmation whose exclusion is justified inasmuch as phenomenological analysis of *givenness* finds no ground for it.

The question here concerns the correct understanding of the intentional object as "meant," as "that which counts for the act." Does this mean that *concreteness* is abstracted from, leaving the phenomenologist confronting—under the title 'intentional object'—a pure meaning? Does the abstractive exclusion of the real leave the intentional object as a purely ideal entity?

Three additional clarifications of the intentional object must be made in order to deal with this question. We maintain, first, that the intentional object is not an abstract or ideal entity; second, that it is not an image or a sign; and, third, that it is not a middle term or mediating entity through which the knowing relation is established.

§ 7.1. The Intentional Object Is Not an Abstract or Ideal Entity

Although the being-real of the object has been suspended, the intentional object remains the sole object of the act in question and is not *different*—phenomenologically—from the object intended in that act. If the act in question is a perceptual act, the intentional object that is the necessary correlate of this act is intended as a perceived particular object.[12]

The argument here—contrary to Dagfinn Føllesdal's interpretation—is simple and follows basic phenomenological principles: perceptual objects are given through perceptual intentionalities; ideal objects are given through ideative intentionalities; and abstract objects are given through abstractive intentionalities. The region of phenomenological data may be revealed through an act of methodical abstraction, but this does not lead to the conclusion that the objects of the intentional acts thereby delimited are themselves abstract entities. Abstract (intentional) objects are the correlates of intentional acts of abstraction. And acts of abstraction, which have abstract entities as their intentional objects, are merely one kind of intentional act to be found within the phenomenological domain.

In the perceptual form of the intentional act, reference to the inten-

---

12. In "Husserl's Notion of the Noema," *Journal of Philosophy* 66 (1969), 680–87, Dagfinn Føllesdal argues that the intentional object, purified of "real" ontological status, is an "abstract entity" in principle that is not perceived through the senses. Many other commentators have followed Føllesdal in this.

tional object only takes place through the interpretation of sensations. Its essential character is that of yielding its object "in person." Husserl says: "Every perception is characterized by the intention of grasping its object as bodily present" (365/542; see 457/608).

However, as De Boer points out, this does not mean that the representative content and the represented object coincide here, for the one is immanent while the other is intentionally transcendent: "the object *itself* appears via the representative which could therefore better be called the *pre*-sentative; it is a 'self-presenting content.'"[13] That is to say, the object in question is the object as it counts for the act in question, not as it may be determined by reference to some particular metaphysics or ontology. This means that, regardless of the fact that the object in question is no longer *taken* as real but rather as an object for which real being may be *claimed*, the intentional object of the act of perception certainly has the character of being *intended* as a reality; it is *given* in the way realities are given. Clearly, it is not legitimate for phenomenology to *presume* that such an object *is* real, for it is just this *intending* (cognizing) of reality that is in question. But the methodological exclusion of "reality" does not *by itself* mean that one can simply determine the intentional object of an act of perception as an "abstract entity," since it is the object of a *perceptual* act and not an act of *abstraction*.

A distinction must be made here. On the one hand, it may emerge *as a result* of phenomenological analysis that the objects of perceptual acts do in fact prove to enjoy a particular "ideal" mode of being. According to our interpretation, this is precisely the result of Husserl's later transcendental investigations. But this would not be *as a result* or *an implication* of the procedure of methodical abstraction from the real. Rather, it would only be justified as the result of rigorous phenomenological investigation of the act of perception and of the object of the perceptual act—which certainly does not have the sense of being an "abstract entity" or ideal entity intended through abstractive or ideative acts. On the contrary, it has the sense of being a claimed reality and is investigated *as the object of such a claim*.

On the other hand, genuinely abstract entities are investigated by phenomenology, but their mode of being—as transcendencies—is no less problematic than that of realities. Thus they are also investigated as the objects of certain acts in which such objects are intentional entities. Yet these acts are not acts of perception (in the narrow sense: they may be acts of intuition). They are not acts that intend their object perceptually but that intend it abstractly. Thus there can be no good phenomenological sense to the claim that the investigation of an object as *intentional* is equivalent to investigating an abstract or ideal object. For unlike 'abstract', 'intentional' does not function at this stage as a

---

13. De Boer, *Development of Husserl's Thought*, 146.

specific ontological determination of the object. It is simply a way of limiting the mode in which the object of *any* intentional act can be assumed by phenomenology: it cannot be considered as an "in itself" but only "as it counts for this act." And some intentional objects—the objects of perceptual acts—count not as abstract entities but as individual particulars given through the senses.

§ 7.2. The Intentional Object Is Not an Image or a Sign

Just as the intentional object is not an ideal or abstract entity, neither is it an image. For the similar reasons, Husserl denies that there can be any talk here of an "image theory" of perception, which would say: "The thing itself is (or is at least under certain circumstances) 'outside'; in consciousness there is an image that does duty for it" (*LI*, 436/593).

Husserl deals with this issue in two ways. On the one hand, consciousness of an image presupposes a possible self-givenness both of what functions as the basis for the image—the photograph, the statue—and of the object of which we have the image. He says:

> Since the interpretation of anything as an image presupposes an object intentionally given to consciousness, we should plainly have a *regressus in infinitum* were we again to let this latter object be itself constituted through an image, or to speak seriously of a "perceptual image" immanent in a simple perception, by way of which it refers to the "thing itself." (437/594)

Therefore, image-consciousness can only be understood and analyzed on the basis of a more fundamental analysis of the non-imagined intuitive presentation of objects in their bodily self-presence. There certainly is a particular mode of intentional relatedness which is that of the mediate relation through the image. But to construe the perceptual act as being of the same form as the imaginative act is to do violence to the phenomenological character of the perceptual act. Its very sense, by virtue of which it can be distinguished from (among others) imaginative acts, is precisely that it presents its object "in person." The phenomenological investigation of perceptual consciousness is thus the investigation of "immediate" and "direct" consciousness of its object.

On the other hand, it may simply be argued that perceptual consciousness must be a kind of imaging consciousness because the object that exists in itself does not exist in any way "within" consciousness. The object that *is* "in" consciousness must therefore function as some kind of "image" or even "sign" of the real object in itself.

Husserl's response to this is to point out that the form of the problem is illegitimate insofar as it presupposes a naive theory of being and allows it to establish the form of the problem. Such a procedure is simply unphenomenological. A postulate of the kind that sees the intentional object as a sign or image that refers to a real thing in itself "outside" of consciousness finds no *phenomenological* justification for such an interpretation of the role of the intentional object, since in the case of perception there simply is no image- or sign-consciousness given. That is, in the case of perception the object referred to does not have the character of itself referring to yet another ungiven and further object. Therefore, such an interpretation of the perceptual act could serve no genuine *epistemological* interest, for the supposed *relation* between the intentional object and the real object in itself is not susceptible to any phenomenological (presuppositionless) clarification. On the contrary, epistemological interests can only be served through an investigation of how it is that an object comes to be present for consciousness by investigating that How. In the context of his rejection of the "image" theory, Husserl reaffirms and summarizes the phenomenological imperative:

> We must come to see . . . the general need for a constitution of presented objects for and in consciousness, in consciousness's own circle of essential being. We must realize that a transcendent thing [*Sache*] itself is not present to consciousness merely because a "content" rather similar to it simply somehow *is* in consciousness—a supposition that, fully thought out, reduces to utter countersense—but that all relation to an object is part and parcel of the phenomenological essence of consciousness and in principle can be found in nothing else, even when such a relation points to some "transcendent" thing. (437/594–95)

§ 7.3. The Intentional Object Is Not a Mediating Term

The intentional object is not a middle term or mediating entity through which the knowing relation is established. Husserl's claim reads:

> It need only be said to be acknowledged that the intentional object of a presentation is the same as its actual object, and on occasion as its external object, and that it is countersensical to distinguish between them. The transcendent object would not be the object of this presentation if it were not its intentional object. (439/595–96)

With this passage, Husserl clearly rejects the notion that the intentional object is a middle or mediating term in the knowing relation. He again has good grounds: a mediating term would presuppose a mediating intentional act, something that perceptual intentionality is not. Perceptual intentionality presents its object *originaliter*, "in person."

It seems, though, that this passage puts the achievement of the reduction at risk. Does it not affirm an identification between the intentional object and the real object, something the reduction is intended to distinguish?

This reading would be a *realist* interpretation of the thesis of intentionality and would claim that through the thesis of intentionality Husserl breaks out of the closed circle of consciousness effected by the exclusion of all transcendent affirmations and establishes contact with the real world. Is this interpretation justified?

The first point to make is that it conflicts not only with the general theory of perception in the *Logical Investigations* but also with many of Husserl's explicit statements. But need we find in this statement an internal contradiction within Husserl?

De Boer has offered the definitive interpretation of the passage in question. According to him, the passage quoted above can be used to support a realist interpretation of Husserl (and an interpretation that utterly conceals the motivation of the transcendental radicalization of the reduction) *only* if it is read as a polemic against Brentano, for Brentano maintained a distinction between the intentional and the real object. But Husserl also maintains this distinction.[14]

What can Husserl mean, then, when he affirms that the intentional object of the perception is the same as the actual object of the perception? The key to this is his use of the term *wirklich*—and one should be on guard against any quick (natural and "naive") substitution of 'actual' for 'real'. For *this* particular identification is precisely what the reductive exclusion is designed to disconnect.

According to De Boer the background against which Husserl's troublesome statement of identification is to be read is not Brentano's but rather the Scholastic theory, which is represented here chiefly by Twardowski.[15] Both Brentano and, at this stage, Husserl hold that "behind" the intentional object there is the real thing in itself, the object of the science of physics and presumably the source of the sensations that receive the objectifying interpretation through the intentional perceptual act. This object is ruled out of consideration by the phenomenologist on methodological grounds, an exclusion that can be sustained because—although the nexus of really inherent act-contents establishes from within itself the act as an act of reference and in doing so specifies the *object* of that reference—the object is thematized by the phenomenologist *as* and *only as* it "counts for the act."

Twardowski, however, extends this notion of the term of the intentional relation and claims that "the object existing in itself, which is to be distinguished from the psychical image 'in' us, is the object of the intention." Therefore, continues De Boer,

> he returns to the Scholastic doctrine that we can intend the object outside us. Consequently, he again ascribes to the intentional object its mediating function. . . . It is a point of transition to the real object in the external world. For Brentano . . . the intentional object is the terminus of the intention. Any inner relation between the intentional object and the "real" object is eliminated. For Twardowski, the "actual object of the presentation"

---

14. De Boer points out that: "When he did criticize Brentano, it was on other points: 1) that he conceived of the intentional object as immanent, and 2) that he called this object a 'sign'. He raised analogous objections against the term 'image'; it furthers the confusion between perceptual and significative apperception." *Development of Husserl's Thought*, 194.

15. Kasimir Twardowski, *On the Content and Object of Representations* (1894), trans. R. Grossmann (The Hague: Nijhoff, 1977).

is not the "psychical image of the object" but rather "the object itself. . . . Thus, when someone forms a presentation of an object, he at the same time forms a presentation of a content relating itself to this object. The presented object, i.e. the object toward which the presentative activity, the act of presentation, directs itself, is the primary object of presentation; the content through which the object is directed is the secondary object of the presentative activity." . . . For Twardowski, then, there are two objects of the intention, both of which are presented, albeit in different ways.[16]

This is the doctrine Husserl has in mind when he says that the intentional object of the perception is the same as its actual object. What Husserl means is that, given a phenomenological investigation of the act, there are not two objects given in perception. As De Boer says, "he opposes the doctrine that regards the intentional object only as a mediating term that is presented secondarily, while the primary intention is directed toward another object." Thus the intentional object is the actual object of the perceptual act: "The transcendent object would not be the object of *this* presentation were it not *its* intentional object" (*LI*, 439/595–96). Therefore, De Boer is correct to claim that "Husserl equates the 'object of the presentation' with the 'intentional object'."[17] And because "part of what 'intentional' means for Husserl (as for his teacher Brentano) is 'intended'," Husserl's essential meaning in the passage under discussion is simply that it is absurd to draw a distinction between the intentional object and the object that is *really* intended. "But," De Boer concludes,

> this does not mean that the intentional object is "real" (*wirklich*) in the sense of "existing in itself." For the present, this claim on the part of Husserl is *a descriptive psychological* claim which seeks to do justice to the fact that perception clearly represents a *direct* perceiving of the object without any intermediate term.

§ 8. Phenomenological Reduction as Enclosure

Any realist interpretation of Husserl's statement must be rejected. Rather than seeing this as an *expansion* such that intentionality now becomes an opening to the real world through which the real object then comes to be included within the fund of legitimate phenomenological data, the opposite is the case. In fact the inclusion of the intentional object within the field of legitimate phenomenological data does yield an expansion of the originally conceived "narrow phenomenological sphere," beyond that of the really inherent content of the act. The phenomenological sphere includes the object that is *intentionally* included within it. "*Phenomenology* is accordingly the theory of lived experiences in general, inclusive of all matters, whether really inherent or

---

16. De Boer, *Development of Husserl's Thought*, 192–93. The following quotation is also found here.
17. Ibid., 194–95. The following two quotations also fall on these pages.

intentional, given in lived experiences, and evidently discoverable in them" (*LI*, 765/862).

However, this is only a *qualified* expansion. In spite of Husserl's disagreement with the Scholastics over the *mediating* role played by the intentional object, he is very much in agreement with them regarding the ontological status of the intentional object. For this object is dependent upon consciousness and can exist even if the "real" object does not.

This is a very important result for Husserl. It means that the intentional object of the perception is the actual object intended in the act and that as such the sphere of intentionality is circumscribed through the exclusion of all "transcendencies." After this exclusion (through which the being of the object undergoes a modification and thereby belongs to the sphere of phenomenology) it is hard to see how any "reality"—some entity that exists "in itself"—could come to assert itself within the "narrow phenomenological sphere." For every in-itself that was (somehow) able to assert itself within the phenomenological field would itself undergo the phenomenological modification into an *intended*—claimed—"in itself." Its *genuine* being in itself could thus always be questioned.

The justification—indeed, the philosophical requirement—that the being "in itself," the "reality," of any entity be considered in this way emerges clearly once it is seen that the intentional object is the end-term of perception. Because there is no phenomenologically detectable difference between the intentional object of an act and the object that is really intended by such an act, it simply follows that there can be no phenomenological ground for distinguishing between the actual and the intentional object of perception. Thus the phenomenological exclusion of all "transcendent affirmations" in fact delimits the region of intentionality in such a way that the supposed real being in itself of the object can undergo an abstraction without impoverishing the *experience* of such a perceiving in any way. The question then presents itself as to just what the experiential basis for the attribution of real being could possibly be.

This procedure of reduction yields a strange "all-inclusiveness." On the one hand, the field secured is very broad: it includes intentional life in its entirety, as well as the entirety of objects intended therein. No "datum" given in the experiencing of this intentional life is excluded insofar as it is present as the correlate of the intentional functionary. Thus it would appear that this reduced "all-inclusiveness" does not impoverish experience—in terms of what is experienceable—in the slightest way.

On the other hand, it is also an exceedingly narrow all-inclusiveness. For in spite of the rich supply of objects it includes, it effects a profound ontological impoverishment: no such object has being beyond or other than its being for the consciousness of it. "We must come to see . . . the general need for a constitution of the presented objects for and in consciousness, in consciousness's *own circle* of essential being" (437/594).

As the exclusion of all transcendence, all that is other, the reduction is the establishment of just such a "circle" and is a limitation to that "circle."

The intentionality found through the "proto-epoché" is both very powerful and very weak. It possesses each and every one of its intended objects, and no possible object of reference is forbidden to it. Yet given that each such object is *merely* intentional and given that its attaining of what is real and other than itself is only legitimate as a *claim* to attain in that way, one may wonder whether its intentionality, its being as self-transcending, has not been profoundly weakened, or at least put into question. For it is nothing other than the possibility of such a claim that is now seen to be problematic. Until the problem of the *phenomenological* justification of the attaining of the transcendent has been resolved, the possibility of deceit remains regarding the very being of intentionality, *as* self-transcendence in attaining transcendence. However, the procedure as developed thus far formally and methodologically precludes any such investigation.

Hence two questions remain. First, the being of the transcendent can only be clarified if it in some way shows itself; but the very possibility of the investigation of such a showing seems to be ruled out by the reduction. The question becomes: What would an encounter with the real (phenomenologically) actually be?

Second, if the being of the transcendent, the "in itself," the genuinely other, is in question, then the being of intentionality as the being that *prima facie* transcends itself in attaining the genuinely other must also be in question. For what is the meaning of an intentionality that remains within its own sphere, ignorant of that which is other? The exclusion of the "real" turns out to be another form of closure, one in which the sense of intentional function is already prescribed. In any event, if intentionality is inseparable from that term that, in being attained, reveals intentionality to be a self-transcending, and if all genuine transcendence is systematically excluded from the domain of investigation, then genuinely self-transcending intentionality would be methodologically precluded from showing itself. Investigation would not be possible, then, for the entry of the intentional object into the phenomenological domain is brought at the cost of its transcendence. Once again, it seems as though the phenomenon of intentionality has been obliterated by the abstractive exclusion of all transcendence.

We have shown, then, that the exclusionist moment of the reduction, if taken seriously, precludes the showing of intentionality as genuine self-transcendence and so cannot prepare the way for a resolution of the "riddle of transcendence."

But the abstractive moment is not without difficulties either. As will be seen in the next chapter, a procedure of abstraction cannot help but imply a commitment to precisely the kind of transcendence against which the reduction is directed.

§ 9. Methodological Premonitions of Openness: The Dialectic of Intention and Fulfillment

It is worthwhile to pause here to assess just what Husserl has achieved to this point. We note a somewhat surprising—indeed, worrisome—development. Husserl tells us at the beginning of his investigation that his central problem is that of transcendence. "Transcendence" is now encountered, but only with the ontological sense of being merely "for and in consciousness," constituted—and remaining—in "consciousness's own circle of essential being" (437/594). It seems that in the name of a concern with genuine transcendence—and the nature of the openness that characterizes subjectivity in its relation to that transcendence—Husserl has found himself limited to considering pseudo-transcendencies and to thematizing a subjectivity essentially closed within itself and its own constituted products.

However, such a conclusion must be tempered by a consideration of what James Mensch has called "the dialectic of intention and fulfillment,"[18] which Husserl discusses in detail in the Sixth Logical Investigation. In this phenomenon we find some of the phenomenological resources that will allow Husserl to develop a genuinely phenomenological clarification of "transcendence" and the "openness" of subjectivity to what is beyond it. We also find the resources that will allow us to expand upon Husserl's own self-interpretation and state more clearly the senses in which his phenomenology is a philosophy of openness.

At the stage in Husserl's development currently under discussion, however, he is unable to see the phenomenological significance of this phenomenon because the presupposition proper to the natural attitude is still in play. Only later, as the sense of this presupposition comes to the fore, does he find himself in a position to confront the phenomenological sense of "transcendence" and "openness" that manifests itself here.

Now we shall briefly elaborate the phenomenal dimensions of the dialectic of intention and fulfillment that introduce aspects of "transcendence" and "openness" to the phenomenological investigation and then show the way in which the presupposition proper to the natural attitude operates to conceal the genuine significance of the dialectic.

§ 9.1. "Transcendence" and "Openness" in the Dialectic of Intention and Fulfillment: The Actual Presence of Transcendence "Itself"

Husserl introduces the notion of 'fullness' in the context of the phenomenological clarification of acts that "merely" signify their intended object and those that, by contrast, actually present their intended object—a transcen-

---

18. James R. Mensch, *The Question of Being in Husserl's* Logical Investigations (The Hague: Nijhoff, 1981), 84–85.

dence—"itself." Fullness is a phenomenologically given characteristic that distinguishes intuitive acts; by contrast, signitive acts are "empty." Husserl says:

> What the intention means, but presents only in more or less inauthentic and inadequate manner, the fulfillment—the act attaching itself to an intention, and offering it "fullness" in the synthesis of fulfillment—sets directly before us.... In fulfillment our experience is represented by the words: "This is the thing itself." (*LI*, 597/720)

The group of intentional experiences characterized by fullness are precisely experiences whose very meaning is to render present to consciousness the transcendent object in its actual bodily presence, in its "full" onto-metaphysical being. From the point of view of phenomenological description, fullness is the givenness of the transcendent object. No other experience is available to consciousness that would give, over and above the experiences marked by fullness, "real" or "genuine" transcendence *as meant*.

Furthermore, Husserl again confirms that "transcendence" is marked by—indeed, given as—intuitive fullness when he equates fulfillment with knowledge. Even though a complete coincidence—*adequation*—between a meant object-sense and the intuitive givenness of the meant object precisely as meant is really only a limit case (in this sense, the distinction between indicative and expressive signs Husserl outlines in the First Investigation would be properly speaking a programmatic rather than a phenomenological distinction), the progressive synthesis of identification between the empty signitive intending and the fulfilling intuitive presenting in actuality of the meant sense is nothing other than the ongoing establishment of the *presence* of the transcendent object *itself*. Husserl puts this point as follows: "A concatenation of such relations [of fulfilling synthesis] seems accordingly possible where the epistemic superiority steadily increases. Each such ascending series points, however, to an ideal limit, ... a limit setting an unsurpassable goal to all advances: the goal of absolute knowledge, of the adequate self-presentation of the object of knowledge" (598/720).

In other words, though Husserl maintains that there is always a difference between the sense and the being of the entity, a difference he marks by noting the *inadequacy* of the relation between the intended sense and its intuitive fulfillment, it is still the case that transcendence as such is only given in and through the synthesis of fulfillment. In this progressive synthesis the phenomenologist has found the site where transcendence is manifest: if "knowing" has as its goal the genuine "possession" of genuine "transcendence," then this synthesis is what the phenomenologist must focus his attention on, for epistemic intentionality finds its goal in the ideal limit governing this synthesis. As the object in its fullest disclosure, that limit represents "an unsurpassable goal to all advances." It would be "transcendence itself."

§ 9.2. "Transcendence" and "Openness" in the Dialectic of Intention and Fulfillment: The Experiential Character of Receptivity, Passivity, and Lack

To indicate a second set of issues bearing on the openness of consciousness to transcendence, we briefly turn our attention from the *object* that is intuitively given in fulfilling experience to the distinctive phenomenological character of the *experience* in which the intuitive presence is announced. At this stage Husserl only presents the phenomenological characteristics of these acts in a preliminary way, but we can see here the outlines of a phenomenology of "receptivity" or "passivity" that prepare the way to a rather different—and presuppositionless—investigation into the experience of a "beyond" or "outside." These matters will be taken up in greater detail in the second part of this book when the issue of *facticity* is addressed and shown to provide the basis for a genuinely phenomenological account of the sense of transcendence. For the moment, however, it is enough to draw attention to two remarks Husserl makes in the Sixth Investigation.

The first is that, in discussing the differences between the intending and fulfilling moments of the synthesis in which an object is given as "itself," Husserl makes an observation about the relative *values* of the two moments. He says that "the synthesis of fulfillment involves an inequality in worth among its related members. The fulfilling act has a superiority which the mere intention lacks" (*LI*, 598/720). The question that then presents itself is this: What is the basis of this character of superiority? Is the answer to this question derived from strictly phenomenological grounds or from the implicit or explicit operation of metaphysical assumptions? *Somehow* this experience provides the basis for consciousness's recognition of an encounter with transcendence. Does this experience have the sense of being an encounter with *something foreign or alien*; is it an encounter with a "beyond" via an encounter with a self-limitation? At this point, Husserl offers only the following—and this is the second remark of interest here—*phenomenological* elaboration of the nature of this value difference. He says that in the synthesis of fulfillment the intuitive moment, in having the character of "being the fulfiller" (607/728), manifests a further quality: it *gives* presence, "fulfillment." In this quality of "giving" we may begin to see the basis for an elaboration of the sense of phenomenological transcendence and of consciousness as open; for Husserl goes on to note that the signitive intentions are "in themselves 'empty' and that they 'are in need of fullness.'" In short, despite its interpretative capacities, intending consciousness is in some way characterized by a *lack*—a lack *satisfied* by the givenness of "something" that it is not in the power of intending-interpreting consciousness to produce.

It must be said that Husserl does not develop this investigation along these lines, nor does he take up the directions suggested by the language of description he uses. Only later, after the assumptions proper to the natural attitude have been more fully elaborated and deactivated, can the full import of these descriptions be grasped. As will be seen shortly, the ground for the superiority that Husserl here affirms of the fulfilling intuitive moment is based on metaphysical assumptions still operative at this stage of his development.

§ 9.3. Transcendence and Openness Concealed

It must be stated at this juncture that, though Husserl has arrived—in the dialectic of intention and fulfillment—at one of the most fundamental phenomenological "sites" of the encounter with transcendence and, no less fundamental, at a structure of openness in the being of consciousness, the metaphysical assumptions proper to the natural attitude are still in play. As a consequence a genuinely phenomenological investigation of transcendence and open subjectivity remains blocked. The meaning of 'transcendence' continues to be presupposed and, from a strictly phenomenological perspective, opaque and unapproachable—despite Husserl's identification of the site of openness. To see why this is so, it is instructive to revisit Husserl's analysis of the act of perception and then to place that description back into the context of the metaphysics still in play at the time of the *Logical Investigations*.

We recall that the *Investigations* understands perception as interpretation. As was seen earlier, perception involves the taking of certain really inherent components of the act—the sense data or hyletic data—and "ensouling" them via an interpretative act. Thanks to the latter act, those immanent data come to be taken as "representatives" of an object that appears in and through them. As interpretation, perception thus demands sense contents that are there to be interpreted. It is this fact—together with the essential character of the "givenness" of such contents—that underpins the sense of perception as an encounter with something transcendent to consciousness, something "beyond" and "other" than consciousness, because the presence of such content is beyond the conjuring power of the free interpreting consciousness. It is this sense content or hyletic data that functions as a check of intuition upon interpretation. As Mensch puts it:

> not every significant intention results in perceptual fullness because either the appropriate contents are not present or, if contents are present, they are not such as to sustain its interpretation. One of the essential "characteristics" of actual intuition is, then, the presence of these contents. . . . They are actually experienced contents of consciousness which, by virtue of sustaining a particular interpretation, "point unambiguously to the corresponding contents of the object."[19]

The import of this doctrine lies in a strict distinction between sense and presence: sense is always a result of a act of interpretation, and no object is given

---

19. Mensch, *Question of Being*, 134.

other than as a unity of sense. The fulfilling moment of the act of perception is not the presence of the sense of the object, but rather the experienced indication of the presence of the meant object. In Husserl's terminology these "data" are "representatives" of the meant object, and they act as a check on or limit to the interpretive activity of intending consciousness. Hence possession of the *sense* of the object—even where that sense functions as a moment in an ongoing synthesis of fulfillment—does not *itself* assure us that we have objectively valid intuition, for the fulfilling moments that grant the actual presence of the object are always inadequate to the intended sense; they are only progressively encountered as the synthesis proceeds. In what sense, then, is perceptual—intuitive—consciousness consciousness of transcendence? The answer at this point is because, as Mensch puts it, "sense contents are assumed to have a transcendent source."[20] Why must we assert this? Because, despite the "exclusion" of problematic transcendence from the narrow sphere of phenomenological investigation, the consciousness thereby delineated is still ontologically predetermined as *psyche*, that is, as a part of the (natural) world. *Descriptive* mundane phenomenology abstracts from causal analyses of psychic phenomena but does not put them into question thereby. Though the ontology of the natural attitude is not actually *employed* in the procedure of the descriptive investigations of the *Logical Investigations*, it remains assumed and implied nonetheless.

This allows us to shore up our claim that the meaning of transcendence still remains presupposed and thus phenomenologically opaque, despite Husserl's methodological precautions. Transcendence remains presupposed insofar as the ontology of the natural attitude remains presupposed: transcendence remains unquestioned as *worldly* transcendence, and the opening of consciousness to that transcendence is essentially causal. This can be most clearly understood by referring to an analysis of the subject–object relations in terms of what Mensch calls "the weight of being."[21] It can be stated briefly as follows. In the natural attitude, the attitude of our everyday encounter with the world and the attitude that is still in play in the background of the *Investigations*, the weight of being falls on the objective side of the relation. Here "the object is assumed to have *independent being*, while consciousness—as consciousness *of* the object—is assumed to have *dependent being*." As Mensch goes on to say, this is Husserl's position in the *Logical Investigations*, with the somewhat Kantian qualification according to which the sense of object for consciousness is not a *picture* of the worldly transcendence but the interpreted result of consciousness's interaction with external-causal input. For Husserl, as for Kant, the structuring and perceptual *forms* of knowledge lie within the subject. And

---

20. Mensch, *Question of Being*, 171.
21. Ibid., 86. The next quotation may also be found on this page.

so "the *contingency* of knowledge . . . is overcome by these structuring, *a priori* forms of the subject."[22] However, as Mensch quickly points out, the strength of this position is also its weakness:

> For, according to its schema, the non-relativity of knowledge is bought at the price of an unknowable thing-in-itself. Otherwise put: The necessary *universality* of knowledge is guaranteed, but not its *objective validity* as Husserl defines the term. Thus the *object* or thing *in its own categories* is said to be unknowable. The forms of experiencing consciousness can be said to *cover up* rather than *reveal* these categories.[23]

Thus at this stage Husserl fails to seize the opportunity presented by the dialectic of intention and fulfillment in the *Logical Investigations* for a genuinely phenomenological investigation of the sense of transcendence and the structure of the openness of consciousness. On the one hand, the meaning of 'transcendence' still remains presupposed: thanks to the abstractive nature of the phenomenological reduction, transcendence is still worldly transcendence—outside, yet ontologically comprehending, the psyche. Intentionality is a mode of (worldly psychological) being, which in its intentional functioning "constitutes" objects of knowledge through an interpreting act. Objectivation is interpretation. Given that objects are only present via a *sense*, and given that this sense only arises as a result of an act of interpretation, it can no longer be asserted that the objects that this intentionality knows, as it knows them, are the genuinely transcendent "things" of the natural world whose actual being is necessarily and essentially implied by the abstractive reduction and against which the reduced region attains the (metaphysical) meaning of being a *part* of a more originary and all-encompassing whole, the world. And this holds, despite the descriptive characteristics of the act of intuition outlined above which attempt to give acts of intuition their due as acts of self-transcendence.

Furthermore, the person in the natural attitude, the founding attitude of the scientist as well as the everyday person, already knows in advance what the relation is between this regional intentionality and worldly transcendence. It is one of causation. The object-senses may be the result of an interpretative act on the part of regional intentionality, but genuine transcendence "makes its mark" on the psychological subject through causation, primarily through the senses. These "marks" then function as the data that enter into the interpretations, which render the marks "representatives" of worldly transcendencies.

This whole metaphysics, which Husserl will soon come to identify as the standpoint of the natural attitude, is still presupposed by the thinking found in the *Logical Investigations*. As an operative predetermination of the meaning of transcendence, it prohibits a genuinely phenomenological investigation; the meaning of transcendence remains presupposed.

---

22. Mensch, *Question of Being*, 87.
23. Ibid., 88.

This leads to two problems. First, given the commitment to a causal relation to the genuinely transcendent, the objectifying act that presents itself for phenomenological description cannot be understood as a genuinely *constitutive* act in which genuinely transcendent objectivity comes to presence. These senses are subject-dependent and thus not genuinely transcendent; hence, "genuine" transcendence remains phenomenologically opaque insofar as, functioning through causal relations, it does not present itself as a phenomenon but only as an explanatory term.

Second, the aspects of the experience of "fulfillment" that will later come to reveal a genuinely phenomenological understanding of transcendence—and hence of the openness of consciousness—remain hidden in their significance. Since transcendence is still worldly, the meaning of consciousness's openness to that transcendence is also predetermined: consciousness is open to transcendence as a subject of causation—but the entities that operate causally on this consciousness are not available for *phenomenological* investigation. Consequently, consciousness qua *intentional* is still closed. Only with the transcendental turn, in which the understanding of transcendence proper to the natural attitude is overcome, will Husserl at last acquire the methodological position from which a genuinely phenomenological understanding of transcendence will emerge, along with a genuinely open subjectivity. This will become clearer once what Husserl calls 'facticity' has been discussed.

Chapter Four
Examination and Critique of the Reduction as a Procedure of Abstractive Exclusion

As a methodological procedure intended to establish a rigorous "science" of knowing, the epistemological—now referred to as the phenomenological—reduction seeks to achieve two things: first, freedom from presuppositions regarding both the meaning and possibility of transcendence and the meaning and possibility of intentionality; and, second, the provision of access to intentional functioning. Together these two achievements will bring to light the very emergence of what is now posed as a problem—namely, transcendence—by showing how it is that intentionality effects a going beyond itself.

But does the reduction succeed? Our examination of Husserl's claim that it provides access to functioning intentionality showed that it failed to do so—at least in an unambiguous manner. It remains to determine whether it achieves freedom from presuppositions.

§ 1. Presuppositions Underlying the Procedure of Abstractive Exclusion

We have seen that the phenomenological method developed up to this point is best described as a procedure of abstractive exclusion. However, such a method can genuinely achieve its intended goal of freeing the investigation from presuppositions only if no preacceptances regarding transcendence and intentionality are *already operative* in the *application of that method*. Is this the case?

§ 1.1. Presuppositions Underlying Abstraction

First of all, abstraction requires that a distinction be made within a range of elements and that a division be established between the relevant and the irrelevant, the significant and the insignificant, the valuable and the worthless, the problematic and the unproblematic. But abstraction is not simply this process of making distinctions. Next it is a leaving out of consideration of the irrelevant, insignificant, worthless, or problematic elements. Abstraction thereby achieves a *narrowing of focus*, through which a sub-domain of elements corresponds or through which a sub-domain of elements is given, "purified" of the other kinds of distinguished elements. In this way abstraction suggests itself as a methodical device for delimiting a region, which could in turn offer itself for clarification.

In Husserl's pretranscendental or mundane phenomenology, the first sorting is that of evidences into the categories of 'immanent' and 'transcendent'. Focus is then narrowed to the domain of immanence. Transcendencies do not "disappear" but are "put aside." After the sorting, Husserl indicates the leaving out of consideration by saying that, after reduction, transcendencies "count for nothing" for the phenomenologist.

What is presupposed by such a procedure can be seen by noting a precondition for its application. The region sought by delimitation is first encountered through the process of *sorting*. It is a *subset* of the range of evidences available *prior* to the operation of sorting. That means that the domain delimited through the process of abstraction must always have the ontological meaning of being a part of a larger whole. Were the domain sought not pregiven with the sense of necessarily being a part, that is, a region within a larger whole, then, as a method of providing access through effecting a delimitation, abstraction would not suggest itself.

Abstraction does not *reveal* its secured subject matter to be a region; rather, it seeks to isolate for theoretical investigation a subject matter that is *already* pregiven with the being-sense 'region'. It is by virtue of this presupposition that abstraction is deemed an apposite method. But that means that such a method expresses a prior ontological determination. If intentionality is the domain sought through the method of abstraction, then we face the inescapable conclusion that—irrespective of the hopes of the investigation to proceed in a manner free from presuppositions—the application of such a method not only reveals but also *demands*—as the condition of its application—that the domain of intentionality be pregiven with the unquestioned ontological predetermination of being a "part." Insofar as this determination is not then placed in question by the investigation—and how could it be without entailing the very disappearance of the subject matter?—a presupposition regarding the being of intentionality, as the subject matter of the abstraction, can be found to underlie and motivate the methodical reduction through which it is isolated.

This is a preacceptance that vitiates the claims of the investigation to place all transcendence in question. For insofar as the intentional function is predetermined as a *part*, the existence of a range of being other than the domain of such intentional functioning is necessarily affirmed. The method attempts to isolate an intentional functioning in such a way that all "being other than it" is placed in question. Yet as an abstraction the *method itself* necessarily affirms a domain of non-immanence as that whose being and being-such is left out of consideration by the investigation. It affirms, in other words, a domain of transcendence. The goal of presuppositionlessness regarding the affirmation of transcendence therefore is not met. This "being a part," which is endorsed by the method chosen to isolate it, is what might best be called a *minimal* ontological predetermination of intentionality, for it says nothing about the being of the *whole* that the method of abstraction begins with and then differentiates. The *enrichment* of this minimal determination takes place when the mode of being of the prior whole—in which the abstracted part is originally found—is elaborated. So it is not only beyond the scope of the science of the delimited region to question the ontological status of its region as *part* but also, because the particular ontological predetermination of the prior whole precedes (or is independent of) the sorting of that whole into its parts, the specific ontological determination that the part receives *by virtue of its belonging* to that whole can itself *never* be clarified by the science devoted to that part "in itself"—for the science of the part is not the science of the whole. This means that as long as the subject matter of a science is ontologically determined as a region, which finds its place within a prior whole, there remains an ontological predetermination of that *part* upon which, paradoxically, the special science of the part cannot investigate or pass judgment. That is, the science of the part cannot investigate, or justify predeterminations of, that whole to which the part belongs and in whose being-sense it necessarily "takes part." Thus there must remain a (possibly indeterminate) range of ontological predeterminations and preacceptances regarding any region identified through abstraction, which the science of that abstracted part is powerless to investigate.

The science of the part must therefore always remain provisional. Its results are neither completely adequate to its region—for its region shares in the ontological preacceptances that characterize the whole and that therefore escape the scrutiny of the special science of the part—nor are they final. They await a clarification that can only emerge with the investigation of the preacceptances through which the prior whole is determined to be what it is.

§ 1.2. Presuppositions Underlying Exclusion

The co-functioning of presuppositions in spite of the methodical intention to arrive at freedom from presuppositions can also be seen in the fact that the reduction takes place as an *exclusion*. The presuppositionless domain is to be established by the exclusion of transcendence, after which the genuine sense of 'transcendence' is to be clarified by the investigation of functioning intentionality. But how can something be excluded unless the method of reduction first possesses a notion of what is to be excluded? This is a deep problem for the presuppositionless phenomenology: either transcendence is properly in question, in which case no notion of transcendence is available for use by the reduction, and no transcendence is included, or a notion of transcendence is available and is employed in the delimitation of the region for study, in which case the investigation does not achieve freedom from presuppositions. Rather than allowing transcendence to be clarified first through the investigation of functioning intentionality, the procedure of reduction intended to bring functioning intentionality into view already employs a notion of transcendence.

§ 2. The Actual Practice of Abstraction in Mundane Phenomenology: The Attempt to Establish "Purity" within the General Thesis of the Natural Attitude

These presuppositions become perspicuous in a consideration of the way in which Husserl speaks of reduction as abstractive exclusion.

At this stage he accepts that the intentionality in question is human intentionality. As such it is a part of the whole real world. The task is thus to delimit a part of this real world—the intentional.

He proceeds by speaking, in the *Logical Investigations,* of the unity of body (*Körper*) and lived experience as the "empirical ego" (*LI*, 367/543). As De Boer points out,[1] Husserl also speaks of such a unity as the "empirical person" and identifies the empirical person with the human, thing-like being in the world:

> The ego in the sense of common discourse is an empirical object, one's own ego as much as anyone else's, and each ego as much as any physical thing, a house or a tree, etc. Scientific elaboration may alter our ego-concept as much as it will, but, if it avoids fiction, the ego remains an individual, thing-like object.... (*LI*, 363/541)

Hence for Husserl's epistemological purposes there exists an ontological equivalence between all real worldly transcendencies and the empirical ego. It follows that the domain of non-transcendence Husserl seeks as the starting point for his presuppositionless epistemology *cannot be identical with that defined by the empirical ego*: "If we consider the self-evidence of the *Cogito, ergo sum*, or rather of its simple *sum*, as one that can be sustained against all doubts, then it is plain that what here passes as ego cannot be the empirical ego" (367/543). Clearly the ego-body and its delimiting principle is ruled out as the measure of immanence. But, as we saw above, so is the "purely psychological" stratum, insofar as this is a domain accessed by inner perception. Yet the method of reduction as abstractive exclusion affirms the domain of genuine immanence still to be a component part. But of what is it a part? The only option is: a part of the human being. And this is just what Husserl affirms. *Adequate* perception—the kind of perception that, in yielding the indubitable, is understood as yielding the genuinely immanent—is not identical with "inner" perception. Nevertheless, it is a subset of the range of inner perceptions:

> In the judgment 'I am' self-evidence attaches to a *certain central kernel* of our empirical ego-notion that is not bounded by a perfectly clear concept. If we now ask what could belong to this conceptually undemarcated and therefore unutterable kernel, what may constitute the self-evidently certain, given element in the empirical ego at each moment, it becomes easy to refer to judgments of inner (i.e. adequate) perception. (367/543–44)

This is a very illuminating passage. Certainty—always of interest insofar as it is the mark of genuine immanence—is here asserted to be the mark of the

---

1. De Boer, *Development of Husserl's Thought,* 212.

"central kernel" of the empirical ego, the human being. The sense of the reduction thereby becomes clearer. It is a narrowing of focus, so as to disclose a central kernel of the empirical ego, through the exclusion of all that does not belong to the central kernel. The principle of demarcation is that of adequate givenness.

What we have called 'the minimal ontological determination of functioning intentionality'—its determination as being a part—is clearly affirmed here. But as a kernel of the empirical human ego, a far richer ontological determination of that part is also given *de facto*. With the transcendental turn, this determination is referred to by Husserl as the being thesis of the natural attitude in terms of which the *exclusion*, as part of the reductive method, is enacted.

§ 3. Exclusion

As abstractive exclusion the reduction secures access to functioning intentionality predetermined as a part, as a "central kernel," of a wider, more bountiful, and more primordially given whole. To begin with, this wider whole is the human being itself. Relative to it, reduction secures the adequately given with the pregiven sense of being a peculiarly central or immanent ontological moment of the human being. But more than this, to be human is to be in turn a part of a wider whole; it is to be situated within the world—and precisely as a part of the world.

Despite all abstractive reductions, the intentionality in question is still a human intentionality, and the overarching metaphysical determination implicit in this sense acceptance continues to dominate the meaning of the problem of transcendence. As Eugen Fink says: "It is still a human subjectivity which is at issue when a definite and abstract method purposely disregards man's empirical and concrete being.... Man, at least minimally, is still the basis for abstracting to the epistemological ego."[2] This means that the investigations are always carried out within, as Fink puts it, a "horizon of prefamiliarity"—the ontology within which "human being" is situated. This ontology is pregiven. The normal resistances to psychologism and subjective idealism testify to the evidence of this pregivenness and, though they remain naive so long as they do not issue from a transcendental phenomenological clarification, express a fundamental truth: to be a human subject is *necessarily* to have a world of transcendencies that exist in themselves. The human *is* a being defined in relation to the world. As Fink writes:

> belief in the world is the unique way in which one being, namely man, exists within the world.... To call myself or someone else "man" already implies being certain of myself as one man among others and hence a

---

2. Eugen Fink, "The Phenomenological Philosophy of Edmund Husserl and Contemporary Criticism," in R. O. Elveton, ed. and trans., *The Phenomenology of Husserl: Selected Critical Readings* (Seattle: Noesis, 2d ed., 2000), 70–139, here 133.

knowing of myself as existing within the world as a being related to the world in a conscious manner. Existing-within-the-belief-in-the-world and believing oneself to be a man are one and the same.[3]

In this belief in the world, however, "the world is not objective . . . as if the world stood over against man as a universal unity of acceptances, but rather is man, within the context of his intending of the world, included within this belief itself and encompassed by it."[4]

§ 4. The General Thesis of the Natural Attitude

As a part, the intentionality secured by this reduction is ontologically predetermined as, in Husserl's words, "a little tag-end of the world" (CM, 3). This in turn carries essential and unavoidable implications for the meaning of both intentionality and transcendence:

> Knowing (in the widest sense) is a one-sided relationship of one being (existing in the manner of consciousness) to another being. Being-known is of no concern to the being which is itself known. It is what it is whether it is known, meant, valued, believed, or not. In other words, the being-given of a thing within the consciousness of another being does not touch its reality; it is ontically independent of the knowing being. So certain is it that we can only encounter beings in our experiencing and intending (in one word: in our believing in the world), nevertheless this being does not originate *out of* this belief. This means that the experience of the world, the having-the-world-in-acceptance thematized by psychology, is in itself impotent. To the essence of the natural attitude belongs the differentiation of beings in themselves from beings for us, or, as we say with less precision, the differentiation of the world from our "representation of the world." . . . Developed as a positive science, psychology moves from the start within the self-explication of human experience as being only receptive and impotent. Psychology can now also degenerate into "psychologism" if it should attempt to reduce beings to their being-given, if it should discount the evidence of outer experience and proclaim the transcendent to be a mere acceptance-image, a mere correlate of subjective meaning, or if it should orientate the concept of all non-immanent being along the lines of a "merely intentional object," thereby making the reality of the world an illusion in order ultimately to end with the absolutization of immanence.[5]

If this prior whole, the world, is thematized as Nature, then intentionality, if revealed through abstractive exclusion, is demarcated as a domain of Nature. It is then known as 'psyche'. Thus 'psyche', when used by Husserl, carries what is fundamentally an ontological significance. As such the domain of the psyche is determined according to the general ontological structure of Nature. This in turn must surely establish the meaning of the "intentional" relations effected through the operations of the domain of the psyche, irrespective of any ab-

---

3. Ibid., 103.
4. Ibid., 104.
5. Fink, "Phenomenological Philosophy," 112.

stractive exclusion, for methodological purposes, of being that is transcendent to the psyche.

The ontological meaning of the objectivity that remains within the delimited region is established by reference to that implicitly still-given—though methodically excluded—transcendence. This is a transcendence given along with the apperception that constitutes the intentionality in question as human. The epoché excludes this transcendence but never places it in question. Thus the "purity" established by this reduction remains ever artificial.

§ 5. Conclusion

From the foregoing we can draw the following conclusions. First, in spite of the intention to achieve utter freedom regarding the meaning of the being of transcendence, the reduction, as a method of abstractive exclusion, presupposes the being of a domain of real transcendence whose actuality is never placed in question and whose possibility is never established.

Second, in spite of the world of real transcendence that remains presupposed, the reduction as abstractive exclusion still effects a closure of intentionality upon itself. When thematizing pretranscendental phenomenology as a "phenomenological psychology," Husserl clearly affirms this. To be sure, intentionality is thematized after a fashion, for the intentional pole, the "meant" that is other than the meaning itself, is a legitimate moment of the field from which all "presupposition" has been excluded. Yet, as Husserl says, the only reason for this is that these particular objects are found to inhabit the domain of "pure immanence." They are merely intentional objects; they are nothing more than "transcendencies in immanence." The methodological meaning of the reduction, as abstractive exclusion, is nothing but a denial of any being "in itself" to such "transcendence"; these objects, Husserl says, are "thinkable only as a moment belonging to an ego-subject's own essence" (*Crisis*, 245/242).

Therefore Husserl is not quite correct in saying that in the operation of the reduction transcendence is retained in such a way that "nothing at all can be lost," if by that he means—as he surely does—that the reduction preserves for investigation intentional functioning in the universality of its life. For in fact the meaning of such a reduction, which is effective in bringing about a delimitation, a constriction, is that the phenomenologist could never investigate two vital things: first, the ontic determination of the "transcendence in immanence," a function of the affirmation of the being of a domain of real transcendence that is the ontological (and biological) precondition of the domain of "transcendence in immanence"; and, second, any intentional function that attains a *real* transcendence. Because of the ontology against which the reduction receives its meaning, no "attaining of being in itself" can *in principle* ever be tolerated or acknowledged by the investigation. But we know in fact that as human there are intentionalities that *do* manifest themselves as just such an attaining. Were this not the case, we would not know ourselves as human. What is in fact lost is that range of intentionalities that attain real transcendence, that "break out" of the "narrow sphere" of the purely psychical.

Therefore we can say: the intentionality that is secured through the reduction as abstractive exclusion—the "psychological reduction"—is an intentionality closed in upon itself. Its objects are its own constitutive achievements and are ontically predetermined as mere correlates of a psychic act. This raises questions: Can such a "transcendence in immanence" be called an *object*? In no fundamental—that is, ontological—sense is it *transcendent*, for its being, while not identical with the constituting intentionalities themselves, is nonetheless only what it is as a product of such functions. Its being is utterly assimilated in its intentional possession. Equally, what kind of intentionality is it that does not transcend itself? Insofar as the intentionality secured by the reduction as abstractive exclusion does not show itself as attaining any "otherness," no genuine self-transcendence makes its appearance. Thus, this form of the reduction fails to secure access to its intended domain and is to be rejected as a way of establishing a presuppositionless epistemological investigation.

Chapter Five
The Transcendental Reduction

§ 1. Restatement of the Epistemological Problem in Light of the Ontology of the Natural Attitude

Any phenomenology that conceives intentionality as psyche moves within a "horizon of prefamiliarity," which consists of a particular predetermination of the ontic meaning of both intentionality and transcendence. This horizon provides the conditions that constrain and legitimate any procedure intended to enable the investigation of such ontically familiar intentionality, as well as the interpretation of any results gained thereby. As such it is not possible for a psychology to move beyond this horizon. It follows then that no discipline that remains within this horizon can rise to the epistemological problems that served to motivate phenomenological psychology, for this horizon *predetermines* the answer to that problem a priori: the epistemological relation is an intramundane relation between two mundane entities, whose being as mundane is never placed in question.

Husserl deals with this problem explicitly in the *Cartesian Meditations*. He says: "Even when the traditional theory, as empiristic, bases itself on the usual psychology, it intends not to be merely psychology of knowledge but to clear up the essential possibility of knowledge" (*CM*, 115). This essential possibility of knowledge is nothing other than the essential possibility of "transcendence for me." The problem emerges in the following terms:

> Whatever exists for me, exists for me thanks to my knowing consciousness; it is for me the experienced of my experiencing, the thought of my thinking, the theorized of my theorizing, the intellectually seen of my insight.... All my distinguishing between genuine and deceptive experience and between being and illusion in experience goes on within the sphere itself of my consciousness.... Evidently actual, intellectually necessary, inconsistent, thinkable, probable, and the like—all these are characteristics that occur within the realm itself of my consciousness, as characteristics of the intentional object in question. Every grounding, every showing of truth and being, goes on wholly within myself; and its result is a characteristic in the cogitatum of my cogito.
>
> But how can this business, going on wholly within the immanency of conscious life, acquire objective significance? How can evidence claim to be more than a characteristic of consciousness within me? (116)

This statement of the problem is essentially the same as the first expression found in the *Logical Investigations* and *The Idea of Phenomenology*.[1] The difference—and this is a most significant difference—is that Husserl enriches his later account by placing it *explicitly* within the natural horizon of prefamiliarity. What was previously passed over as unworthy of comment due to its "obviousness" is now specifically drawn into the picture. As situated within that horizon, the previously implicit pregiven humanness of the intentionality that wonders about the meaning and authenticity of its cognitive achievements is now made explicit: humanness is "a fundamental property of my psychic life, is a real property belonging to me, as a man, and to every other man in respect of his purely psychic inner being" (*CM*, 115). That is to say, the abstraction that serves to *isolate* human intentionality does not, in spite of the fact that all extra-psychic predicates are left out of consideration, effect a change in the ontic status of that intentionality.

Therefore the fullest form of the epistemological problem can be expressed as follows: How can I, this man, know whether the activities of my intentional life ever achieve any objective significance, where 'objective' clearly has the sense of 'existing independently of my consciousness of it'? In knowing transcendencies that make their appearance in and through my intentional life, how can I be sure that the claim of these transcendencies to exist independently of this intentionality is not itself an "intentional invention" and, by extension, what could be called an 'intentional deceit'? Is the "being in itself" of the world merely an intentional determination of a being that in the final analysis is nothing more than a "transcendence in immanence"?

However, with the benefit of the explicit statement of this "natural" predetermination of the being of the intentional, Husserl now rejects the very possibility of posing the problem of transcendence in this way. For in terms of the horizon of prefamiliarity "the whole problem is inconsistent" (116). To be human *is* to exist, as Fink points out, "within-the-belief-in-the-world."[2] Thus it is appropriate to wonder:

> Who . . . can rightly ask such "transcendental" questions? As a natural man, can I rightly ask them? As a natural man, can I seriously and transcendentally ask how I get outside of my island of consciousness and how what presents itself in my consciousness as a subjective evidence-process can acquire objective significance? (*CM*, 116)

Husserl immediately answers negatively, recognizing that an intentionality so determined already carries with it, as a function of its very meaning, a commitment to the being of transcendence as being in itself:

> When I apperceive myself as a natural man, I have already apperceived the spatial world and construed myself as in space, where I already have an

---

1. Compare the foregoing passage, e.g., with *Hua* II, 36/28: "transcendence is both the initial and the central problem of the critique of cognition."
2. Fink, "Phenomenological Philosophy," 103.

Outside Me. Therefore the validity of world-apperception has already been presupposed, has entered into the sense assumed in asking the question—whereas the answer alone ought to show the rightness of accepting anything as objectively valid.

The term 'human' is thereby revealed to be an *ontological determination*, a necessary implication being that of real transcendence. That world about which the human epistemologist believes himself to be uncertain and whose being he attempts to investigate and grasp is just as certain and unquestionable as his own humanness. A determination of intentionality as 'human' is equivalent to a determination of the meaning of 'transcendence' vis-à-vis this intentionality as "in itself." Yet surely the epistemological question has a genuine urgency about it. The issue now is to give the problem its correct formulation.

§ 2. The Dual-Directedness of the Horizon of Prefamiliarity

We note first the mutually implicated ontic ordering to which Husserl refers in *Ideas I* as the 'general thesis' of the natural attitude (see *Id. I*, 52).

To qualify 'transcendence' as 'being in itself' is to determine transcendence by reference to an intentionality against which that transcendence is independent. To qualify 'intentionality' as 'human' is to qualify it in such a way as to necessarily implicate it in a belief in transcendence as "being in itself": to be human is to be worldly, to "live, move, and have being" within a domain that has its being *independently* of that intentionality. Thus the ontic determination of intentionality as human does not take place without implicit—and necessary—reference to transcendence.

Nor does the ontic determination of transcendence take place alone, and this mutual reference is nothing other than the "general thesis" proper to the natural attitude. The naiveté of the natural attitude is therefore the taking of this ordering for granted. It is characterized by two moments: on the one hand, it determines intentionality as human and thus as an intramundane, dependent part of the real world; on the other hand, it determines transcendence in relation to this intentionality, which is well defined as psyche: transcendence is that which is external to this inner dimension of the psychical; this transcendence is real and exists in itself.

It thus emerges that the power of the presupposed—as that which, precisely in its familiarity, predetermines—does not ultimately lie in the presupposition of a meaning of 'transcendence', where this transcendence would be considered in abstraction from the intentionality to which that transcendence refers. For such transcendence receives its being-sense as "in itself" only as a partial moment within a more fundamental and all-encompassing ontological precommitment, through which is established an ontic sense of 'transcendence' and 'intentionality' with mutual reference to one another.[3]

---

3. The problem with the psychological reduction was that it only recognized the nat-

This dual-directedness of the horizon of prefamiliarity thus indicates the scope of the transcendental epoché. The suspension of an ontically predetermined transcendence alone is no longer sufficient. Rather, the transcendental epoché must be directed toward the ontological ordering that is deeper than and precedes any exclusive determination of transcendence alone, an ordering that mutually predetermines a meaning of both 'transcendence' and 'immanence'. Husserl now refers to this general, all-embracing prefamiliarity as 'worldliness'.

§ 3. Worldliness as the Presupposition of the Natural Attitude

'Worldliness' is therefore an ontological signifier. It refers to the particular ontological determinations that the terms 'intentionality', 'immanence', and 'transcendence' already have "naturally," prior to any theorizing.[4] As such, worldliness is not a *particular and individual* transcendence, given in an act of actual or possible intuition. As Fink points out: "In the belief in the world . . . the world is not objective . . . as if the world stood over against man . . . but rather is man . . . included within this belief itself and encompassed by it."[5]

Nonetheless, worldliness offers familiarity regarding the being of both transcendence and intentionality and their being in a mutually dependent fashion. Thus, not only is transcendence something *for* the intentional functionary; it is now clear that, as a complex ontic determination, worldliness *itself* is "something" that is "for me thanks to my knowing consciousness." It is a "truth of being" that is accepted and affirmed by me.

With this clarification we are now in a better position to identify the presupposition that has thwarted the development of the investigation thus far. As accepted and affirmed by me, the entire ontic complex referred to in the term 'worldliness' indicates an intentional functioning, an intentional achievement,

---

ural predetermination in one direction, that of transcendence. It failed to see that the determination of transcendence as 'in itself' is only one moment within a more general and fundamental ontological ordering. However, because the predetermination of the meaning of transcendence as 'in itself' is *essentially* implied by the predetermination of the intentionality in question as human and because the psychological reduction does not place this predetermination of the meaning of the intentionality it sets out to investigate into question, the predetermination of the meaning of transcendence that is necessarily part of the meaning of the predetermination of intentionality as human also remains implicitly in operation. And this sense reenters whenever the question of the capacity of phenomenological psychology to resolve ultimate epistemological questions is dealt with.

4. Psychology, phenomenological or otherwise, remains a "worldly" discipline. It studies a region of the world, never "worldliness" itself. And how could it ever not be worldly? To be no longer "worldly" would be no longer to know what the being of the region to be investigated could be; to lose the object-region of study in this way would render one unable to develop a method of approaching that region; and no longer having a method, a way of proceeding, would mean no longer having any such science at all.

5. Fink, "Phenomenological Philosophy," 104.

through which it has come to be for me. In that case, though, just the same epistemological problem arises for it as arose for particular transcendencies. That is: How can something going on inside me—in this case, the intentional functioning through which the set of mutually implicative ontic determinations referred to in the term 'worldliness'—come to have objective significance?

Thus a certain disquiet comes to surround worldliness itself. Its objectivity now becomes as uncertain and as mystifying as the status of transcendence considered by itself. Worldliness itself does not escape the epistemological problem. More than transcendence alone, worldliness is now recognized to conceal a fundamental obscurity regarding its very status. Thus it has itself become problematic.

To affirm worldliness without first clarifying it as an intentional achievement—without, that is, overcoming the obscurity inherent in every "thing" considered as mere positivity—is to affirm a meaning-determination that is itself obscure. As Husserl says, "world is for me a continuous-living pre-judice and is, in certain sense, the totality of my prejudices in my natural life."[6]

Worldliness, more fundamentally than transcendence, becomes the presupposition whose predetermining power must be deactivated so as to enable its phenomenological clarification.

§ 3.1. A Remark on Foundations

Without entering into a full discussion of the meaning of 'foundation' in Husserl's phenomenology, it is nonetheless important to consider briefly the implications of the foregoing analysis. It is clear that the characterization of phenomenology as 'foundationalistic', meaning that it attempts to isolate an absolutely certain foundation upon which all other claims are to be grounded, is no longer really true of the transcendental form of phenomenology. This can be seen from our development of the deepest problem of phenomenology, despite Husserl's misleading use of language in certain instances. This is due to the fact that, despite his criticism of Descartes (e.g. in the First Cartesian Meditation), Husserl is more a captive of Cartesian ways of expressing his problems and procedures than he is aware. This tendency obfuscates the deepest intentions of his own thinking, which, though inspired by Cartesian motifs, is not really Cartesian at all. Descartes's problem concerns *what* is given; Husserl's concerns *how* what is given is given, and the genuine meaning of the being of what is given. That is why Husserl's opening move in the *Cartesian Meditations* is a discussion of various kinds of evidence—adequate and apodictic—and why,

---

6. Edmund Husserl, Ms. C 3 III, p. 9 (cited from Gerd Brand, "Intentionality, Reduction, and Intentional Analysis in Husserl's Later Manuscripts," in Joseph Kockelmanns, ed., *Phenomenology: The Philosophy of Edmund Husserl* (Garden City, N.Y.: Anchor Books, 1967), 197–217, here 206.

employing that distinction, Husserl can announce that, although the "transcendental I-am" (*CM*, 62) is given apodictically, it itself—in contradistinction to objects given non-apodictically—is still not a certain ground in the sense intended by Descartes, because it is not clear how far the apodictic evidence for the transcendental I-am extends. As Husserl says, "at any particular time this experience offers only a core that is experienced 'with strict adequacy,' namely the ego's living present . . . ; while, beyond that, only an indeterminately general presumptive horizon extends. . . ." Husserl quickly draws from this phenomenological fact the conclusion that "a new idea of the grounding of knowledge . . . becomes disclosed: the idea of it as a transcendental grounding" (66). And what is this idea? It is the clarification of givenness rather than the deduction of axioms and the subsequent building, piece upon piece, of the whole edifice of scientific knowledge: "instead of attempting to use *ego cogito* as an apodictically evident premise for arguments supposedly implying a transcendental subjectivity, we shall direct our attention to the fact that phenomenological ἐποχή lays open . . . an infinite realm of being of a new kind as the sphere of a new kind of experience: transcendental experience." In short, the phenomenological reduction leads not so much to an axiom as to a "field of work" (70) that is to be investigated rather than possessed and put to use.

Thus 'grounding' in Husserl's thought develops its own peculiar meaning. Here, the possible senses of 'ground', 'being grounded', and 'need for grounding' must all show themselves through phenomenological analysis. A presupposition is a problem not because it is a claim that is "not grounded" but because its ontological status is not yet clear. Such a lack of clarity, such ambiguity or obscurity of sense, is for Husserl what constitutes its being a presupposition. The reason why a presupposition ought not to be affirmed—which in this context means: taken by the philosopher with the definite sense of *not being in need* of clarification—is not because it lacks an axiomatic "ground" but because, as its sense is obscure, unclear, ambiguous, such an affirmation would be an affirmation of something whose meaning and possibility remain obscure, unclear, or ambiguous. As such, transcendental reduction cannot be understood as the exclusion of presuppositions because such a procedure would require for its effective execution a clear and unambiguous notion of what is to be excluded. Yet it is just this that is now seen to be lacking.

§ 4. Transcendental Reduction

'Worldliness' is the title for a fundamental and determining presupposition that necessarily remains in operation when, despite best intentions, the search for freedom from presuppositions takes the form of an abstractive exclusion. Worldliness must thus *itself* be investigated as an intentional achievement. But how is it possible to investigate worldliness as an intentional achievement without thereby investigating, as a matter of fact, *human* intentional achievement?

In answer to this problem Husserl offers the transcendental reduction. Born of the failure of reduction as abstractive exclusion, it is a method very different from the psychological-epistemological reduction, both in the meaning of its reducing and of what undergoes reduction. It has two moments. One is recognized as epoché and could be called "negative" insofar as it is a moment of abstention, of "loss" (though this word must be used very carefully here). The other is reduction proper and could be called "positive" insofar as it is a reclaiming of the originally obscure transcendence and intentional functioning through phenomenological clarification.

§ 4.1. The Negative Moment: Transcendental Epoché as a "Defamiliarization of Ontic Predeterminations"

Two themes are in need of clarification here. First, *what* is it that actually undergoes epoché? Second, *how* does this take place; or, more simply, what is the properly transcendental epoché?

The clue to understanding the properly *transcendental* form of the epoché lies in Husserl's claim that it is both "universal" and "limited" (*Id. I*, 56). Let us attempt to decipher this qualification.

We have already seen that one *cannot* exclude the term of the act from a study of the act as intentional; it now becomes clear that transcendence is not the fundamental problem. Problematic is rather a particular and predetermining ontic ordering that we call worldliness, which, beyond providing an ontic determination of transcendence, also ontically determines intentionality as human. The idea is this: the epoché is universal in that it is a deactivation of worldliness itself; it is a deactivation of the fundamental—and for that reason "natural"—ontic ordering. The entire "natural" ontic ordering of the world is to be deactivated.

But the epoché is "limited" in that it is *limited to* that ordering of the world and does not affect the being or the being-given of the world itself. It thus generates a *defamiliarization*, though not an exclusion or loss of being. Husserl clarifies this in very explicit terms in a marginal note from 1929 to *Ideas I*: "The modes of acceptance operative in naive experiencing, the naive effecting of which is one's 'standing on the basis of experience' (without having put oneself on that basis by a particular purposing and decision), I put out of operation, I deny myself that basis."[7] The phenomenologist exercises epoché regarding

---

7. *Hua* III/2, Beilage 35, 585; cited by Kersten in his translation on p. 61 n. 30. Husserl continues: "And yet the old course of my experience goes on as it always has, except that this experience, modified by the new attitude, no longer supplies the 'basis' on which I was standing up to now. In this manner I exercise the phenomenological epoché...." (The 1976 edition of *Ideen I* [*Hua* III/1-2], ed. Karl Schuhmann, establishes the corrected text of the three editions published during Husserl's lifetime; the second volume contains revised and corrected texts of the supplementary material found in Biemel's edition along with material

worldliness, the ontic ordering as such, not regarding single transcendencies. Because the general thesis *mutually* implicates its predetermination of both transcendence and intentionality, Fink offers the following methodological stricture:

> It is important here to guard against a possible misinterpretation. One does not perform the transcendental epoché in two steps, first disconnecting the belief in the being of the external world, and then, by means of a supplementary disconnecting, the self-apperception of the subject of beliefs as man. The reverse order is equally incorrect.[8]

Because it is worldliness itself that has been recognized as the fundamental presupposition, *both* natural predeterminations—those of transcendence and of intentionality—fall under the epoché at one and the same time. Fink writes:

> In one act, which cannot be made more radical, and with one stroke, the absolute and concrete apperception of the world, or the belief in the world located within it, is bracketed. Included within this bracketing is the constant self-apperception of the "human ego" with respect to its being and its possession of a particular nature. All single and natural human acts, together with the pregiven world which is their constant acceptance-background, are *eo ipso* subject to the reduction.[9]

But though worldliness may no longer function as ground for the philosopher, the world is not thereby lost. As Husserl says: "The world is and remains for me the one I always accept at face value—the reduction does not alter this fact in the least."[10] Thus under the scope of the epoché the world is not lost or excluded. This investigation *remains* concerned with "every sort of existent itself, real or ideal...."[11] After the epoché, Husserl says, the "whole natural world"—the archetypal transcendence—"is continually 'there for us,' 'on hand,' and ... will always remain there for consciousness as an 'actuality' even if we choose to bracket it" (*Id. I*, 56).

Because of the inseparability of the intended object from the act in which it is intended, this thematization of functioning intentionality in the universality of its structures now has the following implication: no real transcendence can be excluded from the field of transcendental phenomenological investigation. Husserl affirms this unequivocally: "likewise everything *meant* in such accepting or positing lived experiences of consciousness (the meant judgment, theory, value, end, or whatever it is) is still retained completely" (*CM*, 60).

---

not found in that edition, including Husserl's marginal notes in his personal copies of *Ideen*—identified as Copies A, B, C, D.) References to *Hua* III/2 are followed by corresponding references to Kersten's translation.

8. Fink, "Phenomenological Philosophy," 105.
9. Ibid., 106.
10. Husserl, Ms. B I 5 ix, pp. 27–28 (cited from Brand, "Intentionality," 207–8).
11. Ibid., p. 85. Note how different this statement is to that of the first, exclusionist form of the reduction.

We thereby *limit* the applicability of the epoché *to an ontic ordering* of the world, with the result that by this limitation the world itself remains given. But how is this limitation to be understood? On our interpretation, it is intended to indicate the peculiar way in which *nothing is lost* in the universal epoché—or, more precisely, to indicate the precise meaning of the way in which something is lost. Husserl gives us the key when he says: "We put out of action the general thesis that belongs to the essence of the natural attitude; we place in brackets anything and everything that this thesis encompasses *in an ontic respect*" (*Id. I*, 56).[12] 'In an ontic respect'—*only* with respect to being is something lost, though not, as we saw, the being of those real transcendencies themselves. But what is it to bracket with respect to being—and universally so—while not losing this being? The key lies in the clause Husserl adds to the passage just cited: "*thus the entire natural world* that is continually 'there for us,' 'on hand.'"

The word to note here is 'natural'. It determines both the universality and the limitedness of the transcendental epoché: the epoché applies to the particular ontic ordering designated by the term 'worldliness' and is *limited* to that ordering. Although the entire real world remains given just as it was before, the natural predetermination of its being is now identified as the presupposition to be investigated. The revocation of complicity is thus limited to complicity in the set of ontological predeterminations referred to in the term 'world'. Thus the meaning of transcendental phenomenology's depowering of presuppositions can be defined as the deactivation of the general thesis proper to the natural attitude and is nothing other than this. It is not "the real world" that is the presupposition phenomenology must deactivate but the *natural ontological predetermination of* that world. It is this natural ontological predetermination that is "lost," and never the world, which continually remains given. It is thus a particular determination of the real, and not the real itself, that is the presupposition to be deactivated.

Therefore what undergoes epoché is not the world itself but a particular positing that gives the world a particular ontic meaning. The transcendental epoché, this "putting out of action," is *not* directed against the *term* of the intentional function but against the *thesis in which* such terms receive a particular ontic determination.

§ 4.2. The Meaning of Epoché

We have just seen what the transcendental epoché is directed against. But what is the actual operation of the epoché? To this we now turn.

The transcendental epoché retains real transcendencies, but with a "change of value" (*Id. I*, 55). The change of value is this: from unproblematic to problematic, hence from what is present as taken-for-granted to what is

---

12. My emphasis.

present as "dogma." Worldliness, now problematic, can no longer function as ground, the reduction

> only prevents me from taking the real world in the way in which it always seems to be real, and continues to pass for ground, as pregiven being-horizon. . . . But when in reduction I deny myself the ground of all my questioning about concerning the natural world . . . this does not alter the fact that it continues to seem what it was before, in all its foundations from which this being took shape for me. How are we to understand the retention of all that is naturally given, yet with a change of comportment? Let us try to clarify the meaning of this change of comportment in terms of just what it is that is no longer available to the philosopher as unquestioned, as, therefore, foundation.[13]

Epoché does not signify the *exclusion* of the world, much less the loss of its being. Rather, it signifies a *change* of the natural *comportment* toward it. Detecting a problem with worldliness, the phenomenologist no longer has it present with obviousness or clarity.

Worldliness now takes on a moment of *unfamiliarity*. The said change of comportment is nothing but a methodological recognition of this, that what was once obvious and clear was unproblematic and therefore *simply believed* in. Now, however, the element of unfamiliarity demands a "de-activation of the belief"[14]—and the epoché gives this its due. This means that the transcendental phenomenologist *revokes complicity* in worldly ontic ordering.

In particular, this means, on the one hand, that all "natural" transcendence is defamiliarized. It is no longer to be taken for granted that "being in itself" is to be investigated under the title of 'transcendence'. That is why Husserl says of the epoché, again in a marginal note to *Ideas I*, that "with a single stroke we bracket the in-itself and everything in itself."[15]

On the other hand, the deactivation of the general thesis can only occur through the deactivation of the natural predetermination of this intentional life as human. In Fink's words:

> As the persistent and radical deactivation of the belief in the world, the epoché is the disconnecting of the belief in the human performer of beliefs, that is, the bracketing of the world-belief's self-interpretation by which it apperceives itself as being in the world.[16]

The most precise account of this deactivation is to be found in the *Cartesian Meditations*, where Husserl points out that in its securing of functioning intentionality the transcendental epoché, unlike Descartes's procedure, does not rescue something that remains "a little tag-end of the world" as the dimension of presuppositionlessness. For such a "tag-end," no matter how abstract, how

---

13. Husserl, Ms. B I 5 ix, pp. 27–28 (cited from Brand, "Intentionality," 207–8).
14. Fink, "Phenomenological Philosophy," 104.
15. Insertion from Copy A of *Ideas I*. See *Hua* III/2, 485/61 n. 29.
16. Fink, "Phenomenological Philosophy," 104.

purely formal, how attenuated, already sustains an essential reference to the world of which it is a tag-end; its attenuation presupposes and expresses this. Only the peculiar doubly directed transcendental epoché deactivates the being-sense of intentionality as such a "tag-end." Husserl says as much in no uncertain terms (distinguishing the transcendental epoché from the mundane psychological reduction, which he regards as an abstraction):

> This ego, with his ego-life, who necessarily remains for me, by virtue of such epoché, is not a piece of the world; and if he says, "I exist, *ego cogito*," that no longer signifies, "I, this man, exist." No longer am I the man who, in natural self-experience, finds himself *as* a man and who, with the abstractive restriction to the pure contents of "internal" or purely psychological self-experience, finds his own pure *"mens sive animus sive intellectus"*; nor am I the separately considered psyche itself. Apperceived in this "natural" manner, I and all other men are themes of sciences that are objective, or positive, in the usual sense: biology, anthropology, and also (as included in these) *psychology*. (*CM*, 64)

However—and this is the circumstance that makes transcendental phenomenology possible as an actual investigation of a field of experience—this deactivation of the natural predetermination of this intentionality does not result in the disappearance of the intentional life, it does not compromise its being-given. Just as the transcendencies that have become subject to the universal epoché remain, likewise the intentional life that has also fallen under the epoché *remains*. Husserl says: "The epoché can also be said to be the radical and universal method by which I apprehend myself purely: as ego, and with my own pure conscious life, in and by which the entire objective world exists for me and is precisely as it is for me" (60).[17]

As a deactivation of these natural predeterminations of the transcendent and the intentional, both the transcendent and the intentional are *retained*, but rendered unfamiliar. As Fink states: "The reduction . . . does not

---

17. This is an intentionality whose self-transcending—whose presenting of the transcendent—is itself the matter of investigation. As such it is not human intentionality. The defamiliarization effected by the transcendental epoché bears on an intentionality understood in a much more radical sense than can ever be the case in psychology. Husserl writes: "It is necessary to dismantle everything that already pre-exists in the sedimentations of sense in the world of our present experience, to interrogate these sedimentations relative to the subjective sources out of which they have developed and, consequently, relative to an effective subjectivity. This is not the subjectivity of psychological reflection, of a subject perceiving itself situated in the presence of this world as already complete. It is, on the contrary, the subjectivity whose operations of sense have made our world that is pregiven to us what it is, namely, *our* world. . . . We then understand ourselves, *not as a subjectivity that finds itself in a world* ready-made, as in simple psychological reflection, but as a subjectivity bearing within *itself, and achieving, all of the possible operations to which this world owes its becoming*. In other words, we understand ourselves in this revelation of intentional implications, in the interrogation of the origin of the sedimentation of sense from intentional operations, *as transcendental subjectivity*" (*EJ*, 47–48/48–49).

lead to a being already known in its general structure.... The reduction leads us into the darkness of something unknown, something with which we have not been previously familiarized...."[18]

§ 4.3. Defamiliarization of the Epistemological Problem

Thanks to the defamiliarization of the ontology of worldliness effected by the transcendental epoché, the epistemological problem can no longer be posed in terms that derive their meaning from that ontology. Fink says: "In contrast to the psychological 'epoché,' the phenomenological epoché is not a method for delimiting an area within the world, but is rather a method for going beyond the world by *removing limits*...."[19] These limits are nothing other than the ontic predeterminations effected within the natural attitude. Therefore, the transcendental defamiliarization means:

> Within the context of the belief in the world which has become its theme, phenomenology cannot in principle distinguish between the simple givenness of that which is accepted and a "something" which might be independent of it. In other words, the *transcendental* acceptance-relation is not identical with the intramundane acceptance-relation which alone is relevant to psychology.

The defamiliarization of the epistemological problem can best be seen in noting the distinction between the psychological and transcendental intentional correlates or, in Husserl's technical terminology, "noemata." In an intentional psychology, the intentionality in question is human. Considered as the correlate of such intentional functions or "noeses," the noema is not genuinely transcendent: it is a "meaning" that is related to the genuinely transcendent object in some way yet to be specified. These distinctions follow necessarily from the ontology of the natural attitude. But the transcendental concept of the noema can only be understood within the horizon established by the transcendental reduction. As Fink says:

> Just as the epoché does not disconnect the intramundane belief and is not a reduction to the inner sphere of the psychical (together with the "representation of the world" lying within it) but discovers, by bracketing the world, that belief in the world which is to be bracketed ... so also does the epoché present the possibility of determining the correlate of this belief, which, formally expressed, is its "noema." In other words, the transcendental noema is the world itself viewed as the unity of acceptances contained within the belief which belongs to transcendental subjectivity's flowing world-apperception. If the psychological noema is the *meaning* of an actual intentionality which is to be distinguished from the being itself to which it is related, then by contrast the transcendental noema is this being itself.[20]

---

18. Fink, "Phenomenological Philosophy," 120.
19. Ibid., 113. The next quotation in the text also falls on this page.
20. Ibid., 117.

The question of the relation between the noema and something that exists in itself and that somehow corresponds to it no longer is the focus of the transcendental investigation. It thus becomes clear that the noema's relation to its object must be considered differently according to whether the investigation takes place within the natural predetermination of being or the unfamiliar horizon established by the transcendental reduction. Again, we cite Fink:

> The psychological noema refers to an object which is independent of it and which announces and exhibits itself within this noema. The transcendental noema cannot refer to a being beyond and independent of the infinity involved in such endless identification; the transcendental noema is the being itself, and is so in the hitherto unknown depths of its hidden meaning of being as transcendental acceptance. Here "relation to the object" only has the sense of referring an actual noema (i.e., the correlate of an isolated transcendental act) to the manifold of act-correlates which, through the synthetic cohesion of constant fulfillment, first forms the unity of the object as an ideal pole.[21]

Therefore the phenomenological problem of transcendence no longer has the meaning of the traditional problem of knowledge. The reduction is no longer a delimitation to a particularly privileged region of immanence, but is rather a *revelation*. That Husserl sees this aspect clearly is attested by a marginal note to *Ideas I* in which he alters his original statement that the reduction leads to the "acquisition of a new region of being never before *delimited*" to "acquisition of a new region of being never before *exhibited*" (*Id. I*, 58).[22] And in this mode of exhibition lies the key to phenomenology's way of dealing with its newfound field of unfamiliarity.

§ 4.4. The Positive Moment: Reduction Proper

That the reduction allows a vital supplement to be seen and then investigated becomes clear from the following.

The defamiliarization it effects is not loss of world or transcendence but only of a naive comportment to world or transcendence. It is the retention of what has finally been recognized as phenomenology's true problem. Worldliness is no longer obvious and unquestioned regarding its status or meaning; it enters the purview of phenomenology as a mere claim whose genuine sense is now to be established. In fact, insofar as the reduction reveals worldliness to have its ground in something *other* than itself, Gerd Brand is justified in saying that "the reduction does not make the world disappear but, on the contrary, makes it come to the fore; it is the positive bringing to light of the original world."[23] This can be seen when it is realized that such a way of taking the pre-

---

21. Ibid., 118.
22. My emphasis. The last word was inserted in Copy A. See *Hua* III/2, 486/63 n. 4.
23. Brand, "Intentionality," 207.

supposed supplies it with something. To consider worldliness as something *claimed* is to consider it in relation to the *achievement* in which such a claim is made—that is, to consider it in relation to the intentional achievement through which it comes to be present to the intentional functionary. Hence this radical alteration of its naive acceptance is actually the first step in a genuine *recovery* of worldliness, because in thematizing it as a "unity of acceptances lying within the life of the reductively disclosed transcendental subjectivity"[24] the reduction supplies "the accepted" with something that in fact always accompanies it. The reduction brings back (reduces) the transcendent—the accepted—to its origin in the intentional life of acceptance. By disclosing worldliness—as unity of acceptance, as the object of an (implicit) intentional affirmation—as only naively conceived of as without origin, the reduction helps it, as Michael Theunissen says, "to become what it is."[25] Theunissen writes further:

> As the discovery of the origin, phenomenology remains an overcoming of naiveté as the forgetfulness of origin. On the other hand, that which has to be reduced is not in any way altered insofar as it is only that which has arisen from the origin and is therefore still contained within it. The only effect that the reduction has upon it is that it locates it in the origin in which it is intrinsically rooted.[26]

Thus one must recognize a "positive kernel within the negative shell of the epoché."

Husserl's procedure is to allow the recognition of worldliness as a *claim* to illuminate this *claiming itself*. In so doing, one is to be *led back* to the functioning through which what appears shows itself: we "reduce" it. This operation provides 'reduction' with its meaning in Husserl's phenomenology: to reduce is to lead back. Thus worldliness is to be clarified regarding its meaning and possibility by investigating how it is that worldliness originarily comes to be claimed, to be affirmed. Everything that is for me, Husserl says, "gets its sense and acceptance or status in and from me myself" (*CM*, 60). The task then is to investigate precisely this accepting in order to determine how it is that the accepted legitimates or shows itself. Having attained a properly phenomenological comportment,

> I do not simply accept the pregiven world in its being and being-thus, but I thematize the pregivenness of the world and of this concrete world as being and being-thus, exactly in the flowing modes in which consists this being, pregiven-to-me, having this or that meaning for me, and verifying itself in this or that way.[27]

---

24. Fink, "Phenomenological Philosophy," 113.
25. Michael Theunissen, *The Other*, trans. Christopher Macann (Cambridge, Mass.: MIT, 1984), 24.
26. This and the next passage cited may be found on ibid., 25-26.
27. Husserl, Ms. C 3 III, p. 9 (cited from Brand, "Intentionality," 205-6).

Through reduction the naiveté with which worldliness functions and predetermines meaning in the natural attitude is overcome by the explicit addition of its "supplement": the intentionality through whose functioning it comes to presence. We shall now seek to clarify the *status* of the worldliness of the world and its objects by considering the relation of that achieved significance to the intentionality that achieves it—by considering, in other words, how "the achieved" is related to its "ground."

This positive kernel grants transcendental phenomenology both its method and its subject matter. Having allowed the supplement of worldliness (where worldliness is considered as an acceptance) to reveal itself, the procedure for resolving the status of that worldliness suggests itself: one must investigate the How of its acceptance, by investigating the intentionality that, in its functioning, achieves that acceptance. The appropriateness of this method derives from the fact that any transcendence can only be for an intentional functionary as an achieved meaning—which presupposes in turn the functioning through which acceptance of that meaning takes place. In Husserl's words: "No being or being-thus for me, whether as actuality or as possibility, except as *accepted by me*" (*FTL*, 207).[28] Husserl points to the investigation of this supplement in the following:

> I begin . . . by questioning that which has in me, under the heading 'world', the character of the conscious, the experienced, and the intended, and which is accepted by me as being; I ask what it looks like in its being accepted thus; I ask how I become conscious of it, how I may describe it, how I can designate it . . . how what is subjective in this way manifests itself in different modes, what it looks like in itself, as experienced or as intended as this or that, or what this experiencing itself as experience of the mundane looks like, how it is to be described, what kind of achievement it is that brings about in me a world of this typical existential character. I ask how all these manifold experiences of our consciousness of world meld into the unity of a common achievement by which, across multiple subjective [elements], a unity of one supposedly objective thing is found and by which . . . a unity of one objective universe continuously manifests itself. That is the general theme opened up by the reduction. . . .[29]

---

28. This holds equally for the affirmation 'being in itself' and, most importantly, for the affirmation 'transcendent being'. Otherness must show itself originarily at some point. As Gerhard Funke puts it in his "A Crucial Question in Transcendental Phenomenology: What is Appearance in its Appearing?" (*Journal of the British Society for Phenomenology* 4 [1973], 47–60, here 48), after the phenomenological revolution, "[m]etaphysics . . . is no longer a knowledge of provinces of being and things hidden behind the phenomena: on the contrary, if the problem of constitution has been firmly grasped, it is understood to deal with the acts to be supposed prior to all having of objects—acts in which an intentional correlate of meaningful processes comes into view, unfolds itself, so that a 'something' can at all be spoken of. Even the so-called metaphysical object is a phenomenon, since it exhibits itself as this and that."

29. Husserl, Ms. B I 5 ix, p. 31 (cited from Brand, "Intentionality," 209).

§ 5. Thematization of Transcendence and Intentionality through the Transcendental Reduction: Transcendence as Transcendental Acceptance; Intentionality as Transcendental Acceptor

§ 5.1. Transcendence as Phenomenon: The Extent of the Phenomenon

As Husserl puts it, "nothing exists for me otherwise than by virtue of *the actual and potential performance of my own consciousness*" (*FTL*, 207). This enables us to establish the phenomenological sense of the phenomenon: the posing of the transcendent (the world) in terms of its origin—which is to say, in terms of the performances through which it comes to presence—is nothing other than the rendering of the transcendent as "phenomenon," for to do so is to pose it in terms of its appearing. As such the term 'phenomenon' does not signify any impoverishment of being but an enrichment; the phenomenon is the transcendent located in the origin in which it is intrinsically rooted. In short, all transcendence is now thematized by transcendental phenomenology as "transcendental acceptance." Therefore worldliness, as the givenness of worldliness to me thanks to the intentional achievement of its meaning as worldliness, also comes to be thematized as transcendental acceptance.

Equally, any presence that has its presence as an acceptance, as the result of an accepting, an intentional achieving, is now understood by phenomenology as transcendent; for as accepted it manifests an ontological difference from the intentional accepting. Phenomenology becomes *transcendental* upon the commitment of the philosopher to thematize all possible transcendence in this way. Yet it is not only transcendence "pure and simple" that falls under the heading of 'phenomenon', but subjectivity as well insofar as it is also present as acceptance-correlate. 'Intentionality as human' is definitely an acceptance-correlate; 'intentionality as human' thereby falls under reduction and is thereby rendered as phenomenon:

> For an understanding of the true and genuine sense of transcendental philosophy it is decisively important to lay hold of the fact that *human being*, and not *only human organism* but also *human psyche* (no matter how purely the human psyche may be apprehended by internal experience), are *worldly* concepts and, as worldly, apply only to objectivities of a *transcendent apperception*, which therefore are included, as constitutional problems, within the universal transcendental problem, the problem of the transcendental constitution of all transcendencies, nay, all objectivities of whatever sort. (223)

The *phenomenological* meaning of the distinction according to which it is recognized that "I, the constituting ego, am not identical with the ego who is already worldly" (211) is simply the recognition of the demand that the subject as worldly, as achieved significance, indicates, in its very status as something *given through meanings*, an actual intentional performance of my own consciousness through which subject-as-meaning receives its whole being-sense.

The sense of the phenomenological problem is such that this very functioning must be "consulted" (207) if the status of subject-as-affirmed (i.e. human being) is to be legitimately understood. Only by an uncovering of the "performance" (215) that constitutes the being-sense of this worldly intentionality can the philosopher legitimately know what can be assigned to that being-sense. As a legitimacy, human being points back to a "pertinent intentionality" from which it has received that legitimation. "I must," Husserl says, "turn back and seek out the configurations and contents of the actualities and potentialities that function as sense-constituting for this being-sense" (214).

The meaning of the transcendental reduction's establishment of a difference within subjectivity is thus not that of denying being to the transcendental functionary—by dis-identifying transcendental and human subjectivity. Rather, it is the radical freeing of the "mode" of subjectivity that is present as originarily affirming intentionality from "everything that gives it the significance of a reality in the world" (227). Husserl uses the transcendental reduction to dis-affirm the identity between worldly subjectivity and subjectivity in whose functioning worldliness receives legitimation in order to isolate worldliness as an intentional clue.

§ 5.2. Intentionality as Transcendental

'Phenomenon' names the new way in which transcendence is held after the transcendental defamiliarization effected by the epoché. But what can be said of the way in which that originarily functioning intentionality is present for the investigation? It is to be characterized as 'transcendental'.

At first this term carries a "purely negative and prohibitive"[30] meaning. 'Transcendental' refers to the fact that, upon defamiliarization, intentionality can no longer be taken as "a little tag-end of the world." However, a primally positive determination of the intentionality that the reduction reveals is also brought to the fore with this de-familiarization. This intentionality knows itself minimally here as "transcendental acceptor." As Fink says:

> The epoché structures the basic problem of phenomenology, the transcendental problem of the world, by discovering the true "subject" and subjective life out from which the belief in the world emerges (inquiring beyond man as a unity of acceptances lying within the belief in the world), thereby recognizing and breaking with the imprisonment of man as such.[31] In disclos-

---

30. Fink, "Phenomenological Philosophy," 124.
31. Given the current talk of the 'decentered subject' and its role in various attacks upon phenomenology and given the often naive notions of the 'subject' under discussion therein, one could begin to see precisely in this transcendental defamiliarization a prototypical "decentering" of the subject. But this only reinforces the centrality of the "functioning intentionality" through whose life such decentering can occur, and doubles the urgency of undertaking an investigation of the meaning of this "anonymous functionary."

ing the world as a universe of transcendental acceptances, the epoché makes possible for the first time a problematic which does not itself stand *upon the basis of the world* (i.e., which does not stand within the natural attitude's imprisonment within the world, but which is "opposed" to the world). Phenomenology's inquiry into the *being of the world* passes beyond all questions raised by a philosophy with a "natural orientation." This inquiry is not preoccupied with the being of the world itself, but investigates this being by recognizing that the being of the world is "transcendental acceptance" and by tracing it back to the "transcendental subjectivity" in whose life the world is accepted and "held to be valid."[32]

Though unable to affirm humanness of this originary intentional functionary, it is nonetheless actual. This intentionality is "subjectivity functioning as primal source"; it is functioning intentionality "as the primal locus of all objective formations of sense and validity" (*Crisis*, 102/99). It is thus the *ground* of phenomena, of the accepted; in this it is transcendental.

§ 5.3. Transcendental Intentionality as Concrete and Actual

Functioning intentionality "loses" that which makes it "subjectivity in the world" precisely in the sense that the being-determination 'worldly' is now recognized to be a problem. This subjectivity is "no longer worldly" insofar as one can say in a very serious sense that, until "transcendental clarification" has resolved the matter of its status, one would not genuinely know what one was affirming of functioning intentionality when affirming worldliness of it. Clearly, then, this "loss" is not the discovery of yet another and different subject-entity, which would be identifiably distinct from human being in the world, in a worldly sense of distinctness. Rather, it is the loss of a naively taken-for-granted right to affirm that the being of this subjectivity-for-the-world is "worldly."

In affirming a difference between transcendental and worldly subjectivity, Husserl in no way affirms anything of ontological import for transcendental subjectivity: the recognition of this difference is not the positive discovery of a *being* whose mode of being is "unworldliness." The transcendental epoché is utterly impotent to determine the ontological status of transcendental subjectivity, for the epoché is not a clarification of the achieved significance 'worldliness' but is the *recognition* that worldliness *is* an achieved significance. In this sense Heidegger is fully justified when, in commenting on the distinction Husserl draws between transcendental and mundane subjectivity, he asks: "what is the kind of being in which the 'world' is constituted?"[33]

The justification consists in the fact that the distinction in question, which is made here solely at the level of method, does not yet even pretend to know

---

32. Fink, "Phenomenological Philosophy," 107.
33. Cited from Walter Biemel, "Husserl's *Encyclopedia Britannica* Article and Heidegger's Remarks Thereon," in P. McCormick, and F. A. Elliston, eds., *Husserl: Expositions and Appraisals* (Notre Dame, Ind.: University of Notre Dame, 1977), 286–303, here 300.

such an answer. But precisely for this reason such a question could not be directed to Husserl as a criticism. His answer—which will also be an answer to the question of the exact form of the relation between the transcendental and mundane intentionality—can only be arrived at *through* the phenomenological explication of how the originarily affirming "transcendental" subjectivity intentionally achieves the legitimated significance 'worldliness'. Only such an investigation can bring to light this intentionality in its concrete functioning; only then can the being of this functionary be clarified. For it is the being of intentionality in its *originary functioning* that is at stake here.

It must also be noted that transcendental intentionality's loss of worldliness does not in any way entail a loss of its reference to worldly entities. It simply means that the philosopher is no longer justified in affirming that the originarily functioning intentionality is qualified by a certain mode of being. Or rather, it means that such a being-qualified must be demonstrated—and to do so requires that it not be presupposed. Two things must be philosophically established: first, the meaning and status of 'being worldly' and, second, the being-worldly of the entity in question.

But just as this first methodological distinction between transcendental and mundane intentionality does not entail an ontological *affirmation* regarding transcendental intentionality, neither does it sustain any positive ontological *denial*. No longer having at one's philosophical disposal the general truth that intentionality *is* intentionality-in-the-world is not at all synonymous with the results of the world annihilation experiment. In that case an ontological claim is being made, about which one may argue. But at this stage of Husserl's investigation this difference is not, so to speak, ontologically positive. Therefore, Heidegger's further question on this point—"Does not any world whatsoever belong to the essence of the pure ego?"[34]—is not well motivated in this context. The decision about whether or in what way worldliness "belongs to the essence" of "transcendentally reduced" intentionality must be clarified through the intentional analysis of worldliness and its constitution.

It is clear then that neither the term 'man' nor the notion of 'being in the world' have the same meanings for Husserl as they do for the Heidegger of *Being and Time*. One of the reasons for this is that *Being and Time* is an investigation into the being of the entity that constitutes—an investigation whose ground is prepared by Husserl's first posing of the problem of what is, in terms of its constitution. Husserl never denies that "what constitutes is not nothing" nor that "it is something and exists." And, as is clear from the Fourth Cartesian Meditation, he agrees that "the question about the kind of being of what does the constituting itself cannot be circumvented." As the utter antithesis of abstraction (which seeks to discover the "subsoil"), transcen-

---

34. Ibid. Likewise the quotations in the next paragraph are taken from the same page.

dental purification is not only compatible with the existence of a *concrete* subject, but actually *demands* that its subject be so (see *FTL*, 226 and 217-18). Biemel is simply wrong to claim that "[f]or Husserl, 'is' is synonymous with being worldly."[35] As Jacques Derrida points out in his discussion of a similar temptation in Emanuel Levinas's early work,[36] this is so far from being the case for Husserl that absolute being is recognized to mark the transcendental functionary *alone*; the world's being is merely secondary and contingent. Purification does not rob the transcendental functionary of being but only of naive complicity in a particular ontology.

Husserl simply sees that these questions must be taken only as they become inevitable through the order of phenomenological investigation, and then only with the meaning that accrues thanks to such an "archaeology."

In short, to speak of 'man', of 'human being', is to recognize that the division between acceptor and acceptance is not isomorphic with that between man and world, between "subject" and "object," but in fact permeates intentionality itself. It recognizes that, as "worldly," subjectivity—intentionality—itself emerges as a constitutional problem.

§ 6. Conclusion

Insofar as phenomenology's problem remains that of the meaning and possibility of transcendence (of course, it becomes more than this, as an investigation of the being of transcendental intentionality) and given that phenomenology thematizes transcendence as transcendental acceptance, phenomenology transforms the question concerning the being of the intentionality in whose functioning life this accepting of transcendence takes place. That subjectivity, says Fink, "which ultimately accepts the 'world' and within whose life the belief in the world, together with the meaning of the world's being belonging to it, is constantly being enacted and shaped into the unity of a universal apperception."[37] This accepting of the transcendent by functioning intentionality is thematized by Husserl under the heading of *constitution*. The being of the world, encountered as it is only through this acceptance, is to be clarified by a clarification of this accepting, that is, by a clarification of its constitution in and through functioning intentionality. This acceptance of the transcendent by functioning intentionality is thus the problem with which transcendental phenomenology begins and remains. As Fink puts it: "The true theme of phenomenology is neither the world on the one hand, nor a transcendental subjectivity which is to be set over and against the world on the other, but the *world's becoming in the constitution of transcendental subjectivity*."[38]

---

35. Biemel, ibid., 302.
36. Jacques Derrida, "'Genesis and Structure' and Phenomenology," in *Writing and Difference*, trans. Alan Bass (Chicago: University of Chicago, 1978), 154-68.
37. Fink, "Phenomenological Philosophy," 108.
38. Ibid., 123.

With this, transcendental phenomenology establishes itself as legitimately able to investigate the meaning and possibility of intentional self-transcending, and the meaning and possibility of transcendence in its otherness, its difference, vis-à-vis that intentional functioning. It has freed itself from complicity in a pregiven ontic ordering that would vitiate its claims—and intention—to achieve presuppositionlessness regarding its problem. Yet it has still allowed for the problematic phenomena—transcendence and self-transcendence—to show themselves and thereby to be clarified.

Part Two

Analysis and Discoveries

Chapter Six
Reorienting the Problem

Having established the appropriate methodological meaning of presuppositionlessness as a revocation of complicity in worldliness rather than as an abstractive exclusion of transcendence, we are now in a position to investigate Husserl's response to the central problem of the status of transcendencies and, essentially intertwined with it, the corresponding problem of the meaning of the self-transcendence that intentionality is. We begin by noting a tension at the heart of Husserl's solution.

Intentionality is "consciousness of . . ." The 'of' indicates the peculiarity of this "relation," which consists in a being directed outwards and, in this outward movement, the reaching of something that is "other." Intentionality is therefore self-transcendence. The term of this intending is *other* insofar as it always has the sense of being something encountered only in this self-transcending.

Yet the investigation of this self-transcending yields a confounding result. In *Ideas I* Husserl states the results of his investigations in a way that seems to contradict the sense of the phenomenon in question—and at no point in the later writings does he revoke this claim. He writes:

> Thus it becomes clear that, despite all the assuredly well-founded talk about a real being of the *human* ego and its lived experiences of consciousness *in* the world and about everything that might belong to it regarding "psychophysical" concatenations—that, despite all that, consciousness considered in its "purity" must be held to be a *self-contained complex of being*, a complex of *absolute being* into which nothing can penetrate and out of which nothing can slip, to which nothing is spatiotemporally external and which cannot be in any spatiotemporal complex; it cannot experience any causality by a physical thing, nor exercise any causality on a physical thing. . . . (*Id. I*, 93)

This conclusion is reaffirmed and expanded upon in the *Cartesian Meditations*. There Husserl affirms that the transcendencies attained by functioning intentionality—which he designates in that text as 'transcendental subjectivity'—are inseparable from the processes that comprise the functioning of this intentionality, and in fact have their being as that which goes to make up "the ego taken in full concreteness" (*CM*, 102).

This establishes the ambit of the second part of our investigation. We have considered the development of Husserl's problem and in turn the requirements that this problem makes upon phenomenological method. In now seeking to trace Husserl's answer to his problem, the focus of our investigation is sharpened into the questions: How can the "transcendent" come to be understood as including the concreteness of the intentionality that attains them? If this is the case, what is the sense of their "otherness"? And what is the meaning of intentionality as a "going beyond," a "going out," a "self-transcending," if transcendental intentionality is a self-contained mode of being, "into which nothing can penetrate and out of which nothing can slip"? How is it that Husserl can call the study of *intentionality*—one that embraces the transcending, as well as the transcendent—an "egology"?

The fundamental principle of phenomenology is expressed in the method of phenomenological reduction: it is experience that must be allowed to determine the meaning and status of what is; conversely, no predetermination of the meaning of what is can be allowed to determine the meaning of experience, nor the meaning of what is given experientially. In Rudolf Bernet's formulation: "That which the thing-in-itself is, is to be determined by cognition and not the other way around."[1] For, as has been seen, there is "no being nor being-thus" other than as accepted by me. All determinations receive their meaning and validity-status—for me—only through my affirmation. Thus Ludwig Landgrebe clarifies the fundamental phenomenological principle by saying that "everything which we can in general speak of as 'being' is being for consciousness and must permit the justification for its being posited as 'being' to be exhibited in consciousness."[2]

Our procedure will be as follows. Recognizing that not only is the being-sense of every particular transcendence something that emerges as a result of intentional achievements but also that the very determination 'transcendent' is also such a result, we intend to investigate the meaning and being of the "transcendent" through an investigation of the functionings that have such a meaning as their result. For, properly speaking, the central problem of Husserl's transcendental "epistemology" is not the How and What of particular transcendencies, but rather the How and What of transcendence as such. This problem is approached through an investigation of particular transcendencies, but with an essential concern for them as transcendencies as such.

The key question that will guide this investigation, and to which the investigation will always return, is this: How is it possible that a transcendency can appear? Or, equivalently, what is involved in the being-given of a transcendence? This specifies the object of our investigation, namely the nature of the achieving that has as its result—or that facilitates—the being-given, the appearing, of a transcendence. Again, our interest lies in where and how the "external to me" is encountered. Where does alterity break in upon the

---

1. Rudolf Bernet, "Perception as a Teleological Process," *Analecta Husserliana* 9 (1979), 119–32, here 129.
2. Ludwig Landgrebe, "Husserl's Departure from Cartesianism," in Elveton, ed., *The Phenomenology of Husserl*, 243–87, here 247.

immanence of intentionality; and what precisely is the sense of this alterity? What can 'external to me' and 'alterity' mean now, given that both determinations are themselves to be investigated as achievements?

Since at issue at this point are methodological matters, we note in passing that once within the transcendental reduction a particular abstraction is now effected. We abstract both from "the other" as other functioning intentionality and from the range of "transcendence-constituting" operations and contributions that may be found to accrue to it. This is not in any sense to deny the role of the other—transcendental intersubjectivity—in the constitution of the transcendent. In fact it seems *prima facie* that not only is the other itself a transcendence par excellence but also that, insofar as the transcendencies that are for me are also for the other, such transcendencies take on a profound dimension of transcendence, provided that 'transcendence' is understood as 'being beyond me'. None of this is denied. But the abstraction in question is justified methodologically to the extent that the other—as an other for me, an affirmed transcendence—itself refers back to certain achievements in which its precise sense as 'other intentional functionary' is itself originally affirmed in "me" (though just what a 'me' would be who functioned at such a level, one prior to that of personal pronouns, is itself a deep problem) (see *FTL*, §§ 95–96). This achieving is carried out, as Husserl puts it, within the "sphere of ownness." This abstraction therefore effects a certain impoverishment of the phenomenon in question, abstracting from all determinations that accrue to it by virtue of its being for a plurality of functioning intentionalities. These determinations will be dealt with in due course.

Husserl elects to begin his investigation of the problem of transcendence by taking up the privileged case of the real thing, and we shall follow Husserl in this. The said narrowing is justified on two grounds: first, it is the real thing that functions as the ground and presupposition for all other "higher order" transcendencies and so must be clarified before the investigation of all other transcendencies; second, the investigation of real transcendence takes on exemplary status in relation to the investigation of all other transcendencies. Husserl says, "no matter what its genus may be, transcendent being in general, understood as a Being *for* an ego, can be given only in a manner analogous to that in which a physical thing is given, thus only through appearances" (*Id. I*, 81).

Chapter Seven
Husserl's Preliminary Determination of the Domains of Immanence and Transcendence

To begin the investigation of the constitution of transcendence, Husserl builds on the work of the *Logical Investigations* and presents in *Ideas I* a more detailed and developed account of the domains of immanence and transcendence. This is necessary if the investigation is to begin with a preliminary sense of its subject matter. However, because the investigation has not yet determined the *phenomenological sense* of those domains, this preliminary determination does not have the status of being genuinely grounded in the corresponding phenomena. Two distinct moments can be identified on the path along which Husserl proceeds. The first is the development of what might be called a 'principle of indubitability', which is derived not from the phenomenon of immanence or transcendence but from the sense of the *problem* to which the investigation has responded. The second is the attempted application of this principle to various domains in order to determine the scope of problematic "transcendence" and the location of a domain of "immanence," which provides a point of departure for the investigation precisely because it is unproblematic.

Two principal thematic domains emerge: that of the transcendence of the "real object" and, over against it, that of immanence, understood by Husserl as the domain of consciousness. As the investigation proceeds, however, it becomes clearer that though at first glance the principle of immanence would generate such a division within being in a simple and unproblematic way, the determination of consciousness as immanence pure and simple is untenable. That this holds should become clear in the following discussion.

§ 1. The Principle of Indubitability

Husserl first expresses the problem of transcendence in familiar terms. Transcendence is some kind of excess, an excess of being, beyond and thus other than the being for whom this excess is. However, to recognize that "being more" belongs to or characterizes some being, its excess must somehow show itself, must be revealed as a phenomenon. But how? If transcendence is the "being more" of an *object*, then the meaning of the 'object as transcendence' is that there must be yet more showings of the object itself, showings that are themselves different but in which one and the same object is shown. Thus Husserl comes to understand the being of the transcendent in terms of this necessary requirement of its mode of givenness; he says that the transcendent object is always given only through "adumbrations." That is, adumbrations give the "yet more" of the object; adumbrations meet the excess of being that is more than or beyond any single giving of it. As such no transcendent object is ever given "absolutely." For the *actual course* of what will come to be adumbrated is itself hidden, even though the *being-character* of the object as that of being given through adumbrations is not. Because the actual course of the adumbrative fulfillment remains beyond any "absolute" having, it is always possible for the transcendence in question to be other than it claims or purports to be at any one time. As Husserl says in a marginal note to *Ideas I*: "Indeed, the important point in the subsequent pages, the givenness from a number of sides and, consequently, the open presumption and the possibility of non-being" (*Hua* III/2, 494/96 n. 202).

That is, the excess in question, the peculiar transcendence, is such as to generate the possibility of mis-taking the being that gives itself in adumbrations. This possibility of being in error regarding the "truth" of the being that shows itself is the fundamental phenomenal moment of the transcendence in question. This being-character is what is caught in Husserl's definition of 'transcendent being' as being that shows itself in adumbrations. Adumbration as such is thereby understood as the unfolding, the revealing, of the previously hidden excess. It is by virtue of this excess that error and deceit are possible. This yields what might be called the 'principle of indubitability': wherever error or revision is possible, then the excess of transcendence shows itself.

If the "sign" of the presence of excess is the possibility of error or deceit, then one can see how it is that Husserl comes to determine *immanence* as its opposite. Immanence—and in defining it Husserl struggles to express the peculiar truth of Descartes's insight into the "indubitability of the sphere of immanence"—is not characterized by such excess. Rather, it is the sphere that is exceeded. As Husserl says: "In this absolute sphere there is no room for conflict, illusion, or being otherwise. It is a sphere of absolute position" (*Id. I*, 86). So it is that Husserl comes to understand immanence as "being without excess beyond givenness." The immanent object—so it would seem to follow from the principle of indubitability—is utterly contemporaneous with the act that perceives it and is utterly self-identical with itself as perceived. Because there is nothing more to it than is actually perceived, there is nothing of the immanent object that escapes being brought to presence. As such there is no possibility that any further perceptions could give "more" of the object, and it apparently follows from this that no error or deceit is possible in the sphere of immanence. Husserl next attempts to apply this principle to the domains of object and consciousness.

§ 2. Application of the Principle

§ 2.1. The Domain of Transcendence

Because it is given with a "certain inadequacy," the real object reveals its "being in excess" and thereby its transcendence: "Principially, a physical thing"—the paradigmatic, though by no means only, mode of transcendence—"can only be given 'one-sidedly,' and that does not mean only incompletely, only imperfectly in some sense or other, but precisely what presentation by adumbration prescribes" (80). The perceptual act does not actually contain its object. By virtue of this characteristic, the object is "other" than the act and has a being that is other than the being of the act: "Not only does the perceiving of the physical thing not contain the physical thing itself as part of its really inherent composition; the perceiving-of is also *without any essential unity with the physical thing*" (69). Husserl then generalizes this "inadequateness" for all transcendencies, thereby giving expression to their "excess":

> It can already be seen universally that, no matter what its genus may be, transcendent being in general, understood as a being *for* an ego, can be given only in a manner analogous to that in which a physical thing is given, thus only through appearances. Otherwise it would be precisely a being that could also become immanent; yet anything that is perceivable immanently is perceivable *only* immanently. (81)

§ 2.2. The Domain of Immanence

The principle of indubitability will demarcate a domain of immanent being in terms of being that does not conceal itself in its showing of itself: this will be "being without excess." This means a dimension of being that does not conceal itself in its showing of itself, a dimension of being that is not—to speak in the terms of Husserl's static phenomenology—given through adumbrations. From the fact that such being is not given adumbratively, it follows that its givenness is an indubitable givenness: for no *further givings of the one object are possible* that could subsequently motivate a *revision* of what is, or was, present.

Husserl interprets the "absence of excess" in terms of a particular relation between the immanent object and its "perception":

> In the case of an immanently directed perception, or put succinctly, *an immanent* (a so-called "inner") *perception*, ... *perception and perceived form essentially an unmediated unity, that of a single concrete cogitatio.* Here perceiving harbors its object within itself in such a way that it can be separated from its object only abstractively, only as an *essentially non-selfsufficient moment.* (68)

Only those entities that are given as a "really inherent includedness" (69) satisfy this condition. And only one mode of being is given in such a way: the domain of consciousness, or intentional activity, itself. Thus consciousness and its "really inherent contents" emerges as the domain of immanent being. Husserl then proposes that, because it is not adumbrated, consciousness be considered as "absolute being":

> No *lived experience* . . . is presented. That means that the perception of a lived experience is a simple seeing of something that is (or can be) *given in perception as something "absolute"* and not as something identical in modes of appearance by adumbration. . . . A lived experience . . . is not adumbrated. If I look at it, I have something absolute; it has no sides that could be presented sometimes in one way and sometimes in another. (81)

'Absoluteness' thereby defines 'immanence', and 'immanence' defines 'being as consciousness':

> We therefore emphasize: Whereas it is essential to givenness by appearances that no appearance gives the thing as something "absolute" instead of in a one-sided presentation, it is essential to immanent givenness precisely to give something absolute, which can never be presented by way of sides or be adumbrated. (82)

This determination of the being of the immanent as 'being without excess' generates the principle of indubitability. For there is nothing "beyond," nothing that is not given:

> Every immanent perception necessarily guarantees the existence [*Existenz*] of its object. If reflective seizing-upon is directed to my lived experience, then I have seized upon an absolute self, whose existence [*Dasein*] is principially incapable of being negated, that is, the insight that it does not exist is principially impossible; it would be a countersense to consider it possible that a lived experience *given in that way* does *not* in truth exist. (85)

Husserl then reaches the apparently simple conclusion that the domains of transcendence and immanence readily emerge: intentional objects-for-consciousness, given adumbratively, on the one hand, and the stream of concrete consciousness as the domain of absolutely given immanence,[1] on the other.

§ 2.3. A Premonition of Difficulties

As Husserl's inquiry moves on, and particularly as it moves from static to genetic phenomenology, the identification of immanence with the domain of consciousness becomes more and more problematic. But even at this early stage, where Husserl establishes the extent of the two domains through the application of the principle of indubitability, he immediately recognizes problems and introduces qualifications. Let us briefly draw attention to Husserl's own first misgivings before we investigate the constitution of transcendence. As that investigation proceeds, it will of its own come face to face with these problems.

---

1. The domain of immanence is at first thought naively by Husserl to be coextensive with "the lived experiences of consciousness *in the entire fullness of the concreteness* within which they present themselves in their concrete context—the *stream of lived experiences*—and which, by their own essence, they combine to make up" (*Id. I*, 61).

§ 2.3.1. The Entire Stream

Let us recall the original scope of the determination of immanence. Husserl writes: "Its title reads: consciousness or, more distinctly, *any lived experience whatsoever of consciousness* in an extraordinarily broad sense" (60).

This means that the scope of the determination must cover consciousness in its "entire fullness," the entire stream and its contents; otherwise, the stream would find itself no longer manifest as "immanence," as—naively identified—"consciousness," but as a transcendence in immanence. Consciousness would already be determined, in some way, as an "object." Husserl wants to reject this possibility. But can he?

To answer this question we must first ask: Is it true that the entire stream is immanent being? The answer is straightforward: not if we apply the principle of immanence in the form of the principle of indubitability. For, as Husserl admits, it is by no means the case that, for example, the past moments of the stream are given indubitably. He says: "By its *own* full essence, the present remembering could exist even though in truth yesterday's remembering had never existed" (69). And at another point, immediately after stating the principle of immanence in the form of the principle of indubitability, he introduces a qualification: How far does the evidence of absolute givenness extend? How far, in other words, does the phenomenologist have to go before encountering a dimension of being that, in its givenness, conceals some excess? After speaking of the "guarantee" of the "absolute existence [*Dasein*]" of immanence, Husserl goes on to say: "But, one might ask, is it not conceivable that an ego have only fantasies in its stream of lived experiences, that this stream consist of nothing but intentional intuitions? Such an ego would thus find only fictions of *cogitationes*" (85). Hence, not all regions of the stream are capable of indubitable givenness. It follows from this, from the possibility of being in error, that the past of the stream does not manifest itself as "immanent" being; for error is only possible where there is an excess of being, and a being marked by excess is not "absolute" being. If it is true that "[e]very immanent perception necessarily guarantees the existence of its object" (85), then reflection upon the past of the stream is not reflection upon "something immanent," in spite of the fact that "yesterday's remembering, *if* it actually did exist, belongs necessarily with the present remembering to the one and the same, never interrupted stream of lived experiences, which continuously mediates the two by means of various concretions of lived experiences" (69).

Husserl there and then draws the correct conclusion. If the possibility of error indicates excess beyond, and hence difference from, the dimension of immanence proper (however that may come to be understood), then at least in the case of the stream's pastness there can be no claim to "really inherent includedness" in the reflecting (perceiving) act. Husserl says:

> This sort of *really inherent "includedness"* (which is actually just a metaphor) is a *preeminent characteristic of immanent perception and of the position-taking founded on such perception*; it is lacking in most other cases [of immanent experience and] of immanent relation between intentional lived experiences. Thus, for example, it is already lacking in rememberings of rememberings. The remembered remembering that occurred yesterday does not belong to the present remembering as a really inherent component of its concrete unity. (69)

One can see Husserl becoming increasingly sensitive to this problem in the marginal notes he entered throughout his own personal copies of *Ideas I*. In fact, one can detect the attempt to generate a principle that would distinguish "absolute" being (immanence) from dimensions of the stream of concrete consciousness that do not present themselves as absolute. In the original edition one can find almost casual statements of this principle, such as when Husserl, in speaking of absolute being as indubitably given being, suggests a restriction to the perception of "the flowing life *in its actual present*" (85).[2] He suggests thereby that absolute being is always only available in the "living present." As such, an indubitable being can present itself only in the living present; once beyond the living present, the entity takes on a certain excess, a certain difference from the act in which it is rendered "re-present."

This restriction is then re-made consistently throughout the relevant pages of Husserl's personal copies of *Ideas I*.[3] Thus from the principles of his analysis it can be seen that at least some components of the concrete stream are already "transcendencies," as Husserl implicitly recognizes in the distinction he makes between the stream in its "living present" and those moments of the stream that are no longer "living," no longer "Now."

The conclusion is unavoidable. Husserl simply cannot sustain the equivalence of consciousness with immanence if 'immanence' signifies 'absolute being', being without excess, and if 'consciousness' refers to the stream in its full concreteness. For even within the stream—in the case of the past, for example—we encounter being that manifests excess.[4] The stream content that is not "now" sustains an excess of being that is beyond and other than the con-

---

2. My emphasis.
3. For example, "actual" is changed to "of livingly present" (marginal note from Copy D, *Hua* III/2, 491/78 n. 112); the "lived experience," as something "that is (or can become) perceptually given as something absolute" is qualified by the addition of "in its present, at every point in its Now" (494/95 n. 198); "If I look at it, I have something absolute" is qualified by the addition of "with respect to each point of its continuous present" (494/96 n. 201); "But my emphasizing, my consciousness of whatever sort, is originarily and absolutely given" is qualified by the addition of "as a flowing present" (495/101 n. 221); in "In this absolute sphere there is no room for conflict, illusion, or being otherwise. It is a sphere of absolute positing," the term "sphere" is qualified by the addition of "of the living immanental present" (496/102 n. 225).
4. See Husserl's discussion of the temporality of perception, e.g., in § 16 of *The Phenomenology of Internal Time Consciousness*.

sciousness that re-identifies it. Were this not the case, there could be no re-identification at all, and "pastness" would be utterly constituted in the act of re-identification and fall into non-being as soon as the act itself ceased. Therefore, Husserl's attempt to determine the being of consciousness as "absolute" being—as non-transcendent being, as a "sphere of immanence"—is undermined. Almost without so much as a mention—let alone a consideration of its significance—"consciousness" and "immanence" come asunder.

§ 2.3.2. The Living Present

But does Husserl's "restricted" region of the "living present" fare any better? The answer to this question will concern us later as we follow Husserl's investigations of the constitution of primal identity through the dynamic of originary temporalization. But even at this stage we can sketch certain reservations. We note that the whole tenor of the project of *Ideas I* is shot through with a Cartesian concern for establishing a stable and self-guaranteeing ground, a basis more perfect than that of the world given through natural experience. This search is motivated by a concern about illusion, deceit, and error, and Husserl believes, under Descartes's influence, that the grasp of a certainty—where the possibility of "being otherwise" is excluded—can be the only way of satisfying this urgent desire. Husserl's naiveté here, which is overcome through the investigations of the syntheses of internal time, is to believe that such a ground must still be the *possession of an object*. Thus in *Ideas I* he characterizes the content of the living present as yielding a *"determinate descriptive composition"* (*Id. I*, 75). That is, the living present yields an object, an identity. Husserl believes he finds this "object-ground" in nothing less than the living heart of consciousness itself. Offered as a "secure possession" (144) to phenomenological reflection, Husserl assumes that this object will function as the ground sought for; to be a secure possession, this object-ground must, of course, be nameable—and, indeed, it has been named: it is what Husserl has been referring to as 'hyletic quality' and 'act character'. Of the perception—the possession—of such objects, Husserl says: "In this absolute sphere there is no room for conflict, illusion, or being otherwise. It is a sphere of absolute position" (86). The certainty of the living present consists in the fact that a ground, understood as object, is given absolutely. From the previous discussion of the supposed immanence of the entire stream, however, it has become clear that being temporally distended compromises the principle of indubitability and hence of immanence. If it emerges that identity is essentially a function of temporality, then it would seem that temporality characterizes even the objects of the living present and hence the determination of that domain as immanent being. With this in mind, we turn to the discussion of the constitution of transcendence proper, the real spatiotemporal object. This will lead to a discussion of originary temporalization and the primal constitution of identity.

Chapter Eight
The Constitution and Status of the Real Object

In attempting to resolve the question of alterity in Husserl's phenomenology—which he alternately terms 'the problem of transcendence' and 'the problem of objectivity'—the phenomenologist interrogates objects considered as constituted entities. The task is to establish the very meaning of 'object', which involves noting where and in what sense alterity engages the intentional functionary. The "object" becomes a fundamental theme *because* of, and *in*, its claim to alterity.

It is important to bear in mind that Husserl emerges from his investigations as a transcendental idealist, denying any "outside" to transcendental subjectivity. In what sense is this a system of closure? Two facets of Husserl's analysis of the constitution of objectivity must be clarified if this question is to be answered.

First, the status of the object as a *constituted entity* must be determined. In what sense is this a "transcendence in immanence"? Is "transcendence in immanence" a mere "projection" of constituting intentionality and so something enclosed within that intentionality, or is it in some sense itself open, exceeding the intentionality that nonetheless is its constituting ground?

Second, the meaning of the twin transcendental constitutional moments of hyletic data and the synthesis of identification must be established. It may be that the spatiotemporal object emerges as a constituted entity. But could not the flux-moments, as hyletic data, indicate an "unknown cause of experience" that, as noumenon, exists in itself, independent of the experiencing subject? So understood, the flux-moments would indicate an alterity other than the constituted object. Furthermore, a question could arise about the *rule that governs the synthesis* of identification. Because identity is achieved through synthesis, the nature of that synthesis and the laws governing it emerge as central issues in answering our question. This synthesis has the character, as we shall see, of invariability according to object type. How is the lawful character of this synthesis to be accounted for? Could it not be the case that the synthesis is governed by an external being? If so, the synthesis itself would be a mark of alterity.

Husserl of course rules out both of these avenues for the emergence or even insinuation of alterity and refuses any meaning of alterity implied by them. We wish to test the extent of closure and the possibilities for alterity in Husserl's transcendental phenomenology by investigating, first, the object in terms of its constitution and, second, the principle that any synthesis of identification both expresses and is governed by. The status of the flux-moments that enter into the ongoing synthesis will be examined in the next chapter, when we turn to genetic phenomenology and the constitution of primal identity in what Husserl terms the 'originary temporalization'.

§ 1. The Constitution of the Real Object: Transcendence as Identity

After the transcendental reduction, the reality of the thing as understood within the natural attitude can no longer be presupposed. What an appearing object is must be determined exclusively on the basis of its pure givenness. Thus when an object is approached phenomenologically, it becomes a theme *in its appearing*. The problem of the transcendent becomes the problem of "the transcendent in its appearing," because the transcendent is to be approached by revealing how its *appearing* establishes it as transcendent. This sets up the fundamental contrast—and tension—between difference and sameness, many and one, flux and identity. The transcendent (object) is one and stable; appearings many and changing. Thereby, the problem of the "being of the object" necessarily becomes, in its most general phenomenological formulation, the problem of identity: *how* does identity emerge out of the ever changing flux of appearing and *what* is that identity which does so emerge?

§ 1.1. The Object and the Flux of Appearing

The object appears as a single, self-identical unity. Yet it does so through a continually changing flux of *its* appearances, in which the "present appearance" is continually giving way to something "new," as the present appearance slips into the past. Husserl illustrates this with numerous examples, perhaps the most lucid of which is to be found in *Ideas I*:

> Constantly seeing this table and meanwhile walking around it, changing my position in space in whatever way, I have continually the consciousness of this one identical table as factually existing "bodily" and remaining quite unchanged. The table-perception, however, is a continually changing one; it is a continuity of changing perceptions.... The perception itself... is a continuous flux: continually the perceptual Now changes into the enduring consciousness of the Just-Past and simultaneously a new Now lights up, etc. (*Id. I*, 73–74)

This point is reiterated again and again throughout Husserl's descriptions, such as in the lectures on *The Phenomenology of Internal Time Consciousness*:

> Every temporal being "appears" in one or another continually changing mode of running-off, and the "object in the mode of running-off" is in this change always something other, even though we still say that the object in every other point of its time and this time are one and the same. (*Hua* X, 26–27/47)[1]

---

1. Husserl's radicality consists in the fact that, unlike the tradition, he does not begin

The main contrast in these passages is between the identical unity that appears and the continuously changing flow of appearings in which the Same appears and to which that Same is transcendent. We are attempting to establish just what the being of the identity that emerges in this flux is. But to do this we must first investigate in more detail the formal structure of the flux of appearings.

§ 1.2. The Formal Structure of the Flux: Horizons of Retention and Protention

The most fundamental form of the passively flowing flux of appearances from which identities emerge—the flux that "adumbrates" (*Id. I*, 75) the object—is temporal (*CM*, 79).[2] Its formal structure can best be characterized as a threefold temporal dynamic. Husserl speaks of the changing character of the flux with reference to temporal phases: the Now-moment, the constitutively functioning past or retention, and the constitutively functioning future or protention. He uses these terms to characterize "the flowing conscious life in which the identical ego lives" (70), this domain "so truly the realm of Heraclitean flux" (86), this "flowing subjective process" (73). Husserl refers to the Now-moment of the flux as being occupied by "*actual* subjective processes" (81).[3] Retention is the

---

by thinking in ontological terms the difference between what appears, on the one hand, and its appearing, on the other. His original decentering of the subject in the transcendental reduction means that the ontological status of "appearance," as the "subjective side" of what is, is no longer understandable—initially—as ontologically secondary. For the same reason, neither can what appears be thematized as ontologically primary. The problem of appearance must first be thought phenomenologically, which is to say, in terms of how this difference shows itself; prior to thinking the phenomenon in ontological terms lies the question of how it is possible that an ontological determination of it can even arise.

2. The account of flux Husserl presents within static phenomenology is much less developed than the one that emerges in his genetic phenomenology. At this point, we shall give an account sufficient to the analysis of the constitution of the spatiotemporal real object. A more subtle account will emerge in the next chapter in a discussion of the originary temporalization.

3. At its heart, the problem of the flux presents the problem of identity as such—in particular, the problem of the identity of the stream itself, as well as the problem of the identity of the respective "moments" that, with their "determinate descriptive content," make up the particular "lived experiences" that Husserl calls 'immanent objects' and that, via a synthesis of identity, go to make up the full appearing of the real worldly object. However, this can only be properly dealt with after the turn is made to genetic phenomenology, where the problem of identity per se becomes paramount and the principle focus of the investigation. We shall deal with this in the next chapter, where the question of the status of the immanent object will be considered. At this point, we remain within the ambit of constitutive phenomenology and shall treat the flux as already comprised of identities. Husserl himself recognized that the elements of the flux cannot be reduced to and explicated in terms of "identical elements that might be apprehended by means of fixed concepts" (*CM*, 86). Such an exercise would be "pure folly," not because of our "imperfect ability to know objects of that kind," but because "lived experiences of consciousness have a priori no ultimate *elements*

originary givenness, the "presence" of the past, and protention is the originary givenness, the "presence," of the future. The flux yields Nows that are continually going over into "no longer nows" or pasts; and because each Now is continually going over into a "no longer now," the dimension of futurity—of "nows that are not yet"—is inseparable from this dynamic. As continually passing over into the mode of the "no longer now," the Now is being continually replenished; it is a site of the new. Both the past and the future dimensions of the flux are somehow "present" in the Now: the past is not lost and the future is expected.

The protentional and retentional moments of the flux are referred to as the "horizons" of the Now-moment, the contents of which continually alter with each phase of its flow. The actional lived experiences are lodged temporally within a horizon of "potentialities" (81)—which are "not empty possibilities, but rather possibilities intentionally predelineated in respect of content—namely, in the actional lived experience itself—and, in addition, having the character of possibilities actualizable by the ego" (81-82).

Thus there is, on the one hand, the "protentional horizon," the horizon of the future, a vast fund from which ever new lived experiences well up. And though this is the dimension of the "not yet"—which is to say, not yet *actual*—there is nonetheless a kind of "reaching into" it that takes place. The term 'protention' expresses this "pre-grasp" of the "not yet" that allows intentionality its anticipatory moment as the protention grasps the "not yet" in the form of an expectation. A vast fund of *potential* lived experiences offer themselves to the protention, which are bound only by the range of the intentional functionary's potential for experiencing and can be held in the form of expectation. This is a vast field, including all the possibilities of conscious life: the whole range of emotional, intellectual, and affective comportments, as well as the full extent of kinaesthetic and sense-field possibilities "actualizable by the ego."

On the other hand there is the "retentional horizon": no sooner are they actualized in the Now, than those potentialities that actually did come to pass move out of the Now and into the "no longer now," the past. As "no longer now," they once again acquire the character of a potential, the "potentiality of awakenable recollections" (82), to be actualized again on the initiative of the intentional functionary.

Given that the flux is multifarious, ever-changing, utterly differentiated, most of it being either "not yet" or "no longer," how is it that the "not yet" and the "no longer" are nonetheless "present"? And, furthermore, how is it that the flux does not yield a simply unmanageable tumult and chaos, but rather a self-identical and enduring identity?

---

and relations, fit for subsumption under the idea of conceptually fixed determinacies." However, "an essentially necessary conformity to type prevails," thanks to which an intentional synthesis, whose products can be "fixed in rigorous concepts," can take place.

§ 1.3. The Gathering of the Flux: Synthesis

Husserl answers the question of how it is that the "not yet" and the "no longer" are nonetheless present in the Now by pointing to the function of synthesis.[4] He offers the example of the perception of a die:

> *this* die is given continuously as an objective unity in a multiform and changeable multiplicity of manners of appearing, which belong determinately to it. These, in their temporal flow, are not an incoherent sequence of lived experiences. Rather, they flow away in the unity of a synthesis, such that in them "one and the same" is intended as appearing. The one identical die appears, now in "near appearances," now in "far appearances": in the changing modes of Here and There, over against an always co-intended, though perhaps unheeded, absolute Here (in my co-appearing body). (*CM*, 77–78)

It is important to note the peculiar kind of unification that combines consciousness with consciousness is what Husserl calls 'synthesis'—"a mode of combination exclusively peculiar to consciousness" (77). Though the flux-moments flow away with their temporal extents and phases, in synthesis these moments come to be taken as continually changing appearances of the one identical thing. The condition for the establishment of the identity that appears in *all* these flux-moments (which all belong to it as *its* appearances) is that the *unity* in which they are gathered is "not merely a continuous connectedness of cogitations (as it were, a being stuck to one another externally)," for if it were they would remain external to each other and not refer essentially to each other as like appearances *of the one object*. Rather, the unity must be "*a connectedness that makes the unity of one consciousness*, in which the unity of an intentional objectivity, as 'the same' objectivity belonging to multiple modes of appearance, becomes '*constituted*'" (79–80). The unity that is constituted in the synthesis of identification is "the unity of one consciousness," a unity of flux-moments—the Now together with its horizons—*held together* in such a way that this distended and temporally differentiated range is co-present within one conscious act. Thus the unity that emerges from the synthesis is the

---

4. We note to begin with that all moments of the flux are unified through an all-embracing synthesis, in which "the *whole of conscious life* is *unified* . . . in its openly endless unity and wholeness" (*CM*, 80–81). We are here concerned, however, with the syntheses that unify *particular* elements, syntheses that occur *within* the flux and yield the unity of an appearing object, a single intentional objectivity. Note also that synthesis occurs not only so as to unify particular lived experiences within the flux, so as to yield particular object-identities. It is also the case that "the *whole of conscious life* is *unified synthetically*" (80), as a condition for any of the object-yielding syntheses of identification. To be sure, such an all-embracing synthesis never yields a completed stream unity (death may mark some kind of unification, as a completion), which is an "openly endless unity." However, such a unity-in-constitution is the condition for the establishment of the particular "completed" syntheses that take place within the stream of the life of the intentional functionary, and whose correlates are particular objects.

"one consciousness" that gathers a "span" of flux-moments. Identity is thus a function of the *unifiability* of flux-moments.

§ 1.4. Achieving Identity: The Character of "Belonging" and the Principle of Harmony

The second question, namely of how it is that the flux can be ordered to an identity rather than simply yielding a chaos, is answered by noting the relation between the moments that are synthesized. The unity referred to is the "unity of one consciousness" and is a function of the fact that various flux-moments are gathered together and in this gathering *refer to each other*. In their having-flowed-away (retention) and in their yet-to-come (protention) a range of such moments are gathered together and, thanks to synthesis, held in and for one consciousness.

Unifiability is made possible by the fact that in those syntheses that successfully yield identities "the constituting multiplicities of consciousness" are gathered in such a way that they bear the characteristic of "*belong[ing] together for essential reasons*" (90; see 90, 91–92, 98). It is because the "genuinely given" Now-content belongs together with other retentional and protentional flux-moments not actually given that the immanent Now refers beyond itself, that each synthesis of identification is a "meaning more of its meant" (a meaning more than is actually given), that a Same can be intended as a one in many. This character of "belonging" refers to the fact that, in a synthesis of identification in which an object is constituted, the "genuinely present" indicates "more." This belonging indicates a reference of the "genuinely given" beyond itself, by being united with a "more" and taken with it in apperception. This belonging—to which Husserl also refers as an "embracing" (80)—presupposes a synthesis in which all that belongs is gathered *together*. Insofar as this gathering is a presenting of what is beyond or more than what is "genuinely given," it is to be understood as achieving a triumph over the immanence of the present and effecting intentionality as such. "Belonging" is "being gathered in synthesis of identification." The distinguishing characteristic of the syntheses that fail to achieve identity—as is apparent from the thought experiment of world annihilation—is precisely that, although the stream-synthesis itself proceeds, the flux-moments gathered in the stream fail to achieve and sustain essential reference to other stream moments.

How do the flux-moments show themselves to "belong together"? Husserl answers: flux-moments "belong together" when the structure of the flux exhibits "harmony."

In *Ideas I* Husserl speaks of the essential characteristics of any flux of multiplicities in which an object comes to presentation. Such a flux must yield a "continuously harmonious" flow of multiplicities.[5] Harmony thus emerges as

---

5. See Husserl's marginal note in Copy A, *Hua* III/2, 491/91 n. 185. That harmony yields a structure is the very possibility of intentional analysis and therefore of phenome-

§ 2. The Being of the Object

We have spoken about the way identity emerges out of the ever changing flux of appearances: there is a synthetic gathering of the flux-moments that are unified in one consciousness through their exhibiting a character of harmonious "belonging together." But what is the being of the identity constituted in such a synthesis?

In the ongoing synthesis that gathers the flux of appearings, consciousness reaches out beyond the Now and is conscious of the "no longer" and the "not yet" in *one act*. The noematic correlate of that act—that "one consciousness"—is the identical object to which all gathered moments belong as its appearances and through which they thus belong to each other. By virtue of this maintaining of harmony among the always changing flux-moments, an identity is established as the objective correlate of the unified flux: "This something, the particular 'intentional object qua intentional' in any consciousness, is there as an identical unity belonging to noetically-noematically changing modes of consciousness" (*CM*, 79).

---

nology itself, for the intentional object can only function as a "clue" if there is a structure that is interrogatable in some way. Intentional analysis takes the objectivity as given and seeks to clarify its status by asking how it comes to be given. In asking this, such analysis seeks to interrogate the flux and determine under what conditions the flux in its passing can sustain the presence of an objective unity. That is why intentional analysis is governed by a *unity*, the "transcendental clue," and results in making *certain* possible flux-moments clear as *just those* that are picked out in following the transcendental clue. The question is: What set of flux-moments must or can come to pass, such that "the objectivity remains intended as *this* one and as of this kind, and as long as, throughout the changes in modes of consciousness, evidence of objective identity can persist" (*CM*, 88)? The point of departure is the object as actually given in the present. "From it reflection goes back to the mode of consciousness at that time and to the potential modes of consciousness included horizontally in that mode, then to those in which the object might be otherwise intended as the same, within the unity (ultimately) of a possible conscious life, all the possibilities of which are included in the 'ego'" (87). In doing this, the analysis explicates the object in its transcendence-beyond-the-actual: by asking after the flux-moments which would maintain the object as a unity, "phenomenological explication . . . makes clear what is included and only non-intuitively co-intended in the sense of the *cogitatum* (for example, 'other side'), by making present in fantasy the potential perceptions that would make the invisible visible" (85). Therefore, intentional analysis brings to light not only the actual (immanent) flux-moments that make up the giving of an object, but also the *potential* (transcendent) lived experiences that "as such are 'implicit' and 'predelineated' in the sense-producing intentionality of the active ones and that, when discovered, have the evident character of lived experiences that explicate the implicit sense." That the investigation proceeds with a "clue" means in effect that it proceeds in *possession of a structure* according to which some but not other possible flux-moments will satisfy the requirement that, should they come to pass, the identity of the object will remain the same. Accordingly, this structure *predelineates* such future possibilities.

The object–identity is the noematic correlate of the one synthesizing consciousness that gathers together ever new appearings in an ongoing and harmonious way. As such the intentional object is a *product* of intentional functioning, an identity that *results* from synthetic activity. That is to say, the process of knowing an identity is not the progressive discovery of an objective reality that exists independently of consciousness and is in itself already determined. Rather, the real object being progressively constituted is the intentional correlate of the unitary consciousness that encompasses the multiplicities of appearances in a continuous synthesis of fulfillment. Through this synthesis, consciousness manifests itself as intentional: it "refers" to an object. Yet this is reference not to a hidden Same, a noumenon or thing-in-itself, but to those flux-moments that have entered, will, or could enter into the ongoing synthesis of identification. This is why Husserl claims that the intentional object—the identity constituted in the synthesis of identification, the gathering together—is "in" consciousness in a completely unique way. The object appears "in" consciousness (if it did not, it would not be for consciousness as all): it is "continuously immanent in the flowing consciousness, *descriptively 'in' it*; and likewise the attribute 'one identical'" (80). However, this is a "being in" of a unique kind: not a being-in-consciousness as a *really inherent component part*, as are the flux-moments, but rather a "being-in-it 'ideally' as something intentional, something appearing," a being-in as something *adumbrated* progressively by the streaming flux-moments, through the dynamic of retention and protention. The one self-identical object can be intended in many different modes of consciousness, through many different flux-moments. In that sense, the one identical object is transcendent to any of the actual flux-moments, and to any set of flux-moments, because an object is open to infinite adumbration. However, it is the synthesis of identity that, "as a unitary consciousness embracing these separated processes, gives rise to the consciousness of identity and thereby makes any knowing of identity possible." Husserl concludes that "precisely thereby every sort of existent itself, real or ideal, becomes understandable as a 'product' of transcendental subjectivity, a product constituted in just that performance" (118).[6]

This is a strong affirmation of transcendental idealism on Husserl's part, and it seems unavoidable. It appears as if the phenomenologist is left with saying that in knowing, the knower—the intentional functionary—really only knows its own products. To understand the object as the product of a syn-

---

6. Therefore, the object, as just this unity, the object as having identity with itself during the flowing lived experience, "does not come into the lived experience from outside; on the contrary, it is included as a sense in the lived experience itself—and thus as an '*intentional effect*' of the synthesis of consciousness" (*CM*, 80). The expression 'actually existing object'—and here we affirm Husserl's transcendental idealist conclusion—"can have sense only as a unity meant and meanable in the nexus of consciousness" (97). Such a unity has no sense other than as the correlate of a synthesis of possible lived experiences.

thesis effected by the transcendental functionary is to see object-being as secondary, and as having no being other than as product, as a unity of actual and potential subjective processes. It is in this sense that Fink speaks of the creativeness of the transcendental functionary. The threat of closure looms large at this point. But more must be said of the being of the object before it is possible to investigate the sense of the closure suggested by such an idealism.

We have spoken of the flux of experience and of the problem this poses for the appearing of any fixed and abiding identity. We have shown how it is that such an identity is accomplished in a synthesis of identification that gathers the flux-moments in the unity of one consciousness. And we have noted how—although this resultant unity enjoys a different mode of being than that of the streaming flux-moments making up the actual concrete immanent content of the intentional functionary—it nonetheless remains "in" consciousness. The intentional object itself can be further determined in two ways: as rule for the harmonious gathering of flux-moments and as unity-pole or "X."

§ 2.2. Object as "Rule" or "Index"

At any time the total horizon of *possible lived experiences* that in principle can be undergone by the intentional functionary is vast and multifarious. However, *only some* of those possible lived experiences can, or happen to, exhibit a relation of harmony between themselves: not all moments that come to pass within the flux are so unifiable within a synthesis of identification. It is not a *necessary* character of the flux-moments that they exhibit this quality of "belonging together." Expectations can be disappointed; judgments need revision; things can turn out to be "not what they seemed to be." In fact, as Husserl points out in the "world annihilation experiment" of *Ideas I*, it is possible that the flux could collapse into complete chaos and that no object or world would manifest itself:

> It is quite conceivable that experience, because of conflict, might dissolve itself into illusion not only in detail, and that it might not be the case, as it is *de facto*, that every illusion manifests a deeper truth and that every conflict, in the place where it occurs, is precisely what is demanded by the more inclusive contextures in order to preserve the total harmony . . . that experience might suddenly show itself to be refractory to the demand that it carry on its positing of things harmoniously. . . . (*Id. I*, 91)

Where this happens, there no longer *is* "any harmoniously positable and therefore existent world" (*Hua* III/2, 497/109 n. 19).[7]

---

7. Of course, all flux-moments are unified in one sense, namely in the originary synthesis of the one stream in which the ego is itself constituted. Here, however, we are concerned with the synthesis of identification in which objects for the transcendental functionary are constituted.

The "belonging together" of the flux-moments (of the kind in which an intentional object is constituted) is not achieved in such a case. The question therefore becomes: How is the difference between those syntheses that yield identities and those that fail to do so to be understood?

§ 2.2.1. Order and Disorder within the Flux

Every synthesis of identification has a determinate structure, according to which only a specific set of the entire range of possible experiences open to consciousness can actually be joined in the synthesis. Only some are capable of exhibiting mutual relations of harmony, and it is the sense of the object that prescribes this. Notwithstanding the *indeterminacy* (*CM*, 83; see *Id. I*, 80) or imperfections with which a particular object is intended, any synthesis of identification signifies "a determinacy that has a rigorously prescribed style" (*Id. I*, 80). This determinate structure is inviolable and is an index for the essential and invariable structure of an object (when synthesis is considered noematically) or of the flow (when considered noetically) of a given synthesis of identification. This index is normative in character. Because it points to a structure that *specifies* how Sameness is to be maintained, this index is "governed by a rule" (*CM*, 90). Husserl says:

> The fact that the constituting multiplicities of consciousness—those actually or possibly combined to make the unity of an identifying synthesis—are not accidental but, as regards the possibility of such a synthesis, *belong together for essential reasons*. Accordingly they are governed by *principles*, thanks to which our phenomenological investigations do not get lost in disconnected descriptions but are essentially organized. Any "objective" object, *any object whatever* (even an immanent one), points to a *structure, within the transcendental ego that is governed by a rule*. As something the ego objectivates ... the object indicates forthwith a universal rule governing *possible* other consciousnesses of it as identical. ... Transcendental subjectivity is not a chaos of intentional processes. (89–90; see *Id. I*, 314, 311, 297)

The index thus specifies what may enter the synthesis and still exhibit the character of "belonging," thereby maintaining the unity of one consciousness. The *expectation* of such flux-moments as will maintain this harmony establishes a kind of preemption of the future—the protentions. They are "'also meant'—not yet perceived, but anticipated and, at first, with a non-intuitional emptiness (as the sides that are 'coming' now perceptually: a continuous protention . . .)" (*CM*, 82).

As a unity of sense, then, the object functions as a "*rule*" that outlines expectations, the fulfillment of which will continue the constitution of the object in question.[8] It is an index that identifies those experiential possibilities

---

8. See *Hua* III/2, 493–94/92 n. 186: "as long as the harmony is not interrupted and as a consequence carries with it the necessary presumption that it will continue to follow its style, it presents the . . . thing. . . . "

that belong or could belong to the unity in question and that can thereby be considered as belonging to and characterizing the object-correlate of that synthesis. As such a sense, this object "*points ahead* to possible perceptual multiplicities that, merging continuously into one another, join together to make up the unity of one perception" (80).

Thanks to the object's functioning as an index for consciousness, the synthesis that *yields* such an object is intentional, for through this index the intentional functionary is able to reach out beyond what is "actually presented" and preempt, through protention, the "more" of the object that, though yet to come, nonetheless is "given," and given precisely as "belonging" to what *is* actually given.

'Object as rule' is the rule for those experiential possibilities that belong to the transcendental functionary and that will maintain the harmony of the synthesis in question. As such the object has no sense at all without reference to such possibilities. Not only is the object a *dependent* product, but its very sense is to be a unifying principle for a certain course of pure lived experiences, for "potentialities of consciousness that belong to the lived experience itself" (82) and that are "included in the 'ego'" (87). The object is nothing other than a principle—a "rule"—of harmonious "putting together." By virtue of this rule, future experiential possibilities of the object in question—its protentional horizon—attain some content.

§ 2.3. Object as a Pole of Identity or the "X"

We have said that the object is, first, a unity resulting from a synthesis—that is, a product—and, second, that that unity prescribes the content that may enter into synthesis and not compromise the identity under constitution. However, we note, third, that the object is more, though not other, than any range of moments that enter into synthesis: it is "transcendent" to any actual or possible consciousnesses of it. Husserl considers this aspect of the object when speaking of it as a "pole of identity" or the "X" (see *Id. I*, § 131). What can this mean?

If the synthesis is to achieve the constitution of an identity, a Same, then it must bring about, through the gathering of the flux, a "central point of unity" (271). But this central point is in no way a unity of predicates in the sense in which any complex or combination of predicates would be called a unity. "It is necessarily to be distinguished from them, although not to be placed alongside and separated from them; just as, conversely, they are *its* predicates: unthinkable without it, yet distinguishable from it" (271-72). The one identical object is intended in the continuous or synthetic course of experience, but always presents itself differently; it is "the same," though "given in other predicates with different determination-content" (271). Though the object may undergo a continual *enrichment* of sense or value, it is still always *this one* object that is now more beautiful, now more valuable, etc. It is evident then, that, pursuing this line of phenomenological investigation, the "identical intentional 'object' becomes . . . distinguished from the changing and alterable predicates." Husserl says:

> It becomes separated as the *central noematic moment*: the *"object,"* the *"identical,"* the "determinable subject of its possible predicates"—*the pure X in abstraction from all predicates*—and it becomes separated *from* these predicates or, more precisely, from the predicate-noemata.

Thus in no synthesis—nor in the noema that is its achieved result—can "it or its necessary center, the point of unity, the pure determinable X, be lacking. No 'sense' without the '*something*' and, again, without '*determining content*'" (272). But what is that "X"?

First, it is the "something" that is determined in predication: as such, it is therefore to be distinguished from such predicates. However, it is not separated from them. It is not a something-in-itself *beyond* the object's intuitably presentable sense. The X only exists *within* the senses—the moments of the stream gathered in the synthesis of identification—that one entity has for us.

The language Husserl uses in elaborating himself here is, as Mensch points out, distinctly Kantian. He goes on to ask whether or not the "empty X" could be a Kantian thing-in-itself, where the X may be taken (on a certain interpretation of Kant) to be something beyond the object's intuitably presentable sense. However, Husserl clearly rejects this possibility. "Stated most generally," as Mensch says,

> Husserl's position is that the X is empty, but it is not beyond what we can experience. It is empty when considered *in abstraction* from experience. Yet as something set up by the connections between experiences, it has as *its condition* the presence of these experiences. Thus, to think of the X as something beyond experience—and, hence, as beyond the senses which are also part of experience—is to give it a certain misplaced concreteness.[9]

Though the terminology Husserl uses to discuss the object as a product of synthesis bears great similarity to Kant's, there are significant differences. The Husserlian X is not the Kantian noumenon, a thing-in-itself *beyond*, or considered in abstraction from the conditions of, the domain of knowledge. Rather, the X *only* exists *within* the senses that an entity has *for transcendental consciousness*. As Mensch puts it: "It is only something for consciousness since it is only posited when the senses which we can predicate of the entity close up together in an individual unity, a unity in which something identical is recognized."

The thesis of the "object as X" allows us to understand Husserl's claim that an individual real existent is a unity of sense (*Id. I*, 106). Husserl makes apparently contradictory statements here: in intending an individual existent, the

---

9. James R. Mensch, *Intersubjectivity and Transcendental Idealism* (Albany, N.Y.: State University of New York, 1988), 63. The next quotation may be found here also.

glance must pass through the given, appearing sense, which can be described in general terms, to the identical "*this*," the "X." But Husserl rejects the notion that the X, the actual particular entity, is something *other* than or beyond the unity of the gathered together flux-moments that, in being gathered together, form the *sense* of the object. As Mensch says: "The key, here, is Husserl's genetic understanding of sense."[10] Remember that a sense is a *one* in many that has been synthetically constituted, and that the X is the "point of unification." Therefore, though the X, as the point of unification, is not the same as any of the moments that enter into the synthesis, it is not something outside of or beyond the process of synthesis. Thus we can say that the thesis of the X, which is the thesis of the object's individual existence, is *also* the thesis of its sense, because in positing a *same* we posit a one-in-many—but to posit *this* is *also* to posit the X as a point of unification.

However, there *is* a sense in which a distinction must be made between the two whereby, with a certain change in emphasis, we can "speak of passing beyond the object's sense in intending its existence." The world—and all particular objects—has being as a sense, therefore, which arises in consciousness as the field for sense-bestowal (*Id. I*, 106). This sense is the object in the What of its being and is described by giving an account of the various modes of consciousness in which it would remain given. Yet the apprehension of the object as a *sense*, in *general* terms, is not the apprehension of the individual existence or This-ness of an object. So in talking (as we have so far) only of the object in terms of its being a constituted sense, we have not done full justice to the object as given in intuition. For Husserl the thesis of individual existence concerns not the sense but the "bearer" of this sense, for the sense is not what we intend when we focus on the This-ness of an object, on its individual existence. If we conceive of sense genetically, as the result of a process, then the "point of unification" becomes a "point of connection." Here, as Mensch points out, the notion of the object goes beyond its sense—considered as something achieved or arrived at—to include the *ground* of that sense, which is nothing other than the ordering of the stream-moments in such a way as to allow a unifying synthesis to succeed, to "allow sense to be generated as such a point."[11] Considered in this way, it is correct to say that in intending the object as a This—as an individual existent—we do pass beyond its sense. For to intend a particular, we must intend it not only in its What-ness, but also in its This-ness; we must intend "the point of connection between the predicates."

This reinforces the conclusion established in our discussion of the object as an achieved result. The lived experiences that enter into synthesis are *prior*

---

10. This and the next passage cited may be found on ibid., 65.
11. This and the next passage cited may be found in Mensch, *Intersubjectivity and Transcendental Idealism*, 65.

to the individual existence that exists only as a synthetic unity of such experiences. They are the constitutive elements out of which objects arise. But it is not just their actual being that gives us the object; it is rather their mode of interconnection—their being successfully gathered together in a synthesis of identification to yield a unity of one consciousness—that allows for the constitution of a unitary X, which is the actual being of the particular object. Thus Husserl says: "the object is 'constituted' . . . in certain concatenations of consciousness that in themselves bear a discernible unity insofar as they, by their essence, carry with themselves consciousness of an identical X" (*Id. I*, 281). And further: "The title 'actual object' is . . . a title for certain eidetically considered rational connections in which the unitary X present in them retains its rational positing" (302). The individual existence of an object, then, is a function of the unity established within and among the moments of experience and is *nothing more* than that. "Everywhere 'object' is a title for eidetic concatenations of consciousness."

The thesis of the object as "identical X" is the thesis of the *ideality* of the object. Only as such can the object sustain, as an essential moment of its ontic meaning, the *openness of conception* that actually marks it. In fact the proper conception of the thing is not given by a closed or final concept, nor by an "in principle" list of predicates, but rather by a "Kantian idea." No object is ever perfectly or "adequately" given:

> Again and again the intuitions are to be converted into intuitional continua and the pregiven continua amplified. No perception of the physical thing is definitively closed; there is always room for new perceptions, for determining more precisely the indeterminacies, for fulfilling the unfulfilled. With every progression the determinative content of the physical-thing noema, which continually belongs to the same physical-thing X, is enriched. It is an eidetic insight that *each* perception and multiplicity of perceptions is capable of being amplified; the process is thus an endless one. Accordingly, no intuitive seizing upon the physical thing-essence can be so complete that a further perception cannot noematically contribute something new to it. (311–12)

The reality of the object is a function of harmony being maintained throughout the ongoing synthesis: it is a function of the unifiability of the flux-moments, not their being appearings of a preexistent unity. The X therefore is not—even in principle—a determinate list, nor is the "rule" in any sense a *complete* list of the moments making up the essence of the object. This limitlessness is not without "determinate direction" (what this could possibly mean we will investigate soon); but *"perfect givenness"*—which would correspond to the final and definitively actual being of the object—"*is nevertheless predesignated as 'idea'* (in the Kantian sense)" (297). Thus the *identity* of any object is never a really *inherent moment* (a lived experience) of the streaming conscious life. And yet the object—with its open endlessness—*is present*, in a certain sense, *within* the consciousness that knows and attains it. How? When Husserl says that "we have here an *ideal immanence*" (*CM*, 95),[12] he is referring to the mode of presence of the object, which, though always subject to a "more," is nonetheless given as an actual and self-same identity. Such a being, however, can have no being other than as ideal.

§ 3. The Presumptiveness of the Object

We note, first, that the identity of the object is an achievement and that, second, identity consists not in the achievement of a *fixed definitude* or a *static entity* but in the ongoing maintenance of harmony within the flux. For Husserl constitution is *essentially* genetic, always in process. Thus a peculiar result emerges: an identity can be constituted—where the X, as a unitary point of connection has been established—but not completed. We can say that an object has been constituted once a unitary point of connection has been established—but given that "being an object-identity" consists not in the total set of elements that are so connected but *instead* in the fact and possibility of their *connection*—even though there is still more of the object that is yet to be given and still other possible determinations that may *never* be given. In short, because the thesis of the object as X understands the laws governing constitution of being as the laws governing the unifiability of flux-moments, the being of the object is always only presumptive. This is because the givenness and successful synthesis of no matter how many experiences up to some point in time does not in any way guarantee that the course of experience will *continue* to present that object. No set or number of synthesized stream-moments can bring about the end of the process of originary synthesis. The perception of a perspectivally given object can never be completed; there is always more yet to be given.

Because the X is not *equivalent to* its appearings, no appearance or set of appearances can adequately present it. Thus the being of any actual object is always only presumptive because the synthesis can go on and on *in infinitum*, offering further—and possibly non-confirmatory—evidence regarding the object in question. Husserl says:

> Principially something physically real, a being with such a sense, can appear only "*inadequately*" in a closed appearance. Essentially connected with this is that *no rational positing that rests upon such an inadequately giving appearance* can be "*ultimately valid*," "insurmountable," and that no rational positing is equivalent in its singularization to the unqualified 'The physical thing is actual', but is only equivalent to 'It is actual'—assuming that the further course of experience does not give rise to "stronger rational motives" that show the original positing to be one that must be "crossed out" in the broader context. Here the positing is only rationally motivated by the appearance (the imperfectly fulfilled perceptual sense) in and of itself, considered in its singularization. (*Id. I*, 286–87)

---

12. Husserl says elsewhere in that text that the index "is never present to actual consciousness as an actual finished datum" (*CM*, 82).

§ 3.1. "Actual Being" is Successful Synthesis *in infinitum*

Though any actual object is always only given presumptively, this is not ground for either skepticism or realism. It does not follow from the fact that there is always more of an object to be given that there are rational grounds for doubting the truth of judgments about the being of any object that presents itself to intuition. It is not possible to give an account of a non-presumptive givenness of an object, a "better" account that would allow the presumptiveness to be overcome, for to be a transcendent object *is* to be given in this way; this character of givenness establishes the meaning of its transcendence. To be given in this way is *essential* to the ontological excess of the object, and, because of this, the experiential inadequacy is not a reflection on the fallibility of knowing.

Nor does this presumptiveness provide grounds for the postulation of a real object existing in itself, whose existence would be induced or inferred from the fact of experience, so as to provide a "solid anchor" in reality for an experience that fails of its own accord to provide a guarantee of the being of its object. As was said above, presumptiveness is not a function of perceptual limitations, but of the very being of the object itself.

Rather, the object is real *if* the course of experience goes on in such a way so as to allow successful synthesis *in infinitum* (see *Id. I*, 87, 92-93). Mensch elaborates upon this point by noting that Husserl's thesis of the being of the object means that *existence* cannot be a judgment of perception, because the object cannot be identified with any actual perceptual experience or sum of any such experiences. Existence is not a function of the *contents* of individual experiences, but rather their *unifiability* within a single referent.[13] As for Kant, likewise for Husserl it holds that knowledge of an object is knowledge by means of connected perceptions. "For both," as Mensch puts it, "an object is defined as 'that in whose concept there is unified the multiplicity of a given [total] intuition.'"[14] As we have seen, Husserl thereby understands the object as a synthetic accomplishment of consciousness—that is, "as a unity formed by synthesizing (or 'connecting') perceptions. Its appearing sense, or 'concept,' is a function of its being . . . a unity of the 'multiplicity' of perceptions that form an ongoing 'given intuition.'"

§ 4. Real Object as Transcendence-in-Immanence

The conception of the object as the "empty X" is precisely where Husserl recognizes the *transcendence* of the object, as well as the device through which the *meaning* of the transcendence of the object is established. Because in the flow of experience the object continually presents itself differently, with yet

---

13. The principle governing this unifiability will be investigated shortly.
14. This and the next passage cited may be found in Mensch, *Intersubjectivity and Transcendental Idealism*, 60.

new and other determining content, the object that remains the same *cannot* be identified with any one, or any set, of the individual experiences in which it is given, or with any one or any set of the senses that the object-as-index may prescribe. The X is a point of unification; therefore, it cannot be identified with any particular set of flux-moments or intentional acts that could actually be unified in its concept.

Thus because the being of the object is a function of unifiability of flux-moments that, once unified, give it in intuition, the X is transcendent to any set of its appearances, or any set of intuitions in which it is given. This is because the series of appearances or intuitions of the object is limitless (see, e.g., *Id. I*, 311). No perception in which an X is given is ever so complete that a further perception cannot noematically contribute something new to it. The process of constitution is thus an endless one. We shall have more to say about this when discussing how Husserl's idealism maintains its own kind of openness. Suffice it to say at this point, however, that the transcendence of the object is expressed in this limitlessness. Insofar as Husserl understands the object as the X, he conceives of it as an entity that surpasses or transcends the finite sum of any actual views of it. In this its transcendence is not only affirmed but the sense of that transcendence is clarified:

> the physical thing is transcendent to the perception of it and consequently to any consciousness whatever related to it; it is transcendent not merely in the sense that the physical thing cannot be found in fact as a really inherent component of consciousness; rather, the entire situation is one into which we can gain eidetic insight: it holds with *unqualifiedly unconditional* universality or necessity that no physical thing can be given in any possible perception, in any possible consciousness whatsoever, as really inherently immanent. (76)

The being of the object is placed *not* in the appearings that are had of it but in the *ongoing unity established by their connections*. Therefore, the object itself, understood not as the noematic sense (our *present* understanding of the object), but as the X, the "bearer" of that sense, *can never* exhibit the finality of a *closed concept*, "that of a completely conceived and defined sense which is not open to addition or revision."[15]

We note also that, in establishing the transcendence of the object beyond any particular act or set of acts, it has been established that the being of the object is not the same as the being of the acts in which it is given. When those particular and individual acts pass, the object does not pass with them, because it is not identical in being with them. This means that one of the prime requirements for transcendence is met: due to this transcendence, it is in principle possible for such objects to be re-identified, to be given again in different acts of intuition.

---

15. Mensch, *Intersubjectivity and Transcendental Idealism*, 74.

However, this transcendence is a transcendence-in-immanence. Though the X can never exhibit the finality of a closed concept, it itself is always only a function of the unifiability *in infinitum* of the purely subjective flux-moments, which are not themselves real objects.

Thus Husserl says in *Ideas I* that object-being "is a being that consciousness posits in its experiences, that principially can be determined and intuited only as something identical belonging to [harmoniously] motivated multiplicities of appearances: *beyond that*, however, it is nothing" (*Id. I*, 93). And in the *Cartesian Meditations* he states his position in a way that draws attention especially to the implications for any desire for alterity:

> The "object" of consciousness, the object as having identity "with itself" during the flowing lived experience, does not come into the lived experience from outside; on the contrary, it is included as a sense in the lived experience itself—and thus as an *"intentional effect" produced by* the synthesis of consciousness. (*CM*, 80; see 85)

Furthermore, it follows from this that phenomenology becomes an "egology" (76): all of the possibilities for object-being are contained within the intentional functionary itself. Thus Husserl says: "The concrete ego itself is the universal theme of the description. Or put more clearly: I, the meditating phenomenologist, set myself the universal task of *uncovering my self* as a transcendental ego in my *full concreteness*—thus with all the intentional correlates included therein." This self, which becomes the full and complete domain for phenomenological investigation, is "a *self-contained complex of being*, a complex of *absolute being* into which nothing can penetrate and out of which nothing can slip" (*Id. I*, 93). For it is the transcendental functionary, the field of sense, that "contains within itself, 'constitutes' within itself, all worldly transcendencies."

The "metaphysical" implications of these results are well known. Husserl himself pronounces them: his transcendental phenomenology yields a transcendental idealism. Furthermore, it seems that this idealism, in the final analysis and in spite of the persistent affirmations of the intentionality of consciousness and of the restoration of the "genuine" meaning of transcendence to objects, falls prey to the specter that haunts every idealism and that fuels the arguments of its critics. That is, it seems that in knowing its object the intentional functionary does not meet any genuine alterity. What it knows are its own creations: to be an object is to be a one-in-many—to be a sense—and the field of consciousness is the field of sense-giving. The very sense of 'object-being', which phenomenological investigation reveals, *demands* the denial of the alterity of any known or knowable object.

§ 5. The First Aspect of Openness: "Facticity"

The tentative conclusion we must draw at this point is that transcendental phenomenological analysis results in a certain collapse of the theses of sense and being into each other. The constituted sense of the entities of the real world *is the very being* of the entities of the real world, at least insofar as there is no phenomenological difference between the *constituted* real being that shows itself in intuition and the *real being* of the real object that shows itself in intuition. The real object, which we have an interest in knowing, is nothing beyond the being itself that is constituted through the functioning of the intentional act. Does this mean that transcendental consciousness is closed upon itself, knowing as it does only its own intentional "productions"?

Certainly transcendental consciousness does not know a *world of real things* that would be "outside" it and would have to "come into" consciousness from beyond. But Husserl's analysis begins here to broach the openness of consciousness in a genuinely phenomenological way. We shall begin our account of this openness by considering the phenomenon that Husserl refers to as 'facticity'. This will prepare us to see that transcendental consciousness's openness is not to "real things" (only psychological-human consciousness is open to real things, it being a real thing itself) but to a certain "being determined" by what "comes to pass" as comprising the stream of experience. But what "comes to pass" and thereby "determines" the stream by making up its living actual content is not "reality," understood as the domain of constituted sense-identities. What, then, are we to make of the discovery of a stream in which all reality is constituted but that nonetheless continues to be characterized as being determined by some kind of "alterity"? We shall now investigate this in more detail.

§ 6. The Law of the Synthesis

The object has been clarified in terms of its constitution and has emerged as a transcendence-in-immanence. Idealism is affirmed. Yet does the denial of the alterity of the *object* by itself imply a closure of intentionality? How is what might be called the 'law of the synthesis' to be understood? What are we to make of the "essential determination" of the form of synthetic process that characterizes identification? What is the source of the *constraint* that the "idea" imposes upon the process of synthesis? What determines the inviolability of the "rule," as which the object has emerged? Why is the synthetic function bound in just the ways it is? Might it not be possible, when confronted by these questions, to find in such lawfulness the influence or function of alterity? To move in that philosophical direction would leave Husserl's transcendental idealism intact insofar as it concerned the *products* of synthesis; but it would not entail the total closure that would otherwise be associated with it. Husserl may well have demonstrated that the world is constituted "purely within the transcendental ego" (*CM*, 89), but are the conditions governing that constitution also purely within that ego?

§ 6.1. The Dynamic of Originary or Constitutive Verification

Until what we have termed 'the law of the synthesis' has been clarified, the status of the object remains uncertain—specifically, the possibility of the object's law being grounded in some alterity. We have seen that a whole range of horizonal potentialities are indicated by the object and that such a referring expresses a certain invariability (*CM*, 88). But until the sense of this invariability is fully grasped—in short, until the principle of synthesis in which the Same appears is grasped—the status of the Same will remain uncertain.

What governs the possibility of this "reaching out," this synthesis that unifies? How is it that only *some* potentialities and not others can come to manifest the relation of "belonging together" characterized by harmony among the various moments—the "belonging together" in which the "intending beyond itself" consists? (84).

In § 20 of the *Cartesian Meditations* Husserl offers a clue. He notes that this synthesis is something "done on my own initiative" (82).

§ 6.1.1. Particular Evidences and Abiding Being

The task now is to understand the principial difference between the syntheses resulting in the "chaos" entertained in the world annihilation experiment and those in which the real world is constituted. We note first that this difference is not that between no synthesis and synthesis. True, the syntheses typical of world annihilation do not yield real objects or a world. But they do yield a stream of "lived experiences," which lend themselves—if the thought experiment is to work—to a kind of identification. Were this not the case, not even chaos could manifest itself. What Husserl actually says here is that a "host of irreconcilable conflicts" (*Id. I*, 91) manifest themselves, that harmony fails to characterize the order of stream-moments. For this thought experiment, "an annihilation of the world means . . . nothing other than that in each stream of lived experiences . . . certain ordered concatenations of experience . . . would be excluded" (92).

Though without a world, the functionary of the experiment is not utterly without objects: "raw unity formations" comprise the experiential stream of the worldless intentional functionary. They remain immanent, non-real objects, which nonetheless generate conflict and disappointment, the meaning of which is the loss of a world. As immanent objects they do attain the status of what Husserl elsewhere calls a "particular evidence" (*CM*, 96). Particular evidences are purely immanent objects that find their place within the stream, having been constituted through the retentional moment of the synthesis. Thanks to the synthetic function of retention, the evidence that did manifest itself as a Now still remains available for consciousness, co-functioning with the new actual content of the Now so as to provide one dimension of its horizon—the past.

However, the problem with the raw unity formations of the world annihilation experiment is that they do not allow for the constitution of a world. Why? Because "particular evidence does not as yet produce for us any abiding being." Why not? Because particular evidences—immanent objects located temporally within the stream—must be able to be returned to in an originary intuition in order for an abiding being—a being "in itself" that is not just "for me," not just a purely subjective-immanent moment of the stream—to be constituted and not simply to flow away with the stream. To flow away with the stream is to *be* as the stream, to exhibit no difference from it. To abide is to *remain the same*, not to exist as flux-moment. For Husserl, "fixed and abiding being" is equivalent to extra-subjective, extra-immanent object being, because abiding being affirms its difference from the utterly singular flowing of the flux by being able to be *given again*. This is because a being that claims an existence other than purely immanental-subjective must *show* itself to possess that mode of being. That is to say, such a being must be capable of being given again as that self-same identity that was given previously. It must be given not merely non-intuitively, as through a recollection or memory of a thing that once was given originarily. The condition for this is that it not simply flow away as pure flux. As Husserl says, "verification refers ultimately to making evident and having as evident" (92); and "evidence" denotes "the quite preeminent mode of consciousness that consists in the self-appearance, the self-exhibiting, the self-giving . . . of a thing [*Sache*], in the final mode: '*itself there*', '*immediately intuited*', '*given originaliter*'" (92–93). Verification thus has a very definite *constitutional* function: it is not the giving of a being that can be so given *because* it already exists in itself. Rather, verification is the very establishment of the sense of an object as abiding being. Thus abidingness—objectivity—is constituted whenever the transcendental functionary can "'always return' to the itself-beheld actuality, in a series of new evidences as restitutions of the first evidence" (95). *Without the possibility of such verificatory returning*, "there would be for us no *fixed and abiding* being, no real and no ideal world. Both of these exist for us thanks to evidence or the presumption of being able to make evident and repeat acquired evidence."[16]

The postulation of the world annihilation experiment is just this: that the

---

16. The order of objectivity in question corresponds to the degree of "open endlessness," the "I can always do so again," of the ability to verify, to return: "Everything that exists is 'in itself,' in a maximally broad sense, and stands in contrast to the accidental being 'for me' of the particular acts; likewise every truth is, in this broadest sense, a 'truth in itself.' This broadest sense of the In-itself refers us to evidence, not however to a particular evidence as a *de facto* experience, but rather to certain potentialities, which are grounded in the transcendental ego and his life: first of all, to the potentiality of the infinity of intendings of every kind that relate to something as identical, but then also to the potentiality of verifying these intendings, consequently to potential evidences that, as *de facto* experiences, are repeatable *in infinitum*" (*CM*, 96).

attempt to establish abiding being—to constitute a world—fails. But how can this failure to establish abiding being, to make evident again, be understood?

§ 6.2. Retrievability of Particular Evidences

What is the implication of the role of verification in the constitution of fixed and abiding—or worldly—being for the distinction between successful and unsuccessful syntheses of identification? Husserl says that the syntheses of verification "belong essentially in the domain of the 'I can'" (93). When the transcendental functionary is able successfully to return, to retrieve "particular evidences," then in this retrieving of "that very same one," fixed and abiding being is constituted. When this ability is thwarted, no such being is manifest; in the language of *Ideas I*, no world is constituted. This can be elaborated as follows.

Note that if the real object is *constituted* in the "having again" and hence does not exist as a real object prior to such retrieval, then that to which one returns in the attempt to constitutively verify cannot be the real object itself. Nonetheless, there must be some *principle of retrieval* that can be operated. If it cannot be the object itself that is retrieved, then just what is "returned to" in the attempt to "present again"? The answer to this question lies in the structure that characterizes the mode of givenness of the first "particular evidence," through which the "apparent aspect" of the particular evidence—for example, the color or texture, or other "sense" qualities of what will become the object—is always given with what one might refer to as a *kinetic or kinaesthetic "co-efficient."* It is this "co-efficient" that *falls under the sway of the intentional functionary's ability to govern itself*—the 'I can'—that enables Husserl to say the verificatory syntheses belong to the domain of the 'I can always do so again'. In *Ideas II* Husserl elaborates this point: "*To the possibility of experience [of a worldly object] there pertains . . . the spontaneity of the courses* of presenting acts of sensation, which are accompanied by series of kinaesthetic sensations and are dependent on them as motivated" (*Id. II*, 56).[17] In all constitution of real entities, then, two different kinds of "sensations" or lived experiences can be found, with "totally different constituting functions" (57). On the one hand, there are: "the sensations that *constitute*, by means of the apprehensions allotted to them,

---

17. Bearing in mind that Husserl is speaking "objectively" when in elaborating the theory of constitution he uses the terms 'Body' (*Leib*) and 'sense organs'—which is to say, speaking in terms that presuppose the achievement of the objectifying self-apperception whereby the transcendental functionary constitutes itself as a thing in the world—he continues: "*given with the localization of the kinaesthetic series in the relevant moving member of the Body is the fact that in all perception and perceptual exhibition (experience) the Body is involved as freely moved sense organ, as freely moved totality of sense organs*, and hence there is also given the fact that, on this original foundation, all that is thingly-real in the surrounding world of the ego has its relation to the Body" (*Id. II*, 56/61).

corresponding *features of the thing* as such by way of adumbration."[18] On the other, there are the accompanying kinetic and kinaesthetic sensations,

> "sensations" that do not undergo such apprehensions but that . . . are necessarily involved in all those apprehensions of the sensations of the first kind, insofar as, in a certain way, they *motivate* those apprehensions and thereby themselves undergo an apprehension of a completely different type, an apprehension that thus belongs correlatively to every constituting apprehension.

This second kind of sensation is peculiar in that they are operated freely by the intentional functionary: through the "Body" in which they are localized, the transcendental functionary "holds sway" and "rules."[19] That is why Husserl says that the syntheses of verification "belong essentially in the domain of the 'I can'" (*CM*, 93).

It is this fact of relation between these two kinds of "sensation" that allows for the establishment of a "rule" for an object, a set of expectations that yields the "harmony" that characterizes successful syntheses of identification or verification. For originarily, in the first givenness of the "particular evidence," the two kinds of sensation are given, along with the fact of their being *correlated* in a particular and definite manner and order. This first occurrence, this first act in which the "particular evidence" is constituted, provides a set of correlated sensations that, having been undergone, are retained in the ego-stream through the dynamic of retention: "every act, carried out 'for the first time,' becomes an 'instauration' of a permanent possession *lasting* throughout immanent time (in the sense of a lasting identity)" (*Id. II*, 311).

The answer to the problem of how it is possible to "have again" is provided by the correlativity of the two kinds of sensations and the fact that one kind belongs within the domain of the 'I can'. Taken together, these factors allow us to understand the attempt to "have again" as a kind of test: *if* I activate the capacities under my control in a certain way, *then* I expect (protend) the sensations correlated with them in the primal institution, to arise. Thus, what is "had again" is the correlation of "sensations," brought about by my free (in principle at least) activity:

---

18. See also *Id. II*, 57: "For example, the sensation-colors with their sensation-expansions: it is in the apprehension of these that the corporeal colorations appear together with the corporeal extension of these colorations. Likewise, in the tactual sphere, thingly roughness appears in the apprehension of the roughness-sensations, and corporeal warmth appears in relation to the sensation of warmth, etc."

19. See *Id. II*, 152: "The ego has the 'faculty' (the 'I can') freely to move this Body—i.e. the organ in which it is articulated—and to perceive an external world by means of it." Husserl also speaks of "the free 'I move'" (310). Of course, to speak of the functioning of the 'I can' in originary constitution in terms of moving the Body is already to presuppose the constitution of the spatial dimension and the mundanizing self-apperception through which the transcendental functionary becomes constituted as a thing in the world. The originarily constituting kinetic and kinaesthetic functioning cannot therefore be experienced as "the moving of a Body in a world."

116   INTENTIONALITY AND TRANSCENDENCE

> In all constitution and on all levels we have by necessity "*circumstances,*" related one to the other, and "*that which is dependent on*" all the circumstances: everywhere, we find *the 'if–then' or the 'because-therefore'*. Those sensations that undergo extensional apprehension (leading to the extended features of the physical thing) are *motivated* as regards the courses they take either actually or possibly and are apperceptively *related to motivating series, to systems, of kinaesthetic sensations*, which freely unfold in the nexus of their familiar order in such a way that if a free unfolding of one series of this system occurs (e.g. any movement of the eyes or fingers), then from the interwoven manifold as motive, the corresponding series must unfold as motivated. In this way, from the ordered system of sensations in eye movement, in head movement freely moved, etc., there unfold such and such series in vision. That is, while this is happening, there unfold, *in motivated order*, "images" of the physical thing that was perceptually apprehended to begin the eye movement and, likewise, the visual sensations pertaining to the physical thing in each case. An apprehension of a physical thing as situated at such a distance, as oriented in such a way, as having such a color, etc., is unthinkable . . . without these sorts of *relations of motivation*. In the essence of the apprehension itself there resides the possibility of letting the perception disperse into "*possible*" series of perceptions, all of which are of the following type: *if* the eye turns in a certain way, *then* so does the "image"; if it turns differently in some definite fashion, then so does the image alter differently, in correspondence. We constantly find here this twofold articulation: kinaesthetic sensation on the one side, the motivating; and the sensations of features on the other, the motivated. . . . *Perception* is without exception a *unity of accomplishment* that arises essentially out of the playing together of two *correlatively related functions*. At the same time, it follows that *functions of spontaneity* belong to *every perception*. The processes of the kinaesthetic sensations are *free processes* here, and this *freedom in the consciousness of their unfolding* is an essential part of the constitution of spatiality. (57–58)[20]

This analysis gives us two things, both necessary to understand the phenomenon of retrieval. First, the retrieval is made possible by the fact that the "motivating" sensations, the kinetic and kinaesthetic sensations, belong to the

---

20. Husserl reiterates this dynamic of correlation later at *Id. II*, 128, saying: "If we hold fast to the visual sphere pure and simple and to the constitutive unities existing in it alone, then to each position of the eyes (to indicate it in an objective expression), the body and head remaining fixed, corresponds a new aspect of the thing seen and especially of its extension. And the same applies to each change of the position of the head which affects the phenomenal orientation (in particular, the one concerning 'distances'). Each of these aspects and the unfolding of the continuously changing aspects are thereby phenomenologically related to corresponding 'circumstances' and are shown . . . to be related to concomitant complexes of kinetic sensations. And this concomitance itself is something constituted by consciousness. . . . The originary or . . . fully intuitive consciousness of the identity of the form within the continuous change of its modes of givenness . . . essentially presupposes the continuous unfolding, played out in the background of attention, of the concomitant kinaesthetic sensation-complexes or of the corresponding transitional phenomena ('kinetic phenomena') of the sensation-complexes which, for example, are different according to whether, objectively spoken, the eyes move from their position at the start to this or that other position."

domain of the 'I can'. I can do this or that, or enact various "bodily" movements, according to an intention and set of expectations. Second, because of the original fact of correlation, or the development of a pattern of correlation in subsequent activations of kinaesthetic and kinetic possibilities, not only does an expectation of the course of sensations ranged under the 'I can' emerge, but also one of the range of sensations that will be correlated with the kinaesthesias and that will be apperceived as qualities of the object. This expectation is the basis for the possibility of *harmony* in the course of experience. The expected correlation forms the basis of the object as rule—which sets the conditions under which the expectation can be satisfied.

In the *Cartesian Meditations*, Husserl, speaking "objectively," gives the following account of the conditionality built upon the expected correlation of the two kinds of sensations:

> the perception has horizons made up of other possibilities of perception, as perceptions we *could* have if we *actively directed* the course of perception otherwise: if, for example, we turned our eyes that way instead of this, or if we were to step forward or to one side, and so forth. In the corresponding memory this recurs in modified form, perhaps in the consciousness that, instead of the sides then visible in fact, I could have seen others—naturally, *if* I had directed my perceptual activity in a suitably different manner. (*CM*, 82)

Because the ordering and course of a lived experience is coordinated with a kinaesthetic function, the possibility of a *repetition* of a sense-course, a pattern of sense experience, is present. Because this repetition is essentially motivated by an expectation, this dynamic has the form of a conditional; it is an 'if–then'. Consciousness can seek to verify, to establish abidingness by activating a particular kinaesthetic possibility[21] that was originally given in coordination with a particular course of sense experience. The *return* is a return to that course, to have it *again*, via the reactivation of the coordinated kinaesthesia.

The condition expressed by the 'if–then' forms the ground of the "essential formations" (*Id. I*, 91) that characterize the constitution of the object. If the condition is satisfied, "the same," that is, the primal "particular evidence," shows itself again. Through the possibility of this return, the fixedness and abidingness of the object, and hence its otherness than the stream, is established. The "being in itself" of the object refers to the ideal possibility of an infinity of intersubjective retrievals:

> This broadest sense [of the object] refers us to evidence, not however to a particular evidence as a *de facto* experience, but rather to certain potentialities, which are grounded in the transcendental ego and his life: first of all, to the infinity of intendings of every kind that relate to something as identical, but then also to the potentiality of verifying these intendings, conse-

---

21. This is something within the range of our freedom: "Everywhere in this connection an 'I can and do, but can also do otherwise than I am doing' plays its part" (*CM*, 82).

quently to potential evidences that, as *de facto* experiences, are repeatable *in infinitum*. (*CM*, 96)

Where this expectation is "disappointed," the essential formation—the "harmony"—fails to manifest itself; Husserl says that, in such cases, no object or world is constituted, because no *return* takes place.

What he is speaking of in the world annihilation experiment is a range of "object analogues," which *are* that just because they (though given as a "particular evidence") cannot be verified as *abiding being*. Were this not the case, a transcendence of some kind or other would be given.

§ 7. The Principle of Synthesis: No Intrusion of Alterity

We can now complete our answer to the question that was raised at the beginning of this chapter regarding the meaning and possible alterity of the identity that is achieved in synthesis.

It is, Husserl says, "a unity of one consciousness" (79). This unity is achieved through the synthetic gathering together of flux-moments that continually pass over into the past. They are held in the retentional horizon. But not all that flows off and is held in retention makes the *particular kind* of unity of one consciousness that manifests an object for consciousness. Only those whose principle of synthesis is that of "belonging together" can allow such a constitution. The principle of "belonging together" is expectation, whose fulfillment generates "harmony." That means: abiding being is constituted where the 'if–then' can be successfully operated, because the 'if–then' is the principle of retrieval. The "unity of one consciousness" is the unity of the *act* that an 'if–then' specifies.

Without the possibility of such a return—that is, the operation of the conditional expectation of the 'if–then'—there would be no manifestation of abiding being at all. And the *scope* of this ability to return establishes the level of objectivity of the entity in question (see *CM*, 96). Only in such returnings is the being in question objectified and determined as it itself. This continual givenness is a constitutional function:

> As given directly and with increasing perfection in perceptual continua that show themselves to be harmonious and in certain methodical forms of thinking based on experience, a transcendent something acquires, more or less mediately, its evident, continually progressive determination. (*Id. I*, 92)

The principle of the synthesis of identification does not therefore reside or come from "outside" the field of intentionality. It does not intrude itself upon the constitutional activity of the intentional functionary in a blind or occult way; it cannot be seen in any way to "represent" the being or ruling power of a noumenal entity, existing in itself over against consciousness. Rather, the principle of synthesis derives from the transcendental abilities of the intentional functionary itself; the conditionality that the synthesis expresses in the form of its 'if–then'—the condition for the establishment of harmony within the flux—is one dependent upon the purely subjective possibilities for experiencing together with the range of "enactions" that are to be found under the heading of the 'I can' and that are at least in principle at the disposal of the transcendental functionary.

This conclusion confirms Husserl's transcendental idealism. Not only are objects the result of the synthesizing activity of the transcendental functionary, but the principle that governs successful synthesis is also "internal" to the transcendental domain. Neither the product nor the principle of the synthesis can be seen to indicate a domain of being in itself or an "unknown cause of appearances." In the case of the intentional analysis of the real object it seems as though Husserl's transcendental phenomenology is truly an egology and must accept that transcendental subjectivity is ultimately closed in upon itself, knowing only the results of its own constitutional activity.

§ 8. Facticity and Openness

Husserl's idealism—understood broadly as the twofold claim that, first, there is no world "outside" the transcendental functionary and that, second, the transcendental functionary is the constituting ground of all identity—has been justified. Identity was seen to be a function of harmonious gathering, and harmony was seen to be function of the exercise of the constitutional powers of the transcendental functionary. Are we then to draw the conclusion that the being of the world refers to and expresses the creative power of a closed and unconditioned transcendental functionary whose constitutional achievements are best understood to express what might be called a 'transcendental voluntarism'?[22] We can develop an answer to this question by considering Husserl's discussion of facticity (*das Faktische*). This will enable us to understand the peculiar dependence of the world-constituting transcendental functionary upon a domain other than its own being, not just for the acquisition of constitutional capacities but ultimately for the very being of the ego itself.

§ 8.1. The Dialectic of Intention and Fulfillment, Facticity, and the Openness of the World-Constituting Ego

Husserl's world annihilation experiment can be understood as a reflection upon the dialectic of intention and fulfillment aimed at bringing out the essentially contingent character of the course of experience that actually comes to pass. As we saw, Husserl claims that the actual being of any intended object is always only progressively constituted in the synthesis of intention and ful-

---

22. Jacques Derrida, *Speech and Phenomena and Other Essays in Husserl's Theory of Signs*, trans. David B. Allison (Evanston, Ill.: Northwestern University, 1973), 53.

fillment insofar as the synthesis proceeds to yield, in its continuous and infinite course, a "harmonious concatenation . . . in which the X, given always as one and the same, is continuously-harmoniously determined 'more precisely' and never 'otherwise'" (*Id. I*, 298). As we also saw, the unfolding of experience in a harmonious (or, equally, conflictual or disappointing) way itself depends upon a difference between, on the one hand, the empty protentional projection of sense and, on the other, the course of experience actually unfolding according to the matter and form of interconnection prescribed in advance by that sense. The essential difference between the empty intending and the fulfilling intuition to which Husserl draws attention here is the *contingency* of the fulfilling course of experience vis-à-vis the empty intended sense. He says:

> The existence of a world is the correlate of certain multiplicities of experience distinguished by certain essential formations. But it *cannot* be seen that actual experiences can flow *only* in such concatenated forms; nothing like that can be seen purely on the basis of the essence of perception as such and of the essences of other kinds of intuition involved therein. (*Id. I*, 91)

It is actually possible that experience, the very "ground" of our encounter with the world, take that very world from us. Husserl continues:

> It is instead quite conceivable that, due to conflict, experience might dissolve into illusion not only in detail and that, as holds *de facto*, not every illusion manifests a deeper truth and that every conflict, in the place where it occurs, is precisely what is demanded by more inclusive contextures in order to preserve total harmony. It is conceivable that in our experiencing there might be a host of irreconcilable conflicts not just for us but in themselves, that experience might suddenly show itself to be refractory to the demand that it carry on its positings of physical things harmoniously, that its context might lose its fixed regular organizations of adumbrations, apprehensions, and appearances—in short, that there might no longer be any world.

Husserl makes this observation so as to point to the phenomenological discovery that the actual being of the world and its objects is a function of the ongoing harmony of the experiences in which it continues to be given. The laws that specify more or less determinately the forms of interconnections of experience that yield harmony only specify the factual conditions that must hold *if* an actual world is to manifest itself—but they do not prescribe the *actual coming to pass* of such specified experiential content. Nothing *given* to consciousness can ensure that experience will proceed in just the ways required in order for a world, or system of identities, to be manifest or constituted. 'Actuality' is therefore a title for *one possible* order of experiential concatenation—i.e. a harmonious order—and not the *only* possible order. The failure of *harmonious* concatenations of experience to come to pass does not entail the failure of other concatenations of experience. In the case of the collapse of the stream of experience into conflict, it could still be, as Husserl points out, that "to some extent, crude unity-formations become constituted," but that "certain ordered concatenations of experience and therefore certain complexes of theorizing reason according to those concatenations of experience, would be excluded" (92). Actuality therefore "lacks self-sufficiency by its essence. . . . Reality is not in itself something absolute that becomes linked secondarily to something else" (93-94). On the contrary, because it depends upon certain *de facto* concatenations of conscious experience coming to pass, the being of actuality has the secondary sense of a founded mode of being.

What founds actuality, then? Husserl's answer is: above and beyond the protentional anticipation, it is the *factual course* of consciousness. This course is the stream of lived experience as it simply occurs. It cannot ever be seen from the actual course of experience just what will continue to unfold in fact; all that can be determined in advance is a specification of the forms of harmony for whatever may progressively unfold. This founding dimension—which provides the "ultimate elements of experience"[23]—is ultimately *factual*. This dimension is nothing other than the streaming life of consciousness in its sheer flowing undergoing. This is the "infinite field of absolute lived experiences—the *fundamental field of phenomenology*" (*Id. I*, 95). The stream in its flowing components is not itself "actual being," and no rules for its *actual* course can be provided. It simply unfolds as it does. This domain is "absolute" in the sense that it itself does not indicate yet further grounds beyond it itself, grounds that are given as determining or conditioning it; it is not possible to inquire back behind it—to "reduce" it—further. It is an ultimate ground because no rational (phenomenological) condition for its factual flowing (essential structure in advance) can be found. For this reason Husserl claims: "The absolute that we uncover is absolute 'fact'"[24]—where 'facticity' refers to the empirically contingent character of flowing consciousness. That is to say, the laws or norms generated and projected by the world-constituting ego merely predetermine in advance the necessary forms of *real* being—*if being is to continue to manifest itself as real*. But what comes to pass in the stream of consciousness cannot be prescribed or known in advance, and so Husserl says: "'Factual' consciousness has no law. . . ."[25]

Therefore, although the actual world is constituted for the transcendental ego in its synthesizing of intention and fulfillment, it remains the case that the being of actuality is not simply the result of the synthesizing activity of that ego. Certainly the manifestation of actuality in its genuine being requires the projection of sense; but it depends equally on the coming to pass of certain ultimately factual and contingent experiences that, in their actual coming to presence, exceed all powers of the world-constituting ego. That ego is therefore an open constituting subjectivity—in the very activity of its world-constitution, in its *waiting upon* the contingent unfolding of experience in which

---

23. Mensch, *Intersubjectivity and Transcendental Idealism*, 134.
24. Husserl, Ms. E III 9, Nov. 13, 1931 (cited from Mensch, op. cit., 118).
25. Husserl, Ms. D 13 XXI, p. 137, 1907–1909 (cited from Mensch, op. cit., 118).

the actual world may or may not continue to come to presence. The noetic correlate, one could say, of the putativity of actual being is the openness of transcendental subjectivity to the contingent facticity of experience. Let us now elaborate the sense of this openness a little further.

§ 8.2. A Deeper Sense of Openness: The Contingency of the Being of the Ego

What can 'openness' with respect to the world-constituting ego mean, beyond the observation that the world-constituting synthesis is dependent upon the contingent coming to pass of certain "factual" experiential concatenations? Our suggestion is this: In its waiting upon what comes to pass, it is not only the actual being of the world that is contingent; the being of the ego is as well—and in two different (though related) ways. First, *what* the world-constituting ego becomes, in its own particular identity and world-constituting capacities, is dependent upon the contingent flowing of the stream of lived experience; second, the *actuality* of the ego itself is dependent upon the contingent flowing of the steam. We shall now seek to elaborate these ideas.

§ 8.2.1. The Noetic Correlate of the Horizon Structure of the World and its Objects

We recall that every intentional presentation of an individual object takes place against the background of the world and that therefore consideration of an object in and for itself is always already an abstraction. There is no experience of a thing that, as Husserl puts it, "does not already 'know' more about the thing than is in this cognition alone" (*EJ*, 26-27/32). Every experience in which some entity is given only presents *that thing* as itself insofar as this experience employs knowledge of what is *also not present*, or in view. Husserl calls this 'potential knowledge' or 'pre-knowledge', which is "indeterminate as to content, or not completely determined, but never completely empty." It is this kind of "knowledge" that yields any particular entity in the first place, as the entity it is, in the world, as an entity, in short, that has its own "horizon" (27/32). As we have seen, Husserl differentiates an entity's internal and external horizons. The internal horizon belongs essentially to every experience of a real thing and is made up of the further determinations of the thing itself, beyond what is presently in view. Each thing, however, is also found within a more general background, made up of other things that could in turn also be brought into view under appropriate conditions. "This means," Husserl says, "that everything given in experience has not only an internal horizon but also an infinite, open, *external horizon of objects cogiven*" (29/33).

This horizonally structured world is the noematic correlate of a complex noetic system on the part of the world-constituting ego, which itself allows such a world to come to presence in just that way for that ego. The horizonal sense of an object is given through what Husserl sometimes calls 'anticipation'; and this anticipation "turns out to be a variant mode of originally constitutive activities of cognition, of an activity and an original intention, therefore of a mode of intentionality that anticipatorily aims beyond a core of givenness" (28/33). Thus intentionality is not only an aiming-beyond the now-present aspect of the entity to the aspects not yet in view, but it is also an aiming-beyond the thing itself in all its more or less indeterminate determinations to an infinite range of other objects that are "co-given" but are not in view. This means that, as horizonally structured, every experience refers to the possibility of bringing to presence an infinite range of relations and entities not yet in view, if it is in fact to be an experience that presents a worldly entity.

These internal and external horizons—without which this experience is not possible—are operative within cognition as modes of "pre-knowledge" or "anticipation." As such, every experience in which a real object comes to intuitive presence presupposes this anticipatory "capacity" (27/32) of the world-constituting ego. As Husserl puts it: "This original 'induction' or anticipation turns out to be a variant mode of originally constitutive activities of cognition, of an activity and an original intention, therefore of a mode of 'intentionality' that anticipatorily aims beyond a core of givenness" (28/33). The web of anticipations constitutes a horizon that was previously empty and undetermined as to actual content, but within which the actual entity unfold itself in a harmonious (or conflictual) way. As Husserl puts it: "in the case of an object so constituted, its abiding existence and being-thus are a correlate of the habituality constituted in the ego-pole itself by virtue of its position-taking" (*CM*, 102). This raises the question as to how the ego acquires these specific anticipations, a question Husserl answers in terms of the *habitualities* that accrue to the ego as its intentional life proceeds.

§ 8.2.2. The Contingency of the World-Constituting Ego's Sedimented Habitualities

The notion of 'habituality' in Husserl's work is in effect a concretization of the phenomenon of retention. Husserl understands a habituality as an abiding property of the ego, through which it goes into action. A habituality is acquired in the following way. In an act of originary intuition, a sense-determination is achieved; the act in which this determination is achieved passes away, though the sense-determination itself remains in the mode "just-accomplished" (*EJ*, 335/279). Not only is it then "retained in grasp" but, insofar as it is not actually revoked, the ego itself "acquires a *new abiding property*" (*CM*, 100). The act-process vanishes, but the sense achieved for the ego in that act-process remains a constantly available and effective achievement, even if it is not explicitly remembered or focused upon. On the one hand, it may be that what we are dealing with is an abiding ego-determination in the form of an enduring conviction about something and that thus generates anticipations in a more or less explicit way. As Husserl says:

> If, in an act of judgment, I decide for the first time in favor of a being and a being-thus, the fleeing act passes; but from now on *I am the ego who is thus and so decided*, "I am of this conviction." ... As long as it is accepted by me, I can "return" to it repeatedly, and repeatedly find it as mine, habitually my own opinion or, correlatively, find myself as the ego who *is* convinced, who, as the persisting ego, is determined by this abiding *habitus* or state. (101)

On the other hand, we may be dealing not so much with constantly abiding convictions as with sedimentations that no longer explicitly structure the anticipatory horizon. It may be that the retentional deposit becomes more and more a *trace* of an act-achievement, as the sense of the once-present experiential encounter sinks ever further into the background and becomes ever more indistinct and "forgotten." As Husserl says, the once-prominent sense of that originary encounter is

> henceforth incorporated into the passive background, into the "unconscious," which is not a dead nothingness but a limiting mode of consciousness and accordingly can affect us anew like another passivity in the form of whims, free-floating ideas, and so on. ... In this passive modification it therefore represents, like every other passivity that has arisen through the modification of what is originally constituted as a source, a *habituality of the ego*, a permanent possession, ready for new associative awakening. (*EJ*, 336/279)

Thus the "concrete ego" (*CM*, 102), the actual world-constituting ego for whom a world can come to presence, is necessarily a progressively constituted ego, existing for itself in its ongoing life of constitutional achievement and subsequent acquisition of world-constituting habitualities. "It is," as Mensch puts it, "an ego of change and growth which is built up out of a series of successive, yet lasting position takings. In this constitution, one position taking—i.e., one 'validation' or acceptance of a position—serves as a foundation for the next."[26]

§ 8.2.3. Openness as the Contingent Dependency of the Being of the World-Constituting Ego

One of the most important implications of this manner of acquisition is that the world-constituting ego, in both its actual world-constituting capacities *and* its own being *as an effective ego*, is *contingent upon the unfolding of the factual course of experience*. First, the sedimented habitualities that accrue to the world-constituting ego grant to that ego "an abiding style with a unity of iden-

---

26. Mensch, *Intersubjectivity and Transcendental Idealism*, 76.

tity throughout all of them: a 'personal character'" (*CM*, 101). The ego is individualized as a "monad" (102) precisely in the accrual of habitualities that actually do become sedimented. That individual ego would therefore have been different from the one that it actually has become were its sedimented habitualities themselves to have been different. And, of course, it is the point of Husserl's world annihilation experiment to show that such could have been the case. Thus insofar as the ego depends for its actual identity upon the habitualities that actually become sedimented (together with the forms of interconnection that are actually achieved), then the concrete world-constituting ego is dependent for its individuation upon the way the course of experience actually unfolds. In this sense the ego in its concrete world-constituting being is contingent upon something other than the ego itself and therefore is not truly absolute.

Second, not only is the identity of the monad contingent upon the contingent unfolding of the stream of experience, but, more than that, it also emerges that the very being of the world-constituting ego is also contingent. The progressive sedimentation of habitualities is not simply the *addition* of one experience to another, and so on; on the contrary, it is the unfolding of a unity gathered together in *synthesis*. This is a synthesis that "embraces all the particular multiplicities of *cogitationes* collectively and in its own manner, namely as belonging to the identical ego, who, *as the active and affected subject of consciousness*, lives in all processes of consciousness and is related, *through* them, to all object-poles" (100). The synthesis in which "the ego is itself *existent for itself* in continuous evidence," in which the ego is "*continuously constituting itself as existing*," establishes a relation of "belonging" amongst the moments of consciousness that come to pass. But what is this relation of belonging? To begin with, it is the result of a synthesis that has the character of a striving for the establishment and maintenance of unity in the progressive unfolding of the stream of experience. The unity achieved therein means that the "components" that are gathered together have the character of being "mine." They are "unified" in that they "belong to me." To say that "they belong to me" means that "I" have continual access—in principle—to what belongs to me. In short, insofar as I have continual access to my accrued habitualities and the ordered connections that hold between them, I remain the same ego; I have available to me "the same" effective powers of anticipation and futural projection in virtue of which "the same" world remains available to me. The identity of the world-constituting ego thus depends upon the *accessibility* of its world-constituting capacities—in short, the progressively sedimented habitualities—and that accessibility means their availability for that ego in its world-constituting intentional life. That availability, however, presupposes stable and discernable—identifiable—interconnections among and between those sedimented acquisitions, so that they can be affirmed in the form of anticipations "again and again." Only as such are they available as stable structures of anticipation. The ego "thus has within itself a universal unity of life, one embracing both the actual and the possible, one which *is*, with respect to the validities of experience and the experiencing habituality, *a universal and anticipatory unity*."[27] But in order for them to be available in this way, they must have been *actually* constituted *in harmony*, so that they can manifest themselves as "the same" again and again. To the extent that the ego can achieve the goal of that striving for unification—that is, constitute abiding being from originary evidences by satisfying the conditional 'if-then'—then the habitualities that accrue to the ego are sedimented according to connections that can be revivified in the mode "again and again." In short, there is here a certain feedback from the effect of constitution into the constituting ego. Only to the extent that object-senses are effectively constituted as harmoniously ordered can the sedimentations themselves manifest an order allowing of unification.

However, a chaos in the unfolding of experience would not allow *ordered* senses to become sedimented; disorder in original experience, which thus inhibits the institution of unities of sense, remains as disorder in "habitualities." The meaning of this disorder is the unavailability of those sedimentations for the ego's recall and reactivation at a later point. Thus a chaos in the unfolding of the experience of "the world" would deprive the "subject" of those experiences of any effective re-activating assess to them and consequently would inhibit, if not deny altogether, the possibility of ranging those sedimentations under the 'I can'. But then such an "ego" would not itself be a progressively constituted unity or individuality. It would not *possess* any specifications of harmony and so would not actually have any expectations or anticipations. It would not have a "life" that projected or strove for *certain* forms of unfolding actuality, and it would not be an "observer" for whom the world *could appear as a chaos*. The dissolution of the world is at the same time the dissolution of the ordered connections between the sedimentations. Such dissolution amounts to their unavailability for the "ego," which then must face its own progressive impoverishment, disjointedness, and fragmentation. That would be an ego whose own self-same being for itself in progressive self-evidence is no longer available; in this case, it would no longer make any sense to think of that ego's being wrong about cognitive claims. Lacking as it would an anticipatory horizon, there would no longer be any ground for the proposal of any cognitive claims at all. Both noesis and noema are constituted together; as Husserl writes: "In the constitutive sense of all life in which the origin of all being is found, we discover that subjectivities and objectivities constitute themselves in parallel and that subjectivities are constituted unities just as much as their objectivities are."[28] Therefore "[o]ne can also say: a complete dis-

---

27. Husserl, Ms. E III 9, ca. Nov. 15, 1931 (cited from Mensch, *Intersubjectivity and Transcendental Idealism*, 78.

28. Husserl, *Gemeingeist II* (1918 or 1921), *Hua* XIV, 203 (cited from Mensch, op. cit., 80).

solution of a world in a 'tumult' [of experiences] is equivalent to a dissolution of the ego...."[29] Lacking any *available* order within its sedimentations, its sedimentation cannot really be said to accrue to *it*; lacking those "essential types" of connections, the ego is unable to posit definite types of unity within the multiplicity of experience and so is unable to have for itself any "actuality." We conclude that the world-constituting ego is "open" in that its own coherence—as the coherence of its constituting capacities—is *contingent* upon something *other* than its own constitutional-intentional life. As with the "actuality of the world," and the "nature and range of sedimentations," so the very self-identity of the world-constituting ego is dependent upon the contingent unfolding of the stream of experience.

§ 8.2.3.1. The Contingent Dependency of the Pure Ego Pole

What we have been referring to as the 'world-constituting ego' is the ego progressively becoming in the accrual of sedimented habitualities—the 'monad', as Husserl refers to it. This *concrete* ego, which is particularized and individuated in terms of its having-become through its own unique history, is to be distinguished from the "pure ego" or "ego pole" (*CM*, 100-1). The concrete world-constituting ego that acquires its constitutional capacities through ongoing sedimented accrual is "not adequately given in reflection; it points, in principle, to the experiential data related to the infinite horizon of my past life and to an infinitude of advance [in the future] towards the completion of this data...."[30] But this is not the case with the pure ego, that which is identically the same in each and every different act. As Husserl says:

> To know that a pure ego is and what it is, an ever so great accumulation of self-experience is no more informative than a single experience of a straightforward cogito. It would be senseless to think that I, the pure ego, might not actually exist or might be quite different from ego presently functioning in this cogito. (*Id. II*, 104)

The pure ego does not present itself by way of adumbrations, but simply "steps forth" in "absolute selfhood" and "unity" (103-5). The self who has taken a position, and so acquired new habitualities, might change, but the self *of* those habitualities—who remains of a certain opinion or who now has new capacities to exercise—is utterly unchanging. The pure ego is not experienced as a temporally extended being; though its experiences can be regarded as occupying distinct positions within the stream of consciousness constituted in internal time consciousness, the pure ego is utterly one and the same ego in all of its changing experiences. As such it is not constituted in and through certain ordered connections of experience and, in its absolute self-same identity, is actually *different* from any and all of its various experiences.

---

29. Husserl, Ms. F IV 3, p. 57a (1925; cited from Mensch, op. cit., 80).
30. Husserl, Ms. A VI 21, p. 20b (1927? – cited from Mensch, op. cit., 81).

Nonetheless, though different, the pure ego is not *independent* of the concrete being-in-becoming world-constituting ego and in a fundamental sense can be considered as constituted. The difference of the pure ego from its streaming lived experiences is precisely its dependence upon the stream—for its difference is a function of the fact that the pure ego has no specific content of its own. The pure ego "steps forth" and is "awake" only as the ego *of* certain lived experiences and interconnections thereof. Thus, as emptiness, this difference is also its dependence upon the experiential stream for the provision of its "material." As Husserl writes of the pure ego: "An ego does not possess a proper general character with a material content; it is quite empty of such. It is simply an ego of the cogito which [in the change of experiences] gives up all content and is related to a stream of [lived] experiences, in relation to which it is also dependent. . . ."[31] Thus the pure ego is dependent upon the concrete ego that progressively constitutes itself as a unity of life; considered by and for itself, the pure ego is just an abstraction.[32] We must therefore guard against any understanding of Husserl that would hold that the pure ego exists as an unfounded absolute ground, independent of the contingent facticity of the stream.

§ 8.3. The Openness of the World-Constituting Ego as its Dependence upon the "Absolute Flux"

By 'openness' here we intend to refer to the discovery that, despite the phenomenologically unassailable and regularly repeated claim that actual being is constituted by the transcendental ego in its experiences, this world-constituting ego does not "create" the world from out of itself, nor is the world simply a function of a constituting "will" or "idea." Rather, both the actual being of the world and, in turn, the actual being of the ego depend upon the contingent coming to pass of the factual stream of experience, the ground of which is "in excess of" or "beyond" the ego's powers of positing.

This can be elaborated in two ways. First, as we saw, the actuality of the world depends upon the unfolding of the course of lived experience in a particular way. The constituting ego can project the necessary forms of interconnection that must govern the manifestation of an actual world in and through the course of experience, but it cannot *also* determine what will actually come to pass. Its constitutive activity is thus conditioned by the sheer contingency of the coming to pass of the stream according to certain more or less definite specifications. The constituting ego can only *wait upon* the stream and its progressive unfolding, over which it can exercise no power at all.

Second, because the development of the world-constituting ego *itself*—as an ego to which has accrued the necessary habitual sedimentations and capac-

---

31. Husserl, Ms. E III 2, p. 18, (1921; cited from Mensch, op. cit., 84).
32. See Anthony Steinbock, *Home and Beyond: Generative Phenomenology After Husserl* (Evanston, Ill.: Northwestern University, 1995), 35.

ities, in a form in which they are available to the ego *as* the ego's own constitutional capacities—is a function of a particular constitutional history, the actual being of that ego, as the ego of a unified progressive becoming, is itself *founded*. Only to the extent that an actual, harmoniously ordered world has been progressively constituted is there *an ego* subsisting as the substrate of sedimented transcendentally constituting habitualities. Thus that ego is itself likewise dependent for its actual being upon the contingent unfolding of the stream in such a way as to allow the actual manifestation of the world.

In this respect we must say the world-constituting ego—the ego that exists for itself in progressive self-evidence *as* the one who abides through the still-holding of its originary positings, its habitualities—is itself constituted. It is founded in the contingent unfolding of experience—a domain other than its own egological interiority and life. The ego itself, in its unique individuality, as a "unity of its living becoming, a unity of its history" (*Hua* XIV, 36), is something that *arises* and continues to become precisely in its progressive constitution of the actual world. But that constitutive activity, we saw, is not simply the work of the ego; it requires in addition the absolutely contingent unfolding of the stream itself, in such an order that will allow for a harmonious synthetic gathering. Thus the actuality of the world, as well as the ongoing becoming of the world-constituting ego, must wait upon the coming to pass of the stream for their coming to presence in evidence—and then in such a way as to allow its harmonious synthetic gathering.

What is truly grounding, therefore, is not the world-constituting ego, which, as co-constituted along with the world, is itself dependent upon the coming to pass of a particular course of experience. Rather, what is truly grounding is "absolute consciousness"—the flowing stream that just comes to pass. Insofar as in its actual—but contingent—course, it allows the identification of definite forms of interconnection, then a world-constituting ego does come progressively to evidence. But the absolute stream need not flow in just such a way and thus is distinct from what it allows to be grounded in it. This stream is the genuine absolute and is consciousness only in the unique sense derived from the peculiar mode of access offered by phenomenological investigation. This ultimate is subjectivity only in a certain manner of speaking; it is not an *experiencing* subjectivity, because there is no enduring ego here to project anticipations and subsequently to observe the unfolding harmony or conflict that the stream might yield. As Husserl says: "there is no doer here. There is only the absolute" (*Hua* XV, 669).[33] And also: "On the lowest level, we do not yet have an ego...."[34] Here we have the distinction between, on the one hand, the tru-

---

33. Mensch's translation of Husserl, Ms. C I, Sept. 21–22, 1934 (cited from Mensch, op. cit., 149).

34. Mensch's translation of Husserl, Ms. D 13 XXI, p. 124, 1907–1909 (cited from Mensch, op. cit., 175).

ly absolute factical flowing stream-stratum and, on the other, the position-taking world-constituting ego—a distinction that allows us to resolve Husserl's apparently contradictory statements regarding the fate of "consciousness" after the annihilation of the world. The collapse of the world would also be the fragmentation and progressive collapse of the ego that posits the world, but it would not be the obliteration of the absolute factical flowing stream. In Mensch's words: "In itself, the absolute is the possibility of all experiential possibilities; it is the horizon of all possible experiential horizons. As such, it is prior to the intentional acts or *cogitationes* which are formed from definite connections of experience."[35]

However, we have yet to investigate the constitution of the immanent object, that purely subjective entity that makes up the particular appearances that flow away with the flux. It is to them that we now turn.

---

35. Mensch, ibid., 149.

Chapter Nine
The Immanent Object: Primal Constitution of Identity

§ 1. From Static to Genetic Phenomenology

In the preceding chapter we considered the status of the real object and concluded that, though its concept could never be closed, it deserved the title of 'transcendence in immanence'—a well known phrase by which Husserl characterizes his transcendental idealism. We showed that the real object is not, and does not indicate, alterity. Rather, it is a constituted product, a result of synthesis. Furthermore, we found that the law of the synthesis that yields the real object is purely a function of the experiential possibilities of the intentional functionary and does not respond to or conceal an alterity beyond the domain of immanence.

But the extent and kind of closure that transcendental phenomenology adduces for the intentional functionary cannot be established by those investigations alone. We have yet to consider the status of the flux-moments that make up the stream upon which the synthesis that constitutes the real object works. As hyletic data, could these "immanent objects" indicate an "unknown cause of experience" that, as noumenon, would exist in itself, independent of the experiencing subject? So understood, the flux-moments would indicate an alterity other than the constituted object.

The status of the flux-moments that enter into the ongoing synthesis is the central topic of this chapter. In order to provide an account of these moments, we turn to genetic phenomenology and the constitution of primal identity in what Husserl terms 'originary temporalization'. The present investigation comprises three parts: first, a preliminary methodological reflection on the problem of identity and the subsequent transition from static to genetic phenomenology; second, a consideration of the primally constituting temporal syntheses; and, third, a consideration of the kinaesthetic and associative syntheses that provide the concrete "matter" emerging from the originary temporalization.

Before proceeding any further with our investigation, however, a brief discussion of the meanings of and distinctions between "static" and "genetic" phenomenology is called for. As with many other notions developed by Husserl, the senses involved here achieve a genuine clarification only later in his thought; as a rule, problems of genesis present themselves only after phenomenological descriptive analysis is well under way.

One of the most succinct and accurate discussions of static and genetic phenomenology may be found in *An Introduction to Husserlian Phenomenology* by Rudolf Bernet, Iso Kern, and Eduard Marbach.[1] They characterize the distinction between the two as follows:

> Static phenomenology begins from stable objects, both real objects (for example, natural things) and ideal objects (for example, mathematical propositions), and proceeds both noetically and noematically to investigate the complexes of immanent experiences in which these species of objects attain teleologically to givenness. In the course of such an investigation, and within the "phenomenological reduction," these objects are regarded purely as the objective correlates of modes of consciousness. The intention in thus regarding them is to clarify the sense and validity of these objects by means of regressing to their systems of manifestation and authentification within the consciousness within which they are primordially given. The analysis distinctive of static constitution has a twofold character. In the first place, it has stable objects, a stable "ontology" for its guide. In the second place, it inquires into immanent experiences.[2]

To be sure, even within static phenomenology issues of "genesis"—in the form of the historicity of the manifestation of the identical object within the stream of experiential life—present themselves the moment the phenomenologist commits himself to the investigation of "what is, in its appearing." Phenomenology does not "lose" itself in the contemplation of objective unities naively considered as stable identities, but rather investigates that unity as it manifests itself

> within the flow, namely, as the unity of a constituting flow; it follows the movements, the courses in which such unity, and every component, side, and real property of such unity, is a correlative identity. In some measure, this approach is kinetic or "genetic." Every unity of cognition . . . has its "history," its immanent teleology in the form of a regulated system of *essentially* appurtenant consciousness, brought out by questioning it. (*Id. III*, 129/117)

Yet despite this essential interest in the modes in which the object unfolds its manifestation, such a direction of inquiry does not yet open upon genuinely genetic problems, for the altering—developing—courses of experience in which the object comes to manifestation are "only the subjective correlates of a stable identity."[3]

---

1. Rudolf Bernet, Iso Kern, and Eduard Marbach, *An Introduction to Husserlian Phenomenology* (Evanston, Ill.: Northwestern University, 1993). For a more sustained investigation of Husserl's static, genetic, and generative phenomenology—their respective subject matter, methods, and interrelations—see Steinbock's *Home and Beyond*.
2. Bernet, Kern, Marbach, *Husserlian Phenomenology*, 196.
3. Ibid., 197.

By contrast, properly genetic phenomenology in Husserl's mature understanding (he speaks of various dimensions of "genesis" from the earliest stages of his phenomenology onwards) will no longer have as its chief concern the various components—along with their essential relations—of the systematic correlation between stable identities and multiple modes of givenness, but rather the genesis of the systems of correlation as such. For genetic phenomenology, the guiding clue for the analysis is no longer a stable objective or conceptual identity given to the investigator in advance and functioning as a fixed objective sense governing and structuring the lines of investigative description. Now it is the very genesis of the stable objective unity as a stable unity that is the focus of investigation. Genesis proper thus designates "a temporal generation and coming-to-be."[4] Genetic phenomenology is by no means to be confused with an empirical causal explanation. On the contrary, it is intended to provide an account of the immanent motivation within transcendental consciousness that, as it were, projects or impels the intending cognitive will toward a progressive constitution of an identity that, at any particular point in its manifestation, is not yet "for" it and so cannot be encountered as governing the unfolding of its appearings in advance. Static phenomenology is governed by a pregiven and stable object whose sense functions as a rule that governs in advance the possible multiplicities of consciousness in which it could be given. Governance of the flux of appearings is exercised by this stable objective unity of sense. Genetic phenomenology, investigating the very becoming of these rules, these objective unities of sense, finds a different source of the governance of the originary manifestation of identity in motivations inherent to the flux itself.

Thus Bernet, Kern, and Marbach are right in characterizing the basic insight of Husserl's genetic phenomenology as follows:

> The "I" is not an empty "pole of identity," not a mere form in successive intentional acts or experiences. . . . Rather, it is an "I" who possesses his capabilities (in the consciousness that "I can do this or that"), his attitudes, and his convictions. Only in such capabilities and convictions is there a world pregiven as a "horizon of ability" for the "I," a world from which the "I" can, by available means of manifestation and demonstration, bring any objects whatsoever to givenness. These capabilities and convictions point back to earlier experiences and positings. They are *habitualities acquired* by the "I."[5]

It is therefore only with the clarification of the mature conception of phenomenological genesis that Husserl's transcendental phenomenology acquires its true meaning as transcendental *idealism*.

---

4. Ibid., 196.
5. Ibid., 199–200.

§ 1.1. Genetic Phenomenology and the Problem of Identity

The analyses undertaken of the constitution of the real object so far could in no sense be considered truly fundamental, because the concept of identity as such was not posed as a problem in them. In fact the static phenomenology developed in those analyses employs a hylo-morphism that betrays this naiveté quite clearly. It was always taken for granted in those analyses that the synthesis of identification that constitutes such real objects works with stream elements that, though not themselves real objects (Husserl refers to them as 'immanent objects'), are still identities in their own right.[6] Hence the question about the possibility of primal identity emerging from the flux still remains to be resolved, as does the more general issue of its status.

Our investigation here seeks to understand the "original endurances" that static phenomenology takes for granted. As a phenomenological clarification, the inquiry seeks to reveal them in their *coming to presence*, their constitution. This means that the phenomenology in question is now neither a static nor a constitutive phenomenology (which considers entities as products of a constitutive transcendental history, but always sees the contribution of history as the contribution of *identities*), but genetic phenomenology, which has as its task the investigation of the very constitution of identity as such.

§ 1.2. 'Endurance' as Title for the Problem of Originary Identity

It is as *endurance* that the domain of "immanent objectivity," of "hyletic data," of the "primary matter" that arises in passive syntheses, emerges as a phenomenological problem. This is because it is only as something that *abides* that an entity can set itself apart from the flux out of which it emerges and hence be *identified* as itself, while not being something other or nothing. Only as that which abides can an entity remain as itself and be determined in predicates and re-identified, sustaining itself in itself *for* different purely subjective acts.

Thus, because entities come to presence through the flux of experience, the condition for the possibility of, first, the showing and, second, the objectivity (i.e. the difference from the purely subjective act in which it is given) of what is given, is fundamentally one and the same: endurance. For it is only as an endurance that entities maintain themselves against the loss that is threatened in the flux.

But how is this "identity out of flux" to be understood? By definition, we are already talking of an "object" here, something that in offering itself for different acts sustains a degree of transcendence. What alterity is encountered

---

6. The "perceptual multiplicities that interpenetrate and change into one another . . . always have their *determinate descriptive composition*" (*Id. I*, 75).

here? Once again, we come upon the complex problem of "sameness out of difference."

§ 1.2.1. Sameness and Difference

The Sameness in question is that of the immanent object, the particular evidence that emerges out of the flux of consciousness. A more precise determination of it and its ontological status will emerge as the investigation proceeds.

The difference in question is that of the temporal differentiation that is the condition for the possibility of a Sameness that is fundamentally an endurance, a Same that gives itself in the first instance through time (time being the most fundamental dimension of identity synthesis for Husserl). An object given through the flux, if it is not be identical with the flux and thereby flow away just as the flux does, must assert itself against the flux. Yet it is not separate from the flux. It asserts itself against the flux by being not only the Now, but also part of the flux that has passed away, as well as part of the flux that is yet to come. It is made up of these temporal "differences." Husserl makes this point when he says: "The immanent contents are what they are only so far as during their 'actual' duration they refer ahead to something futural and back to something past" (*Hua* X, 84/110). It thus pertains to the essence of the consciousness of any presence that it be

> consciousness of *what has just been* and not mere consciousness of the now-point of the objective thing as having duration. In this consciousness, we are aware of what has just been in the continuity pertaining to it. . . . One notices the steam whistle just sounding; in every point there is an extension and in the extension there is the "appearance" which, in every phase of this extension, has its moment of quality and its moment of apprehension. (32/53–54)

To answer the questions put above concerning the being and status of these primal objectivities requires us to understand them in terms of their constitution. Like static phenomenology in its investigation of real objectivity, genetic phenomenology finds this constitution in a temporalizing dynamic of retention and protention. However, there is a fundamental difference between the way this dynamic operates in static phenomenology, where identity as such is not the fundamental phenomenological question, and genetic phenomenology, where it is. We shall now investigate this difference before examining the constitution of the immanent object proper.

§ 1.3. Retention and Protention in Genetic Phenomenology

Genetic phenomenology still employs the terms 'retention' and 'protention' in explicating the dynamic of the primally constitutive synthesis. However, because the phenomenologist's concern lies now with entities that Husserl says "are constituted in the most primitive way, constituted as unities in the originary time consciousness" (*Id. II*, 24), the constitutive phases referred to through those terms can no longer be understood as particular durations themselves, or as individually identifiable objects. This is because any particular duration is itself already individuated. Thus Husserl draws a distinction between the phases genuinely constitutive of duration and the modes of consciousness that refer to already constituted past and future contents of consciousness. Constitution—original givenness—of the past and the future must be distinguished from the recovery of what is already past (and hence known as such, presupposing its constitution) and the projection of what is future (and hence known as such, presupposing its constitution). As Husserl says:

> From retentions and protentions . . . we must distinguish those recollections and expectations that are not directed toward the constitutive phases of the immanent content but that give past or future immanent contents. The contents endure: they have their time; they are individual objectivities that are the unities of alteration or constancy. (*Hua* X, 84/111)

For this reason Husserl denies that the phenomenon of the primitive temporal entity's temporal differentiation can be understood in terms of a succession of already individuated constituting phases in the sense of a merely contingent "being next to one another." Rather, every such phase "is thinkable only as a phase, i.e., is not to be expanded into an interval which would be identical. . . . We must above all insist that a phase is thinkable only as a phase and without the possibility of an extension" (33/54–55). He then makes the significant remark: "A now-phase is thinkable only as the boundary of a continuity of retentions, just as every retentional phase is itself only thinkable as a point of such a continuum. . . ."

Husserl therefore argues against Brentano—and many others—that there is a fundamental distinction to be drawn between retention or primary memory on the one hand and memory or recollection on the other. The burden of Husserl's argument is this: to claim that the perception of a temporal object in its temporal spread is achieved mainly by memory and expectation—as the modes through which consciousness exceeds the mere Now-content—is to deny, or at least to render incomprehensible, the *perception* of the *temporal object as temporally extended*. For memory, or recollection, is not the perception of the past as constitutive of temporal extension but the presentation of an already temporally extended entity in a non-originary (i.e. non-perceptual, non-intuitive) way. Memory is not presentation but re-presentation. As the re-presentation of a temporally extended individual, memory is not the originary givenness of the past but instead presupposes the originary givenness of the past as that which originarily temporalizes and thereby constitutes the temporally extended individual, which may or may not be re-presented in memory. If a temporal entity is to be perceived, then temporal extension must also be perceived, for the perception of a temporal individual is the perception of a temporal extension. Husserl anchors his argument by pointing to "an evident distinction between the memory of an event or an act that occurred at a moment relatively remote from the actual Now, and the consciousness of the just elapsed phases of a temporal object which one is presently perceiving."[7] This retentional consciousness is perception, Husserl says, because this is consciousness of originary modification that constitutes the temporal difference that enables an originary temporal spread. As such it is that in which the origination of the temporal individual, as a temporal distention, is to be found. Husserl says:

> if we call perception *the act in which all "origination" lies*, which *constitutes originarily*, then *primary remembrance is perception*. For only in *primary remembrance do we see what is past*; only in it is the past constituted, i.e., *not in a representative way but in a presentative way*. The just-having-been, the before in contrast to the now, can be seen directly only in primary remembrance. It is the essence of primary remembrance to bring this new and unique moment to primary, direct intuition, just as it is the essence of the perception of the now to bring the now directly to intuition. (*Hua* X, 41/64)

Memorial consciousness, or recollection, is not originary consciousness, however:

> recollection, like fantasy, offers us mere presentification. It is "as-if" the same consciousness as the temporarily creative acts of the now and the past, "as-if" the same but yet modified. The fantasied now represents a now, but does not give us a now itself; the fantasied before and after merely represents a before and after, etc. (41–42/64)

As John Brough puts this: "Through the 'originary' or perceptual consciousness, the past itself is *perceived* or presented; through the representational consciousness it is simply remembered or represented."[8]

How is it possible to distinguish between retention and protention on the one hand and recollection and expectation on the other? Husserl's suggestion is this: the Now-phase alone does not yield perception of a temporal individual, for such an individual is precisely that kind of thing whose being extends beyond the mere Now: it endures. Retention constitutes the "having just been" through which the intentional act transcends, and thereby achieves differentiation from, the primal impression of the Now; and protention does the same in the direction of the future. Thus retention and protention do not simply supplement the perception of the Now-moment *of the object*; they are the very possibility of the perception of any temporal object at all. Retention does not recollect a temporal object, nor does protention expect one; together they constitute its very possibility. It can truly be said that each Now-perception is necessarily the amalgam of such temporal differences if in the Now-perception a

---

7. John Brough, "Absolute Consciousness," in McCormick and Elliston, eds., *Husserl: Expositions and Appraisals*, 83–100, here 85.
8. Brough, "Absolute Consciousness," 85.

temporal individual in perceived. Such perception is to be understood as an inseparable differentiation yielded by the presence on the side of perceptual consciousness of primal impression, retention, and protention. In this way the entity as temporally distended is present (perceived), and in this way the intentional act's intending beyond itself—its grasping of the "no longer" and the "not yet"—is understood.

On the other hand, recollection and expectation bring to consciousness an object that has already been temporally constituted. That is, they are always modes of re-presenting objects. They do not constitute the object recollected or expected; the identity of the object so brought to consciousness is already presupposed, pre-supplied. In this sense, recollection and expectation are acts of repetition; they are not acts that constitute identity newly, for the first time. Rather, they are acts that yield their object as a re-identified identity. This presupposes an originary constitution of identity, which takes place in originary perception.

This means that the temporally constitutive phases do not possess their contents as temporal individuals; such contents, through which the temporally extended object is rendered present, are not themselves temporal individuals. As Husserl says: "Retention itself is not an act of looking back that makes an object of the phase which has expired" (*Hua* X, 118/161).

In speaking of retentions, primal impressions, and protentions, we have not thereby described any immanent temporal units but only temporal phases or moments of the stream. Such moments actually make up the primal intentionality whereby the temporal individual is first constituted. As Brough says: "Now-perception, primary memory and expectation, forming the intentionality of a dependent momentary phase of consciousness, are not and cannot be independent acts in the sense in which an extended perception is."[9] And as Husserl says: "Retention generates no objectivities of duration (whether originary or reproductive), but merely retains what is produced in consciousness and impresses on it the character of the 'just past'" (*Hua* X, 36–37/58–59).

§ 1.4. The "Phenomenology" of the Originary Givenness of Pastness and Futurity

If originary past, now, and future presents no "identity-content," then how is it given? To answer this, we offer a brief phenomenology of temporal differentiation.

Husserl understands originary temporalization as a dynamic of "modification." In this modification lies the temporal differentiation in which the immanent object is constituted as extended across time, as abiding, and hence as available to intuitive givenness.[10]

---

9. Brough, "Absolute Consciousness," 86.
10. A modification presupposes that which remains the same while undergoing modi-

Let us deal first with the modification that takes place in the direction of the past. How are we to do justice to the two moments of retention, the one establishing a difference, the other a sameness?[11] How is it that this modification yields "the same"? What is its Same the same as? The key to this Sameness—the provision of which is one side of the achievement of objectifying consciousness—lies in the character of retentional consciousness as the holding fast in the Now-consciousness of Now-moments that are no longer now. The coincidence here consists in the fact that the Now that alters with its continually being pushed aside by a *new* Now does not simply become nothing. Rather, it is retained *as it itself*, but not with the character of being actual (122/167). Husserl says:

> The actual tonal Now is constantly changed into something that has been; constantly, an ever fresh tonal Now, which passes over into modification, peels off.... Every actual Now of consciousness ... is subject to the law of modification. The Now changes continuously from retention to retention. There results, therefore, a stable continuum that is such that every subsequent point is a retention for every earlier one. And every retention is already a continuum. The sound begins and steadily continues. The tonal Now in changed into one that has been. Constantly flowing, the *impressional* consciousness passes over into an ever fresh *retentional* consciousness. (29/50–51)

And again:

> We speak here of 'running-off phenomena', or better yet of 'modes of temporal orientation', and with reference to the immanent objects themselves of their 'running-off characters' (e.g., now, past). With regard to the running-off phenomenon, we know that it is a continuity of constant transformations that form an inseparable unit, not severable into parts that could be by themselves nor divisible into phases, points of continuity, which could be by themselves. The parts that by a process of abstraction we can throw into relief can be only in the entire running-off. (27/48)

Husserl accounts for the temporal constitution of identity as the constitution of the Same precisely in terms of the phenomenological fact that the modifica-

---

fication. Otherwise, modification would be annihilation. However, given our discovery that the moments are not presentable as identities, to speak of 'modification' here could be misleading because it suggests that there could be given an unmodified something in and of itself. If, for example, retention were to be understood as such a modification, the suggestion could be made that what undergoes modification is the Now-content, which, as unmodified, could be in and for itself. This is not so, however. Retention does not *add* memory to a something taken for itself; rather, as modification, it constitutes the identical as the retaining of the no-longer-now in the Now. It remains "the same" as the unity of the process of modification. 'Retention' is the title given to that particular mode of possession of a content thanks to which change (the continual running-off of the flux) is not loss but temporal difference.

11. Retention bears within itself both of these moments. If, on the one hand, it did not resist utter change, it could not be what facilitates the showing of what remains the same through difference—the object. But if, on the other, it did not resist utter sameness, no temporally differentiated object could show itself.

tion that establishes this otherness than the Now, otherness than primal impression, is a modification, a difference from the primal impression, which nonetheless *retains* the very primal impression that was once marked as 'actual'. As such, what was actual is not *lost* in its going over into the mode of *retentionally* present. In fact it remains utterly the same, in all respects, other than its mode of presence as 'actual'. How is this possible? Husserl answers in terms of the non-temporality of the constituting flux: though the consciousness that was actual, together with its content, is no longer actual, the retention into which it passes is not itself past. It is nothing less than the very possibility of the Now itself. The retention is not nothing and, above all, is not itself past; the originary givenness of pastness *is not itself past*. Husserl notes that "when the tonal Now, the primal impression, passes over into retention, this retention is itself again a Now, an actual existent. While it itself is actual (but not an actual sound), it is the retention of a sound that has been" (28/50). Thanks to this retaining in modification, endurance is possible and is originarily given thereby.

Husserl enriches his general metaphor for the temporalizing differentiation as flux by introducing the notion of *distance*. Retentional consciousness does not itself flow away. Rather, it is *actual* consciousness making up the atemporal "absolute subject," a consciousness that has its content with the character of 'fading away'. Husserl gives this account:

> Of the interval that has expired we say that we are conscious of it in retentions, specifically, that we are conscious of those parts or phases of the duration, not sharply to be differentiated, which lie closest to the actual now-point with diminishing clarity, while those parts lying further back in the past are wholly unclear; we are conscious of them only as empty. The same thing is true with regard to the running off of the entire duration. Depending on its distance from the actual Now, that part of the duration that lies closest still has perhaps a little clarity; the whole disappears in obscurity, in a void retentional consciousness, and finally disappears completely (if one may say so) as soon as retention ceases. (26/46)

Therefore, the retentional running off, the "changing into the past," is not originarily the passing of what is *already in* an objective or cosmic temporal ordering and whose passing consciousness would merely passively observe. Rather, both cosmic temporality and the being ordered of objects according to such temporality is first constituted on the ground of the originary phenomenon yielded by retentional consciousness. The fading from consciousness is not originarily given as a departure from consciousness into a netherworld where all that has been for consciousness simply finds its way; it is rather disappearance pure and simple. It is not a movement in which the being of the object would be preserved despite its non-presence, but rather the primal phenomenon of the movement into non-presence of being as such. As Husserl points out, the originary givenness of the past, that which retentional consciousness yields, is a changing in the mode of a "running off," a movement "downwards" into "the depths of the past." The retentional modification retains what once was given as new and as "primal impressional," as "the same," yet it retains it across a duration. But being retained across a duration means that some essential moment of "the same" is no longer actual but is constantly sinking deeper into the past (28/50).

Thus we come to one of the mysteries of temporalization. What is past is not now; yet movement into the past is not to be understood as a loss to consciousness. If it were, there could be not even be any presence. Rather, where the movement into the past is understood in terms of what is given—is "present"—through retentional consciousness, the past is not lost because "retention is itself again a Now, an actual existent" (29/50). However, though retention is just what the word means, a *retaining*, it is a retaining through a continual modification of what is retained, a modification whose *limit* is loss. Both in the case of the currently perceived and in that of what has already been perceived and thereby already occupies its place within the continually flowing immanent temporal continuum, there takes place a "shoving back into the past." This continual "being shoved back" is a "modification" that continues until the retained is no longer retained and "disappears"; for "hand in hand with the modification goes a diminution that finally ends in imperceptibility." Thus the temporal modification effected by retentional consciousness is appropriately spoken of as a "dying or fading away" (31/52).

What is to be said of the Now? It has no fixed content that could be identified for itself, because the Now is not extended. Husserl speaks of the Now as a "source point" (28/48, 29/50). It is a fount, a "spring," from which the streaming-off moves. It too is in continual modification: in the Now "a new Now is always presenting itself, each Now is changed into a past" (29/50). It follows from this that the Now, as that which is as continual renewal, is essentially open to the yet-to-come; that is, the Now is a motion, a modification, whose "end" is not yet. Husserl describes the flux continuum of the Now by saying that "in the living source-point of the Now there also wells up ever fresh primal being" (69/94). We thereby come upon the complete temporal horizon of the Now, which is its very possibility. There is, on the one hand, the horizon of the fading-away, the horizon of the past that is actual as retentional consciousness, and, on the other, the horizon of the yet-to-come, the horizon of the future that is actual as protentional consciousness. These together yield the continuous flux that, as temporalization, allows for the presence of temporal distention.

The protentional dimension is originarily given as a "waiting" upon the "to come." Originarily, if we are speaking of the identity-constituting givenness of the future, then the protentional dimension is not yet given through the expectation of a *definite* yet-to-come. Rather, it is an openness to a yet-to-be-determined, a being "subject" to the not yet. It is a vulnerability, an inadequacy of expectation, a "recognition" of ontological contingency.

§ 2. The Constitution of the Immanent Object: Temporal Syntheses

We begin this discussion of the constitution of the immanent object with what Husserl terms a 'reservation' that recalls our discussion above. He says:

> This talk about objects is, to be sure, admissible here only with reservations. For in the natural process of external perception we do not have sense data objectively, but *through* them we are directed toward the "perspectivally shaded" perceived things appearing in them. They first become objects in the proper sense (thematic objects) in reflection by means of an abstractive separation. (*EJ*, 306 n. 1/255)

As Donn Welton says:

> Whereas the early Husserl thought in terms of elements out of which he could reconstruct the perceptual act, the later Husserl reverses his direction and talks of sensations only within a deconstructive phenomenology which takes the full perceptual object as primary.[12]

This noted, we ask: What is the being of the immanent object? In what sense do we, in the case of the immanent object, find a transcendence, a "being other"?

Bearing in mind the methodological qualifications raised above, we are now in a position to investigate the constitution of the immanent temporal object in the originary temporalization. Our guiding question will remain: What is the Same that emerges from the flux, and how is that emergence to be understood?

By 'immanent temporal object' we understand a temporal individual that is other than the stream in which it is given and that, thanks to this otherness, is capable of being given as the Same in different acts. To be given as the Same and to be known as such presupposes individuation; our clue will therefore be the emergence of individuation from flux.[13]

Husserl gives his account of the constitution of temporal objects in terms of what he calls the 'double intentionality' of retention. Why speak of a double intentionality? Because for a temporal object to show itself, there must be

---

12. Donn Welton, *The Origins of Meaning: A Critical Study of the Thresholds of Husserlian Phenomenology* (The Hague: Nijhoff 1983), 219.

13. *Hua* X, 108/143: "If the object has been given once, then it can be given as often as one likes, examined again and in different acts...." And Husserl says later: "Temporal objectivity is established in the subjective temporal flux, and to be identifiable in recollections and hence to be the subject of identical predicates is an essential part of this objectivity" (108/144). To be individuated, and to be thereby capable of determination through identical predicates, presupposes that the subject of such predication is *fixed*, not in constant flux. Husserl understands this fixation as reclamation from the flux through the acquisition of temporal location. If the object is what can be re-identified in many acts, then the precondition for the establishment of such objectivity will be the establishment of individuality. For individuality is the precondition for any "re-consciousness." (Concerning the latter term, see n. 22 below.)

a twofold constitution: first, the unity of the stream of consciousness itself and, second, within that stream, the constitution of the actual temporal object.[14] The intentionality that establishes the unity of the flow Husserl calls 'horizontal', and the intentionality that establishes the unity of the object, 'vertical'. We shall consider these intentionalities next.

§ 2.1. Vertical Intentionality: Secondary Constitution of the Immanent Object

'Vertical intentionality' is the name Husserl gives to the intentionality we have been dealing with up to this point; that is, vertical intentionality is simply the consciousness of the immanent object in the modes now, past, and to come. This intentionality brings about the synthesis that gathers moments of the stream into a unity that is recognized as an object. Husserl now sees the need to qualify it as a certain type of intentionality or synthesis because, though it is the synthesis that yields *objects*, it is not truly ultimate. As we saw previously in discussing the world annihilation experiment, the synthesis that constitutes an object can fail in its intention to yield a unity. The synthesis that attempts to constitute the object therefore works upon a stream that is there *for it* and that is itself already a prior ground irrespective of any particular immanent objects it may yield.[15] However, though the two intentionalities may be distinguished, as the flow's being conscious of the immanent object on the one hand and the flow's being conscious of itself on the other, they are actually inseparable in principle. As Brough puts it: "That the intentionality is termed 'vertical' signifies that the intending absolute consciousness is of a different and more ultimate dimension than of the immanent object which it intends."[16]

§ 2.2. Horizontal Intentionality: Primal Stream-Constituting Synthesis

Husserl introduces the notion of 'horizontal intentionality' to indicate a focus on the constitution of the stream itself, an investigation of the synthesis at the most primal level. This dimension of synthesis constitutes the two conditions for the givenness of an object: endurance, which is the first condition of

---

14. *Hua* X, 80/106: "It is the one unique flux of consciousness in which the immanent temporal unity of the sound and also the unity of the flux of consciousness itself are constituted." And Brough notes that "it is by virtue of the flow's two-fold intentional reference that, on the one hand, the temporal object, in some sense distinct from the flow itself, is constituted in its unity and, on the other hand, the unity of the absolute flow itself is constituted" ("Absolute Consciousness," 95).

15. The stream is, of course, never given as a completed unity but only as a unity-in-constitution.

16. Brough, "Absolute Consciousness," 96.

presence,[17] and individuation, which provides the condition for identification and then re-identification.

§ 2.2.1. Constitution of Endurance

Just as we have encountered the phenomenon of retention vis-à-vis the holding in consciousness of past phases of an object, so, as a condition for this, do we encounter a retentional moment as a constituting phase of the "absolute consciousness" or originary stream. Thereby any actual phase of the stream refers to the just-elapsed phase of the stream. This reference is not simply to the just-past phase, but, because it possesses its own retentional moment, also includes the moments prior to that. This "retention of retention" is what makes possible within the stream an awareness of an extended series of phases in the order in which they emerged into actuality and subsequently elapsed. This retention of retention is the stream's continual self-retention, the condition for its appearing as a unity (or unity-in-constitution). As the stream develops, a steady continuum of retention is engendered, such that every later point is retention for every earlier one. Each ever-new retentional moment is consciousness that continually bears within itself intentionally all earlier memorial consciousness in modification of the past. As Husserl says: "Every past Now retentionally harbors in itself all earlier levels" (*Hua* X, 111/149).

First, endurance is constituted through this primal aspect of the synthesis that yields the unity of the flow itself: its operation overcomes not the loss of the object, as it slips into the past, but that of the stream itself. It is retention of all flowing stream moments, thanks to which all originarily primal impressional consciousness is not lost as it itself undergoes temporalization—the condition for its appearing (see, e.g., *CM*, 80–81). "The most original having" of the stream and its retentional moment—a precondition for the having of an object—is established in

> *the actuality of the original presentation* and in the consciousness of the firsthand presence of this content. The content is in the mode of the Now, is an "actual content" for consciousness, and is in this content individual, the only thing of this content; at least the first and most radical character of individual existence makes its appearance in the form of being-now. (*EJ*, 466/384)

Thus the Now, as well as the "passive synthesis" effected therein, is the originary site of givenness because in it "the whole *is* in becoming" (217/184). This

---

17. As Husserl says in *Experience and Judgment*, every immanent object "has not only the general essence 'duration' but its individual duration, its own time; and all the times of immanent sense data are, in reference to the pure ego, *one and the same* time, which includes in itself all positions, all absolute times proper to individual data already run off, to all individual times" (*EJ*, 305/255).

is a becoming because the passive synthesis through retention establishes a *re-maining*:

> Everything that is, *is* so far as it *becomes in infinitum* and is *engulfed* in the continuum of the corresponding pasts. It is the *identical element in the flux of the change* from present into pasts of continuous gradation. "Enduring" is constituted in the flux of an ever new becoming, of the becoming of ever new being; it is a continual springing-up and passing-away. In the continual springing-up and passing-away (sinking down into the past) of harmonious content an *identical substrate* is constituted as the identical element which always *becomes* and, in becoming, always *is* as the persisting, and which endures through its time: inasmuch as every point lights up the new present in becoming, while, "passing away," it sinks into the modes of the past, it constitutes through all these modes its position in the objective past, its objective temporal position.... (467/386)

This aspect of intentional synthesis is responsible for the constitution of the stream-unity; thanks to it, endurances, though no longer actual, *remain*, as retentional stream moments, in the mode of 'past':

> Each newly appearing datum brings, so to speak, its new time along with it, and this new time is immediately a part of the one time which continues to unfold; all the objects of this "world" of immanent sensibility constitute a single world, and this world is held together by the form of time belonging to this world itself.... (305–6/255)

Before we proceed further, Husserl's distinction between 'active' and 'passive' synthesis should be clarified. Synthesis as such is, according to Husserl, a peculiar kind of "combination uniting consciousness with consciousness" such that what is combined in this way "can be characterized descriptively as *belonging together inseparably*" (CM, 77). Synthesis—"a mode of combination exclusively peculiar to consciousness"—is best understood as the achievement, by and for consciousness, of unity in multiplicity. A changing multiplicity is gathered together in such a way that a temporal flow of experience does not have the character of being an incoherent sequence of subjective processes, but rather flows away "in the unity of a synthesis, such that in them 'one and the same' is intended as appearing." Despite the flowing away of the stream of experiences, where the stream is a stream of appearance, one and the same identical unity remains given. Here we say that the unity of the flux as a unity of appearings of the one entity is

> a unity of synthesis: not merely a continuous connectedness of *cogitationes* (as it were, a being stuck to one another externally), but *a connectedness that makes the unity of one consciousness*, in which the unity of an intentional objectivity, as "the same" objectivity belonging to multiple modes of appearance, becomes "*constituted*." (79–80)

Husserl then distinguishes between active and passive synthesis. Active synthesis is the achievement of a positional ego, an intentionally directed act of determination or constitution. These are the achievements of productive reason. "These include the achievement of real, cultural products (such as art works, tools), as well as that of ideal objects (such as predicates and predicative states of affairs, syllogisms and theories, sets and numbers)."[18] Husserl refers to all these as 'higher order' or 'founded' judgments or acts because they point back genetically to prepredicative experience.

Prepredicative experience proceeds by way of passive synthesis, in which the active position-taking of the ego is not yet in evidence. Such experience is the passive, always presupposed grounding domain of the active production of judgments in which states of affairs are predicatively determined. As Bernet, Kern, and Marbach put it, for Husserl "this foundedness is the very definition of activity."[19] The principle that underlies passive synthesis is association, of which Husserl identifies two main forms: first, as a principle for the formation of unity, whereby various moments of coexistence and succession are gathered and integrated to make up the concreteness of the present, and, second, as a principle for the apperception of objects on the basis of the awakening of an earlier sense and the analogical transference of sense thus enabled.

§ 2.2.2. Constitution of Individuation

The holding-together of the stream as it flows off into the past establishes the first condition for the givenness of an object: endurance. However, endurance alone is not sufficient for the constitution of an object. The endurance must be *particularized* if it is to be an identity and if, as an identity, it is be able to be given as the Same in different intentional acts. Husserl identifies two moments in this, and both are explained in terms of the operation of horizontal intentionality.

§ 2.2.2.1. The First Moment: Place within the Stream

The first moment Husserl identifies as giving effect to individuation is *place or order within the stream*. Any particular duration within the stream is to be distinguished from any other by reference to the absolutely unique place it occupies within the entire stream, which is a function of the moment that it became actual relative to the actuality-moment of all other particular durations. This ordering is then preserved through the retentional structure of the synthesis.[20] Because retention is always "retention of retention" and not an adding

---

18. Bernet, Kern, Marbach, *Husserlian Phenomenology*, 201.
19. Ibid., 202.
20. Speaking of the establishing of order through retention, Husserl says in *Hua* X, 81–82/107–8: "If we keep any phase whatsoever of the flux of consciousness in view (in the phase appears a tonal now and an interval of duration in the mode of just-having-flowed-away), this phase is concerned with a uniform continuity of retentions in the before-all-at-once. This is retention of the entire momentary continuity of continuously preceding phases of the flux. . . . If we now let the flux flow away, we then have the flux-continuum as running-off, which allows the continuity just described to be retentionally modified, and there

on of an already constituted entity, each phase—each "stretch of time" or "endurance"—comes to occupy its own utterly unique place within the one stream and is thereby established in its own unique particularity. We spoke of the most originary being, of the immanent object, as a stretch of time, an endurance. But it is the *place* of this endurance within the stream that gives it its particularity, its "this and not that." It is as a definite and located endurance that immanent objects "are constituted in the absolute flow of internal time consciousness and have in it their absolute position and uniqueness, their unique appearance in an absolute Now, after which they retentionally fade away and sink back into the past" (*EJ*, 465-66/385). Hence, Husserl understands the most fundamental determination of individuality in terms of temporality:[21]

> Its position in time, and then, more precisely, its situationally determined duration, gives for each individual a determination which concerns its existence, its factuality as such. It is ordered according to its own system of pasts and is the identical element that, continually fading away, sinks ever further into the past. It remains *the same fact*, and because of this it is different from every other fact, each being differently determined in time. . . .

§ 2.2.2.2. The Second Moment: Completion of Duration

The second moment in the constitution of individuation is the *completion* of the duration in question. Individuation is not established by retentional consciousness alone, even though retentional consciousness does establish temporal extension or duration. If individuation is the precondition for any "re-consciousness"[22] of the one object, then more must be said about the es-

---

by every new continuity of phases momentarily existing all-at-once in retention with reference to the total continuity of what is all-at-once in the preceding phase. Hence, a longitudinal intentionality [i.e. horizontal intentionality] goes through the flux, which in the course of the flux is in continuous unity of coincidence with itself. Flowing in absolute transition, the first primal sensation changes into a retention of itself, this retention into a retention of this retention, and so on. Conjointly with the first retention, however, a new Now, a new primal sensation, is present and is joined continuously but momentarily with the first retention, so that the second phase of the flux is a primal sensation of the new Now and a retention of the earlier one. The third phase, again, is a new primal sensation with retention of the second primal sensation and a retention of the retention of the first, and so on. Here we must take into account that retention of a retention has intentionality not only with reference to what is immediately retained but also with reference to what is retained in the retaining of the second level. . . . Accordingly, we believe that these retentions, constituted in the flux of consciousness by means of the continuity of the retentional modifications and conditions, are continuous retentions of the continuously preceding ones; they are the unity of the flux itself as a one-dimensional, quasi-temporal order."

21. There can, of course, be co-temporaneous endurances. But if these are to be distinguished from each other—as the phrase 'co-temporaneous endurances' presupposes—then individuation must be a function of more than just temporal syntheses. We shall investigate these other factors in the next section.

22. The term 're-consciousness' is used here to refer to the fact that the originary manifestation of any endurance precisely in its quality of enduring is its being given to another consciousness, again. For Husserl a manifestation characterized by the sense 'the same, again'

tablishment of the temporal individual than has been so far. For if the individual is to be available for a re-consciousness, more is required than the mere constitution of endurance: the endurance must be a determinate one. That is, individuation must yield the immanent object as a *completed* temporal extension. If this did not happen, it would be impossible for that temporal spread to be given *again* in another act; as unfinished, the essential conditions for re-identification would not be met. The entity would itself still be indeterminate, remaining to be determined in its temporal uniqueness, remaining to be determined as this temporal kind and not any other. Thus Husserl says: "it should be noted that it is only past durations that I can, in repeatable acts, 'originarily' intuit, identify, and have objectively as the identical object of many acts" (*Hua* X, 43/66).

This yields a very interesting result: if it is essential to the being of an object that it be available, at least in principle, for a re-consciousness in another act, that, in other words, to be an object is to be individuated, then, at least at the level of the experience of immanent objects, the perceptual act does not *present* an object. This is because in the perceptual act the object, as still "now," is still subject to the yet-to-come of the protentional dimension, as one of the essentially constitutive phases of the act of perception. Perception of the immanent object, one must say, is *constitution* of an object, not its presentation, if the object is necessarily understood as a determinate temporal duration. Only when there is no longer any still-to-come (even when the still-to-come yields "the finish," or "the end") is there a temporal determinateness achieved. But the still-to-come is essential to the very meaning of the Now, of "perception," where perception is an act of consciousness occupying the Now, yielding an originary givenness of an act-content also occupying the Now. Therefore individuation and—to the extent that individuation is constitutive of objectivity—objectivation is properly said to be *achieved* in perception, but not that a temporal individual is itself present *as a temporal individual* in the act of perception; perception does not *present*, or allow consciousness to *possess*, a temporal individual.

This explains Husserl's statement: "After primary memory is past, a new memory [i.e. secondary memory or recollection] . . . can emerge" (35/57). This means that only after perception has passed can a re-consciousness emerge, because retention is constitutive of perception, constitutive of temporal extension, and hence constitutive of temporal individuation.

We have described the way in which the synthesis achieved in the originary temporalization yields a series of "definite durations," which occupy an

---

is part of the very structure of objectivity insofar as, in being (able to be) given again to an act of consciousness different from the first or originary act, what is so given actually manifests its difference from any particular and fleeting single act. This difference is a quality of still being itself, and remaining in itself, despite the passing once and for all of each "single" act of consciousness.

utterly unique position within the streaming flux of absolute consciousness. But how do we justify the claim that such definite durations are primal objectivities? The answer lies in the fact that such definite durations are the most original entities available for re-consciousness or re-identification. As such they demonstrate their difference from, or otherness than, the act in which they are originarily given. The possibility and process of re-identification can be seen as follows.

§ 2.3. Re-identification and Transcendence

How does the constitution of endurance become the constitution of transcendence which, in being identical for many different acts, is thereby different to any one act in which it happens to be given and thus transcendent to any such act? How is it that, in Husserl's words,

> the object is identical and identifiable beyond the time of its intuitive givenness, that what is once given in intuition must still be capable of being kept as an enduring possession even if the intuition is over, and, what is more, in structures that, through indications at first empty, can again lead to envisionment of the identical—to an envisionment whether by presentification or by renewed self-giving? (*EJ*, 232-33/198)

The answer to this question lies in the unique achievements of the horizontal intentionality and the understanding of the meaning of 'being past' that emerges from it. For it is horizontal intentionality that constitutes the most fundamental unity (or, more properly, unity in constitution) of all, the egostream itself. And it is only as moments of the stream that the being, the abidingness, of the primal objectivities—which is presupposed in order for a re-identification to take place—can be understood.

In order for re-identification to occur, the definite duration, as "the identical," must first of all still abide or endure or not fall into non-being, despite its becoming past. We saw that this was the achievement of horizontal intentionality. Secondly, however, it must be available for a re-consciousness of it *as* utterly identical.

Re-identification, recollection, remembering—all are acts of re-consciousness, acts whose sense is not that of originarily constituting a new particular, bringing it into being for the first time, but acts that return to what already exists and that yield it again, as "just the same entity" that was once originarily constituted. The very possibility of such acts consists in the fact that other acts—acts of originary intuition—constitute in themselves entities that abide, and in their abiding resist the threat of continual departure, the threat of non-presence posed by the flux. Such acts, as acts of return, re-address the definite duration, the object that, as an identity, is established in the synthesis of originary temporalization. Thus Husserl does not mistake acts of re-consciousness as acts of origination (although such acts do, of course, constitute new objects of a higher level; but insofar as they do so, they are themselves yet again acts of originary constitution, achieving the presence of the higher order object). Such acts, he says, do not originarily constitute the entity that, though intended in them, was also the identical entity intended in a different act. Rather, they "awaken" such an object, they "vivify" it (see *EJ*, 207–11/177–80). They do this by vivifying the definite duration *precisely as* a duration, "running through" it in its temporal order and spread.

Husserl notes different forms of "recollection." We can, one might say, recollect merely "signitively" by laying hold of the object in question in a "single ray" of regard that does not articulate the temporal determinateness of the object itself. In certain cases, then, "objectivities that are built up originally in temporal processes . . . may be apprehended in a backward glance as if they were objects complete in a temporal point" (*Hua* X, 36/59–60). Given that the object itself as a determinate individual is temporally differentiated and that such temporal differentiation is not articulated in such a mode of recollection, then "what is remembered is indeterminate" (37/59). Such givenness, however, may then undergo a clarification in which the temporal differentiations are themselves explicitly brought to re-consciousness. This kind of recollection would be

> a real, re-productive, recapitulative memory in which a temporal object is again completely built up in a continuum of presentifications, so that we seem to perceive it again, but only seemingly, as-if. The whole process is a presentificational modification of the process of perception with all its phases and levels, including retentions. However, everything has the index of reproductive modification.

It might be thought that such a re-consciousness would reclaim the object itself in the "running through" of the originarily temporalized content of the duration, the content bounded by the temporal beginning of its original running off and the temporal end of its running off. However, because individuation is a function not only of the determinate duration of the essential content in question, but also—and more fundamentally—of the temporal position of the duration itself *within* the one flux-stream of consciousness, such a merely "internal" running through is not enough. Rather, re-identification requires the re-consciousness of the determinate duration *as situated within its own temporal horizon*. That is, genuine re-identification requires the restoring of a stretch of time consciousness that is greater than that of the definite duration of the object itself. As Husserl says:

> Recollection is not only re-consciousness on behalf of the object, but as the perception of a temporal object it carries its temporal horizon with it, so that recollection also repeats the consciousness of this horizon. Two recollections can be memories of like objects, for example, two like sounds. However, they are recollections of the same temporal object not when the mere content of duration is the same, but when the temporal horizon is the same. . . . (108/143)

Ideally speaking, then, a recollection that was to provide itself with an object that was once originarily given, in order to establish the object as self-identical and not merely like another (for instance, with the same essential content, but occurring originarily at two different points within the stream and thus having a different temporal position), would have to "run through" not only the object-content but also, in order to grasp it in its temporal particularity, the temporal before and after of the object itself; that is, moments of the stream that are not of the "object itself" at all.

What can it mean to say that in recollection a duration *itself* is yielded and is the intentional object of the act, thereby demanding that recollection be a "single rayed" act presenting the duration as an identity, and yet also to say that a "real" recollection must "run through" and thereby re-present the duration as it originarily unfolded? Does not the having of the duration itself exclude in the same complex act the investigation of the duration by a "running through" of the duration, having it "as if" originarily given? For having duration itself as an object is to have a fixed duration, while to have it "as if" originarily given is to have it "as if" not fixed, but open.

It is the as-if that is decisive here. The peculiarity of the Now, as we saw, is its newness—and the meaning of this newness is that it forces consciousness to wait upon it. Contrast the genuine Now with the as-if Now of recollection. Here there is still a duration, a temporal spread to be encountered; but, as Husserl notes decisively, this spread is encountered in recollection with a certain "freedom" (47/71). This freedom, strangely enough, is a function of the fact that consciousness need no longer *wait upon the "to come,"* which is now present in the recollected protentional dimension which comprises any now-moment. For the meaning of the as-if is that, while the primordially constitutive consciousness is a "lived experience animated by protentions that voidly constitute and intercept what is coming" (52/76), the same protentions in recollection are not given as empty, as vacancies to be simply waited upon. On the contrary, they are already determinatively fixed. Husserl says:

> the recollective lived experience not only renews these protentions in a manner appropriate to memory. These protentions were not only present as intercepting, they have also intercepted. They have been fulfilled, and we are aware of them in recollection. Fulfillment in recollective consciousness is re-fulfillment . . . and if the primordial protention of the perception of the event was undetermined and the question of being-other or not-being was left open, then in the recollection we have a pre-directed expectation which does not leave all that open. (52–53/76)

This does not mean that recollection does not re-present the future at all. It does, but in a way that only presents an as-if future of the point being run through in recollection. Its openness, its unfixedness, is only "as if."

This merely as-if openness is the possibility of the freedom that Husserl sees as marking the act of re-consciousness. For the fixedness of the protentional dimension means that for recollection there is *no longer the ontological contingency of the intuitive act* that originarily constitutes the Now-presence of the object. The object, as no longer originarily now, has achieved temporal determinateness. Therefore, consciousness no longer has to wait upon the sheer gratuity of the originary showing of the object itself. Presentification is not constrained to merely wait upon the showing of the object, which appears just as it appears. Rather, it "is something free." Husserl writes,

> it is a free running-through. We can carry out the presentification "more quickly" or "more slowly," clearly and explicitly or in a confused manner, quick as lightning at a stroke or in articulated steps, and so on. Presentification is thus itself an occurrence of internal consciousness and as such has its actual Now, its modes of running-off, etc. And in the same immanent temporal interval in which the presentification really takes place, we can "in freedom" accommodate larger and smaller parts of the presentified event with its modes of running-off and consequently run through it more quickly or more slowly. (48/71)

This is an encounter with transcendence, with the immanent object as transcendent in this way: it can be seen that there is no self-identical coincidence between the act of recollection and the recollected identity; for this to be the case, the identity in question would be required to have no being beyond its being for the act of recollection; and this would mean that no act of re-collection, of consciousness-again, could be possible of the object. For it is the very meaning of the act of recollection to attain consciousness of an object that exists independently of it. Only if this is the case can there be identity of objects across different acts.

That this is not a merely formal requirement is seen in the fact that no recollection can yield certainty. The object given in the recollective act is not consumed by that act, is not "immanent" to it, but exceeds it, such that the very same object can still be what it is for yet other acts of recollection. And it is due to this excess, this transcendence, that error is possible. It is always possible that the recollected object is actually not as the recollection presents it. Husserl says:

> If I remember something I experienced yesterday, then I reproduce the occurrence, if necessary, following all the steps of the succession. While I am doing this, I am conscious of a sequence; one step is first produced, then, in definite sequence, the second, and so on. But apart from this sequence, which evidently belongs to the reproduction as the present flow of lived experience, the reproduction brings about the presentation of a temporal flow that is past. And it is entirely possible not only that the individual steps of the occurrence made present through memory deviate from those of the actual past event (they did not happen as they are now presentified), but also that the real order of succession was other than the order of succession as recollected. It is here, therefore, that errors are possible, errors, that is, which arise from the reproduction as such. . . . (49/72)

§ 3. The Constitution of the Immanent Object: Kinaesthetic and Associative Syntheses

As the very constitution of endurance—where endurance is the condition for the possibility of identity—the originary temporal syntheses in which all temporal determinations are constituted make up the most fundamental moment of the "passive synthesis providing all matter" (*CM*, 112).

In light of the preceding analyses of the temporal syntheses, it is clear that the earlier hylo-morphism of the *Logical Investigations* and *Ideas I*—wherein the hyle was held to be mere "dead stuff," not itself constituted and possibly foreign to the ego, thereby raising the possibility of a "something" coming from outside the ego—is no longer tenable. For "the hyle, understood as that which is sensed in the act of sensation, is not itself immediately given but rather mediated through the constituting accomplishments of temporalization...."[23] However, the syntheses of internal time alone cannot account for the constitution of the domain of immanent objectivity. Insofar as Husserl understands the passive syntheses as the syntheses that "provide all matter," then the passive synthesis is a complex function that brings about not only the most fundamental formal structure of any experiential datum whatsoever—the temporal synthesis by virtue of which any endurance whatsoever is constituted—but also the qualitatively distinct and myriad hyletic particularities that as proto-immanent objects are given as endurances. Thus the passive syntheses yield proto-immanent objects in both their formal generality as endurances and their particularizing qualitative determination. The formal structure of temporal endurance establishes both the internal temporality of the proto-immanent object—its own endurance—and its place within the underlying temporal flow, granting it its particular temporal place relative to other proto-immanent objects; however, this alone is not enough to particularize the proto-immanence as "it itself." That requires the manifestation of qualitative particularity as well, and it is the passive synthesis that achieves this. Thus the temporal syntheses are only one abstract aspect of the passive syntheses, and to speak only of the temporal syntheses is to be engaged in an "abstraction insofar as *what* is synthesized in this synthesis of temporalization is left out of consideration."[24]

This gives rise to the question of how the temporal syntheses are related to the concrete datum itself, which in its individuality is much more than a temporal spread. For the temporal syntheses allow only for a comprehension of the unity of the act alone, not for that in terms of which different, though co-temporaneous, endurances are possible. Landgrebe poses this question in

---

23. Ludwig Landgrebe, "The Problem of Passive Constitution," in *The Phenomenology of Edmund Husserl: Six Essays*, ed. Donn Welton (Ithaca, N.Y.: Cornell University, 1981), 50–65, here 58.
24. Ibid., 59.

terms of the relation between originary temporalization and the concreteness of corporeality: Is it not the case that "all concepts of the accomplishments of the constitution of time-formation would be concepts of mere *forms* of functions that would then need a given content before they could come into play?"[25] And would this not imply, or even assert, the intrusion of a foreignness into the stream, of some a-temporal In-itself, a transcendence, an alterity, that would not be clarified through an analysis of its constitution within consciousness, but would merely insinuate itself at the point where phenomenological investigation can go no further?

But phenomenology asserts its right to proceed even here, for what Husserl calls "the primal impressional datum"[26] is only given in such a way that it can become a theme for us.[27] The investigation seeks to uncover the way in which this occurs.

What does this entail? First, that the datum arise as a prominence from a background of less prominence. Thus it presupposes syntheses of contrast and association. But it also presupposes the constitution of the "field" within which such a datum can come to prominence. And the constitution of the field presupposes the kinaesthetic syntheses. We now turn to a consideration of these syntheses, which will show, even more completely than the consideration of the work of the temporal syntheses, how the immanent objects generated therein are properly "transcendencies in immanence," having no being whatsoever apart from this constitution and adducing no alterity.

§ 3.1. Kinaesthetic Syntheses

The most thorough and illuminating discussion of the role and nature of the kinaesthetic syntheses in Husserl's phenomenology is to be found in Ulrich Claesges's work.[28] The following discussion is principally indebted to him, although Welton also has many illuminating observations to make.[29]

What is the importance of the kinaesthetic syntheses in the constitution of originarily given objectivity? What is the role of the kinaesthesan in objectivation?

Husserl turns to the employment of the concept of kinaesthetic synthesis as part of his attempt to do phenomenological justice to the complex phenomenon of originary constitution. Although the temporal syntheses are identified

---

25. Ibid., 56.
26. Ibid.
27. For example, a tone that is given and passes away, or a color that is present with a particular spread.
28. Ulrich Claesges, *Edmund Husserls Theorie der Raumkonstitution* (The Hague: Nijhoff, 1964).
29. Other valuable material is to be found in Welton, *Origins of Meaning*, 212–45, as well as in Alphonso Lingis's "Intentionality and Corporeality," *Analecta Husserliana* 1 (1971), 75–90, and "Hyletic Data," *Analecta Husserliana* 2 (1972), 96–101.

as the most fundamental moment of this constitution, originary experiencing is more complex than merely temporal. The moment of 'quality' must somehow be accounted for, for "objects" are not only differentiated according to temporal differences. How is spatiality, for example, originarily constituted? Husserl answers in terms of the kinaesthetic syntheses.

He proceeds by noting that some kinds of immanent object not only have their own temporality but also a kind of spatiality: visual data have an "extension," they occupy an "expanse" (*Hua* XVI, § 46). As particulars that have "come to attention," such data are already individuals appearing within a "field," and this field is itself already structured. The data appearing within this field indicate this structure and are ordered according to it. This structure is a function of the kinaesthetic syntheses. But the kinaesthetic syntheses that govern the ocular field are themselves part of a greater system of kinaesthetic functions. Thus, as Landgrebe points out, it is not only visual data that are already spatially significant but *all* such "sense" data are. For example, a heard sound presupposes certain kinaesthesan corresponding to the "turning of the head," etc. for it to be given. As such the sound is already given with a spatial determination. We shall now follow Claesges and discuss the kinaesthetic syntheses in relation to the example of the visual datum.

Immanent objects employed in the constitution of real transcendencies, "appearing" transcendencies, are, in Welton's words, "already integrated into a temporal and spatial system 'motivating' their composition."[30] Husserl's question is: How is this possible? He answers that the spatial structure of the particular object is a function of the structure of the field within which it occurs and that this field-structure is in turn a function of what is called 'kinaesthetic synthesis'. This is so in two senses: the kinaesthesan are responsible, first, for the "immanent" spatiality of the datum, its "spread" *within* the field itself, by virtue of the kinaesthesan governing the internal structure and meaning of the field, and, second, also for the situating of the real object itself in terms of its "near" or "far" in relation to the perceiving organism. But how does Husserl claim this?

The term 'kinaesthesis' has two quite different components: the moment of "movement" (*kinesis*) and the moment of "sensation" (*aisthesis*).[31] And, as Claesges points out, the moment of "sensation" has a double determination: on the one hand, it is bound to the notion of the sense datum in the usual sense, to what could be called the moment of quality, which in the case of the visual field is present as "color data"; on the other hand, a moment that Claesges identifies as "sensation of position." But how do the kinaesthetic syntheses account for the experienceability of the sensed datum?

---

30. Welton, *Origins of Meaning*, 229.
31. The passages cited in this and the subsequent three paragraphs may be found in Claesges, *Raumkonstitution*, 64–66.

What qualitatively comes to presence as a datum Claesges calls the 'aspect'. But this aspect-datum is itself in flux, it "runs off." He says: "This running-off of the aspect is in strict correlative relation to a kinaesthetic running-off." Thus there is a structure to the running-off of what comes to actual givenness; although what will genuinely come to actuality is itself indeterminate, is in no way "commandable," there is a structure that governs whatever in fact does come to actuality. One can say that there is an Apriori that governs the "space" within which the actual comes to pass.

This structure brings with it a certain "adumbration," in which certain possibilities for the course of the running-off of the actual content are already implicit within what has already run off. This adumbration is the introduction of the properly transcendental notion of 'adumbration', which also introduces a further instance—beyond the temporal—of "horizon."

Husserl understands the structuring power—the spatial Apriori—of the kinaesthetic syntheses in terms of a kinaesthetic system. But what is this concept, and how does it come to light? The kinaesthesis is originally grasped as a functioning, a "play." At any time, however, this functioning can stop, can come to rest. In this state of rest, one can come to see a "region of function" of the kinaesthesias as a system of other possible kinaesthetic "positions." Husserl understands a kinaesthetic system in terms of the entire range of such possible "positions." Thus Claesges offers the definition: "A kinaesthetic system . . . is the noetic manifold that constitutes the noematic unity of the appearance as its correlate."

The kinaesthetic system—in this case, the oculomotor system, the system of visual sensing—is always a system of possibilities, of which some actual "kinaesthetic situation" is a "partial actualization."[32] 'Possibility' here has the sense of 'ability' (*Vermöglichkeit*). In Claesges's words: "Ability is a possibility in the sense of the 'I can'."

That is, the kinaesthetic system is a system of "ways"[33] of action open to the intentional functionary. The possible range of these ways constitutes the Apriori of the system; these ways, and they alone, are open to the intentional functionary, just as the temporal synthesis is governed by an immutable horizonal structure. This Apriori governs all possible modes within which any actualizable datum can come to presence.

But how are these possibilities themselves present? The clue lies in the notion of 'ability', of the 'I can': these possibilities, as actualizable potentialities, suggest themselves in the "running-off" (*Ablauf*) of the kinaesthetic functioning itself.[34] Speaking generally, at the level of the species, the future course of (for

---

32. Claesges, *Raumkonstitution*, 75. The next passage cited in the text may also be found here.
33. Claesges uses the term *Wege* (ibid., 75), which is justified by Husserl's use of that term in Ms. D 12 I (1931), 5.
34. Claesges, *Raumkonstitution*, 65 and 75–79.

instance, in the case of a visual datum) the range of possible visual showings is bound by the range of the oculomotor kinaesthesan. Further, at the level of the future continual showing or development of some particular datum, only a certain range of possibilities within the more general range of oculomotor possibilities are actualizable if a sustained showing of a unified datum is to take place. This fact establishes the sense of both 'adumbration' and 'horizon'. For example, any appearing within the visual field must be ordered according to the pregiven structure of that field. The most general structure of this field is that of the contrast between its "middle region" and its "outer region": "The field has a small middle region and a large outer region, and this itself has a concentric structure."[35] The phenomenological sense of this contrast is essentially a gradation of clarity and distinctness. The central region offers the greatest degree of clarity, and this clarity steadily decreases with movement toward the edge of the field.[36]

But movement within the field—and hence fixed place within the field—is ordered more particularly with reference to actual kinaesthetic command of the field, a command that enables a given to be brought greater clarity and distinctness. Because this clarity and distinctness is a function of "position" within the field—its being "in the middle"—the order or structure of the field is itself a function of the capacity to bring to clarity and distinctness—that is, the capacity to effect particularization and identification analogous to that effected by the temporal synthesis. Thus it is that the general "inner–outer" determination of the field can be given a more particular determination in terms that are precisely related to, and derive their sense from, the kinaesthetic functioning that achieves the clarification and particularization in question. Position within the field is thereby determined according to the two-dimensional principles of ordering: right–left, over–under, which "cross" each other in the center of the field.[37] These determinations refer precisely to the kinaesthetic syntheses correlated with the visual organs, as the "datum" is brought into the center of the field and thereby to greatest possible clarification, determination, and particularization—in short, identification rendered available for reidentification.

But it is a fundamental mistake to believe that the ocular kinaesthesias govern a merely two-dimensional determination of space. As Claesges points out, the ocular kinaesthesias are also characterized by a peculiar synthesis he calls the "kinaesthesis of accommodation."[38] This particular mode of synthesis gives effect to the depth-dimension of the visual field, through which to the ordered pairs 'left–right' and 'over–under' is added a third: 'near–far'.[39]

---

35. Husserl, Ms. D 13 IV (1921), p. 5 (cited from Claesges, *Raumkonstitution*, 96).
36. See ibid., 69.
37. Ibid.
38. Ibid., 79.
39. Ibid., 80.

These pairs determine the entire "three-dimensional continuum of orientation"; and the kinaesthesan that effect the 'near–far' contrast establish the ground upon which the distinction between 'interiority' and 'exteriority' is constituted: "it is in terms of these coordinates that the perceptual field as a field of action is organized. With this new emphasis perception is seen as a mode of praxis, and passivity, in turn, as a style of possible actions."[40]

The kinaesthesias in question here are typically, in restriction to the ocular kineasthesias, movements of achieving focus. Thus the ocular kinaesthesias are not mon-ocular but bi-ocular. These ocular kinaesthesias are in themselves only isolable through an abstraction that considers them in isolation from their functioning as a part of a total and not merely ocular system. It includes, for instance, the whole range of kinaesthesias involved in the turning of the head and then the whole upper body. Eventually, the whole range of movements comes into play in order for spatial determination to be properly effected. This, of course, presupposes the kinaesthetic constitution of the body as a thing in the world. But this is beyond the scope of our investigation.[41]

This range of possible kinaesthetic "play" constitutes the kinaesthetic system as an a priori capacity for structuring, for the coming to presence of sense-hyle, and hence for the constitution of the sense-hyle as an immanent object. Thanks to this field structure, it can be said that what appears is already structured according to the purely subjective possibilities allowed by the structure of the field within which it makes its appearance. Therefore, contrary to the static hylo-morphism according to which the "content" undergoing apprehension was "formless" "dead stuff," it now appears that the so-called "sense-hyle" already bears within itself an "inner relatedness" (*Hua* XVI, 46–47) to other possible data that could appear within its own field. It is already senseful, regardless of what "representational" role it may come to play. Welton writes:

> In fact, it seems that the "animation" and "projection" taking place are in some sense determined by this inner character: "the physical datum of the species 'tone' cannot exhibit an objective moment of the species 'color'; the physical datum 'color' nor an objective feature of the species 'warm'," etc.[42]

It is due to this Apriori of synthetic possibilities that, Welton believes, Husserl broke with the somewhat occult empiricist account of association, of "tracks 'in the animal spirit' which 'by often treading, are worn into a smooth path.'"[43] Husserl moves at the same time "beyond his own treatment of associations as immediate and passive 'relations' between data, into a description of them as associative *syntheses*."[44]

---

40. Welton, *Origins of Meaning*, 241.
41. For an excellent account of this constitution, see Claesges, *Raumkonstitution*, 90–115.
42. Welton, *Origins of Meaning*, 220. (The quotation of Husserl is from *Hua* XVI, 54.)
43. Welton, *Origins of Meaning*, 221.
44. Ibid.

This "inner relatedness," this "set of possible ways of operation" that the actual brings to light as "possible from here," constitutes the *horizon* within which new appearings are possible. Welton puts this very clearly:

> In each fulfillment what appears and is present is shot through with empty horizons which take the form of a perceptual demand: "A new empty horizon, a new system of determinate indeterminacies, a new system of progressive tendencies with corresponding possibilities . . . belongs to each appearing of the thing in each perceptual phase. The aspects are . . . nothing for themselves, they are appearances-of only through the intentional horizon which is inseparable from them."[45]

This set of kinaesthetic capabilities is structurally bound by what is possible under the 'I can'. That the kinaesthetic movement is itself temporally extended, that it "flows off" through a temporal continuum, according to the originary syntheses of time (the fundamental condition of any identity) and then according to the determinate range of possibilities open to the kinaesthetic operation in question ("this way" and not "that way"), is the condition for the possibility of an appearing unity, that what appears in "one with itself," "the same." Speaking of appearings, Husserl says: "Only as that which is dependent upon the kinaesthesan can they continually move over into one another and constitute a unity of sense" (*Hua* XI, 14).[46] Husserl uses this notion of a kinaesthetic system to clarify the notion of 'field', within which the datum comes to presence: "'Field' in the pregnant sense is a traversable 'continuous' unity due to the functioning kinaesthesen."[47] In Claesges's words: "The field is nothing other than the correlate of a kinaesthetic system."[48] The field structure, the structure that governs the possible appearing of a datum and that establishes the possible sense of "appearing datum" is itself grounded in the structure of the kinaesthetic system—that is, in the a priori abilities that the system maps out. The horizon, within which the given appears and in terms of which its possibilities for alteration are to be spelled out, thus has its ground in a fund of abilities that the intentional functionary can bring to bear, can put into operation.

But how are these syntheses syntheses of *constitution*? Insofar as they are syntheses constituting unification, they are syntheses constituting what appears in its own particularity. They are constitutional syntheses insofar as they constitute a unity above and beyond temporal unity; they are therefore syntheses that constitute an enrichment of the object as the unity that appears. The kinaesthetic syntheses do this since they themselves are first a temporal unity. But this temporal unity, the unity of *one* actual kinaesthetic function that is carried out, is itself a unity as one particular course of "movement," which happens to be correlated with the particular unity of what comes to appearance. In fact,

---

45. Ibid., 235. (The quotation of Husserl is from *Hua* XI, 6.)
46. Cited from Welton, *Origins of Meaning*, 242.
47. Husserl, Ms. 10 IV (1932), pp. 8 ff. (Cited from Claesges, *Raumkonstitution*, 73.)
48. Claesges, *Raumkonstitution*, 72.

one of the determinants of the particular identity of what appears *as a unity*, one of the determinations of its utter particularity as just "that" and not "something else," is the peculiar and utterly particular way in which what appears is given in correlation with a *particular course* of kinaesthetic functioning, which functioning is *itself* a unity. The "aspect" unity—what is given as "sensation"— is something that itself appears in a running-off. It is always temporally and often qualitatively in alteration. But in this alteration, it remains "that one entity that gave itself as altering." How is this extra-temporal qualitative unity possible? What is its principle? The altering quality—for instance, a color datum that may change its shade or may change its "spread" (shape), or both—is constituted as a unity in that it is strictly correlated with a *kinaesthetic unity of one course* of "action," the unity of the "one movement" that enabled its being given. The unity of action is constituted as a unity in the temporal syntheses, and a unity of appearing "aspect," of "given quality," is constituted as the strict correlate of that kinaesthetic unity. Through the unity that accrues to the appearing "aspect" through the unity of the kinaesthetic action, an identity of sensation, a "just that particular one and not another" is constituted and is retrievable through a retrieval of the kinaesthetic unity that has become an immanent objectivity.

This allows Husserl to find a conditionality within the kinaesthetic functioning that he calls 'kinaesthetic motivation'. The 'I can' can be more particularly characterized as an 'if-then'. This 'if' specifies the particular kinaesthetic possibility to be actualized ('if I do X'), and the 'then' specifies the actualized sensory result that is correlated with that particular kinaesthetic facilitation. As Claesges says: "The identical 'then' is the givenness of the aspect-datum."[49]

This, of course, presupposes the constitution of what is specified under the 'then' as an identity. It follows from this that the originary kinaesthetic constitution of an appearing datum as an identity cannot be specified through a conditional 'if-then' structure. As with the originary temporalization, the content of the yet-to-come is still open.

Thus one can see why Claesges claims that "the concept of the kinaesthesis is the fundamental concept of the Husserlian theory of perception...."[50] For in two ways it allows the appearing of the "identifiable"; along with the syntheses of originary temporalization, it constitutes the condition for the possibility of identification. First, where the kinaesthesias are understood as correlated with a "sense organ" (e.g. the oculomotor system), in other words, with a streaming occurrence that is not only that of sheer "movement" (e.g. where there is a "sensation" of color, sound, smell, touch, etc., as well as the "sensation of movement" itself), the kinaesthesias organize the meaning of the

---

49. Ibid.
50. Ibid., 64 n. 1.

"situatedness" of the datum, both within the field itself and in relation to the perceiving organism, in both "pre-space" and "real space." This situatedness is an essential moment of the particular identity of the individual that appears, and it marks its difference from other individuals. Thus the kinaesthesias are not only the condition for the possibility of the being given of such a datum in general, but are also responsible for effecting the particularization of any datum that does appear. They are therefore syntheses of constitution. That is, such syntheses constitute the very meaning of spatiality and hence, in their operation, the very possibility of the givenness of spatial object; in addition, they also constitute the particularity—and hence the identity—of any spatial or pre-spatial object that does come to givenness. This is the second constitutional function performed by the kinaesthetic syntheses: as what is correlated with some particular course of kinaesthetic functioning and specified in the 'then' of the 'if–then', the appearing correlate, the "aspect-datum" achieves particularization as "it itself," as the appearing that is motivated strictly in accordance with some particular and actual kinaesthetic function specified through the conditional 'if'.

Therefore, even at the level of the passive constitution, objects properly emerge that already refer back to syntheses of identification in which they have their origin. Such syntheses are properly a kind of "proto-apprehension" yielding what are already transcendencies-in-immanence, already identities. As Welton points out, a role remains for a static hylo-morphism:

> It seems that when Husserl is speaking of constitution as that which makes possible the *referential* function of consciousness, and when he has the functional contrast between appearances and the various ways of apprehending them in view, he disregards the hyletic constitution of the appearance and takes it as a given upon which the *Auffassung* operates.[51]

But such a framework is distorting and concealing when fundamental questions of genesis are raised. Here a different notion of synthesis must be employed, for the synthesized "data" are no longer dead matter that "come from somewhere into the stream." Then, "when Husserl speaks of constitution as many-layered *synthesis*, as *synthetische Leistung* . . . each datum or complex of data has both a *unity* and a field, and has a 'proto-apprehension' which 'precedes' its apprehension and, in fact, *founds* the perceptual apprehension."

Thus the turn to the genetic analyses generates a new notion of synthesis that "rejects the static picture of sensations as contents undergoing a temporal or spatial apprehension." For, most fundamentally, "it is only *in* the synthetic accomplishments of time-consciousness and the kinaesthesan that such complexes are formed."[52] Husserl's genetic investigations show that the fundamen-

---

51. Welton, *Origins of Meaning*, 236. The next quotation may also be found on this page.
52. Ibid., 231.

tal synthesis of constitution cannot itself be understood to operate with already constituted entities. Thus it does not "have relata in the same sense in which the others do." Welton writes:

> While there is a distinction between synthesis and that which is formed in the synthesis, the relative independence of "content" and apprehension does not exist at this level. Undergoing associative syntheses is equivalent to having sensorial complexes, and there cannot be a single, identical complex which could remain the same throughout various associative syntheses. To put it in a way which clashes with Husserl's static analysis, the syntheses are productive.[53]

Thus there are two notions of synthesis that operate in Husserl's phenomenology, depending upon whether the objectives of static or genetic analysis are in question:

> There is a synthesis as coupling or as combining; such terms point to something separate, to elements which enter into the coupling. But there is also synthesis as blending, as continual fusion; this does not have relata or elements as does the first. Genetically speaking they are primary: "The thing as a formation of aesthetic couplings is built out of sensuous features which originate from continual synthesis."[54]

§ 3.2. Associative Syntheses

However, there is one more moment of constitution that Husserl detects in the constitutional synthesis of identification, of objectification, beyond the originary temporalization and the kinaesthetic syntheses. This is the moment of the "associative syntheses." For beyond receiving temporal and spatial determination, there must be a synthesis that allows the particularization and hence differentiation of individuals that share the same time and space. Husserl identifies these as the syntheses of association and contrast. Such syntheses function to effect a differentiation between, and hence identification and individuation of, "qualities." Landgrebe brings this to our attention:

> That the living streaming present is always a primal impressional present means that these primal impressions are already synthetic unities produced in the passive syntheses of association and contrast. Only in them does the individual datum come into relief.[55]

Welton points to the detailed analyses of these syntheses in Husserl's investigations in *Passive Synthesis*. Three characteristics are needed in order for a particular datum to emerge as an individual that "breaks in" upon consciousness and either attracts or repels. What is first required is a temporal continuity generated in the originary temporal syntheses. Then what is required is the

---

53. Ibid., 239.
54. Ibid.
55. Landgrebe, "The Problem of Passive Constitution," 59.

field constitution effected in the kinaesthetic syntheses, the syntheses that give Husserl's analysis "its roots in existence."[56] Both of these syntheses contribute to the possibility and sense of individuation. But more than this, there is required, finally, a specification of the spatiotemporal particular in terms of its quality:

> there is a synthetic coincidence or congruence of the complex, and this according to the limits of complete congruence (identity) and incongruence (degrees of contrast). In the event of congruence the complex is a "blended" complex said to be "similar"; in the case of incongruence the complex becomes "emphatic" or "lifted out" and is said to be "contrasting" with other elements or with the entire blended field.[57]

The syntheses of association and contrast organize the datum in terms of intensity and quality, using homogeneity and heterogeneity as principle discriminators. Welton refers to these syntheses as "elementary material syntheses."[58] Through such syntheses an individual, a particular, comes to be "lifted out" of a background, a "field," and comes to exert an affective power or tendency: "at the same time that one 'content' becomes prominent the rest of the perceptual field falls away and, while unified, becomes a vague background."[59] As Husserl says:

> The unity of the field of consciousness is always produced through sensuous interconnections, sensuous connections of similarity and sensuous contrast. Without that we would not have a "world" which is there. We could put it as follows: the sensuous similarity and the sensuous contrast ... is the resonance which grounds all which has already been constituted. (*Hua* XI, 131)[60]

The syntheses of association and contrast should not be seen as "autonomous contributors to the perceptual process." Rather, they are properly understood as syntheses of *organization*, which function within the field of possibilities open up by the kinaesthetic syntheses. It is in terms of this set of possibilities that what is present can indicate and point to other moments present within the field, or which are possibly actualizable in the future. Thus, says Welton,

> what we now find is an aesthetic motivation immanent to the appearance and based on the homogeneity and heterogeneity of its complex: the "apprehension" is there in a "modified" form as associations which create tendency, allurement, and anticipations according to a *style* which is both given and indeterminate. The appearance as a hyletic complex is organized in a particular way in and through temporal, kinaesthetic and associative syntheses.[61]

---

56. Welton, *Origins of Meaning*, 240.
57. Ibid., 238. Welton also calls attention to Husserl's discussion in *Hua* XI, 117–25.
58. Welton, *Origins of Meaning*, 238.
59. Ibid., 240.
60. Welton's translation (from *Origins of Meaning*, 240).
61. Ibid., 243.

Thus the immanent object is properly an object, a noematic something, that is not a sheer given but is thoroughly constituted in various syntheses. The immanent object is a transcendence situated within a horizon which is its possibility of coming to appearance.

§ 3.3. The Immanent Object: No "Sign" of Alterity

The discovery of the kinaesthetic syntheses is of great importance for the meaning of the concreteness of the transcendental functionary, the transcendental functionary in its most originary concrete being. For this is the discovery that "the functions of corporeality belong to the functions of passive pre-constitution and together with it to 'transcendental subjectivity.'"[62] The originary syntheses of time-consciousness, though the fundamental moment of any identity formation, are only considerable in themselves through an abstraction. When one overcomes this abstraction by considering the other moments of synthesis that function together in the constitution of the immanent object, one comes to see that the functions of corporeality—though these are not the functions of a "body," for a body is a constituted entity—are located at the functioning heart of transcendental intentionality. In fact, such an intentionality cannot be thought other than as sustaining corporeal functions. For, as Landgrebe says, "without impressions there are no time-constituting accomplishments and without kinaesthesen there are no impressions."[63] The conclusion regarding the corporeality of the transcendental functionary consists in the realization that "the impressions are related to the actual kinaesthetic field coordinated to the sense-capacities."[64] Landgrebe takes this discovery to form the background of Claesges's comment that "the kinaesthetic consciousness is time-consciousness."[65]

This particular discovery is of great importance for our consideration of the meaning of the "transcendence" that, contrary to the Husserl of *Ideas I*, has already been seen to characterize the entire domain of immanent objectivity. Is this a "transcendence-in-immanence," a transcendence that has being only as an accomplishment of originarily functioning intentionality, that in being attained would not signify the attainment of a radical alterity but rather a peculiar "remaining within itself"? Or does the attaining of such a transcendence signify the encounter with something or some region of the foreign, a genuine alterity, an "in itself"?

Antonio Aguirre opts for the first determination: "the hyle arises from me myself, is my own," he says.[66] Surely this is right. The immanent object, as an

---

62. Landgrebe, "The Problem of Passive Constitution," 51–52.
63. Ibid., 59.
64. Ibid.
65. Claesges, *Raumkonstitution*, 120.
66. Antonio Aguirre, *Genetische Phänomenologie und Reduktion. Zur Letztbegründung*

identity, has only the sense of something that arises out of synthetic accomplishments; they are always only results of such accomplishing and always only have the ontological meaning of a result. As such they do not present themselves as entities merely "come upon" by functioning intentionality but exist only as its accomplishment. How can we be so sure of this? Because such entities in their very being-sense ultimately refer, as the investigation has shown, back to the synthetic accomplishments that not only allow them to become present but that establish their very meaning. To be temporal is to be what emerges from originary temporalization, which establishes the very meaning of endurance; to be spatial is to be what emerges as a kinaesthetic correlate. In Landgrebe's words:

> If we only consider that all affection is the primitive affection of the sense organs as organs of my body and that all kinaesthetic movements are the conditions under which the affection of the sense organs becomes possible, it follows that corporeality must be understood not merely as constituted but as constituting. It is a system of constitutive capabilities to which the actual sense fields are coordinated. . . . What can possibly become a datum for me is established by that organization of the sense fields. . . . It is in this sense that "the hyle arises from me myself."[67]

As such the immanent "transcendencies-in-immanence" are just that: transcendencies. For they now have a being that exceeds any act that has them as an object, but they are essentially bound in their ontological meaning to the subjective Apriori from which they arose and whose synthetic accomplishments they are and remain; they have no ontological meaning other than as "constituted accomplishment." Thus, even if—and we will give more thought to this very strange circumstance shortly, inquiring into its "meaning for transcendence"—constitutive synthesis can in no way *command* the yet-to-come to "satisfy" or "fulfill" its expectations, even though what will come to "presence" (even the possibility that presence evaporates) is, as regards its *actual coming to presence*, "beyond the ken" of the synthesizing function, it is nonetheless true that "the hyle is not something that is based in something entirely foreign . . . but rather it belongs to the immanence of transcendental becoming itself."[68]

§ 4. The Status of the Immanent Object

This section revolves around two final questions: What is the ontological status of the definite duration, the primal object, and what is the meaning of its "presence"?

---

der Wissenschaft aus der radikalen Skepsis im Denken E. Husserls (The Hague: Nijhoff, 1970), 167.
67. Landgrebe, "The Problem of Passive Constitution," 60.
68. Ibid., 63.

§ 4.1. The Ontological Status of the Immanent Object: The Most Originary Transcendence-in-Immanence

According to Husserl's original "form–content" schema, present in both the *Logical Investigations* and *Ideas I*, it is the rather mysterious "animating function" that constitutes intentionality proper, in the sense that it is only through the animating "apprehension" of non-intentional and immanent data that consciousness's self-transcending takes place, that an "object" is attained. The hyletic data is located unambiguously on the side of non-transcendence, on the noetic side of intentional function. Welton sums up this direction of Husserl's presentation by saying that

> these data are immanent to consciousness, and they cannot be separated from our *Erlebnis* of them. Whereas we can show that perceiving and what is perceived are functionally and relatively independent of each other, such is not the case for sensations. "With them 'to be' and 'to be perceived' coincide." Sensations are *reell* and thus moments of the stream of consciousness.[69]

But the phenomenology of that period was static, and the question of genesis was left out of consideration. With the explicit posing of this question, however, the turn to the mature and genetic phenomenology is made, and a whole new "immanent" domain of objectivity is discovered. Certainly it remains true that the hyle is still to be distinguished from the real object and is still a dimension employed in its constitutional synthesis. But "apprehension" is no longer limited to the constitution of real objects; the hyle itself is shown to arise from a "pre-apprehension" that is not self-identical with its own product. Rather, as Welton points out, "Husserl came to construe sense-data as hyletic complexes with an immanent organization."[70]

This new understanding, which recognizes the hyle as a constituted apperceptive unity, thereby forces a revision of the old "form–content" schema, which Husserl employed to account for perceptual intentionality in the *Logical Investigations* and *Ideas I*. In Landgrebe's words:

> because the hyle, understood as that which is sensed in the act of sensation, is not itself immediately given but rather mediated through the constituting accomplishments of temporalization, the distinction between hyle as formless stuff and animating apprehension as form is no longer in force.[71]

---

69. Welton, *Origins of Meaning*, 214.

70. Ibid., 212. Note also the following: "I always need two things: on the one hand the streaming field of lived experiences within which there is constantly a field of primal impressions fading into retention and before it, protention; and, on the other, the ego that is affected and motivated to action by this. But is not what is primally impressional already an apperceptive unity, a noematic something which comes here from the ego; and does not the questioning-back lead again and again to an apperceptive unity?" (Husserl, as quoted by Aguirre in *Genetische Phänomenologie und Reduktion*, vii.)

71. Landgrebe, "The Problem of Passive Constitution," 58–59.

The hyle can no longer be adequately understood through such metaphors as 'irrational', 'formless', 'blind', 'dead stuff'. As Husserl says in the *Crisis*, "one must not go straight back to the supposed immediately given 'sense data,' as if *they* were immediately characteristic of the purely intuitive data of the life-world" (*Crisis*, 127/125). As "definite duration," the immanent object, which is available again as a Same for other acts different from the one in which it is originarily given, is therefore a genuine transcendence according to the meaning that has been clarified by phenomenology.

§ 4.2. Dual Implications of the Discovery of the Hyle as Constituted: Hyle as Object; Hyle Brought within the Closure of the Transcendental Functionary

Thus recognition of the hyle as itself already the result of an apperceptive unification moves the hyle from the side of the "non-act," the "non-intentional" and purely noetic stratum, closer to the side of the noema, integrating the hyle into the object itself. Husserl's descriptions require, says Welton, that the hyletic stratum "be taken as essentially intentional formations integrated into the noematic appearances of the perceptual object through [perceptual] meaning."[72]

Because the temporal syntheses make up the "original seat" of the constitution of identity as such, prior to and outside of which there is no identity and hence no transcendence, even the term 'synthesis' can unwittingly mislead at this level. For through his investigation of the identity-constituting syntheses of internal time, Husserl discovers that there is a synthesis that is more fundamental than the one that combines previously separate elements. There is, says Welton, "also synthesis as blending, as continual fusion; this does not have relata or elements as does the first."[73] For this reason Husserl speaks in the *Cartesian Mediations* of "the passive synthesis providing all matter" (*CM*, 112).

---

72. Welton, *Origins of Meaning*, 213. Welton gathers the most explicit expressions of the old "form–content" schema as they continue to be scattered throughout Husserl's writings, and then matches these selections with other observations that reveal Husserl's "misgivings and qualifications" regarding its appropriateness. Typical of this is the way in which *Experience and Judgment* goes on to complicate the apparently simple interpretation of perceptual intentionality as a meaning-bestowing act animating "formless non-intentional stuff," with the recognition that the content that undergoes an objectifying apprehension is itself already an individual and thereby presupposes syntheses through which it offers itself to consciousness as already differentiated. Such "data" is already a "prominence in a field," thus already expressing prior conditions of articulation that lie within the field itself. Such a field, of course, is not ever given as an originary object itself; it is only brought to light in terms of the "non-prominent" field-horizon of the prominence in question. Yet although it is always only available through an abstraction, the field is not given as a "mere chaos, a mere 'swarm' of 'data'; it is a field of determinate structure, one of prominences and articulated particularities" (*EJ*, 75/72).

73. Welton, *Origins of Meaning*, 239.

But although it is an "object," it still is not an alterity, for this originary object *is* only as definite duration. In Husserl's words:

> All individual objects have a temporal duration and position; they are extended with an essential content over the original continuum of time and have . . . a temporal extension of definite magnitude, which is their duration, and a temporal content, which fills this duration. . . . As an individual, the total object is a whole of time. (*EJ*, 217/184)

This duration, however, is always only the achievement of the synthesis—the gathering—of originary temporalization. The primal object is therefore a result, a product, of synthesis. It is not something that would have being in itself merely to undergo temporalization as a form of intuition; rather, it is constituted in the temporalizing synthesis.[74]

Yet it is only a "gathered flux," not an alterity. As determinate duration together with particularizing qualitative content, it is only an object within the domain that yields the very meaning and possibility of a determinate duration, a temporal spread with a beginning and an end. And that domain is the ultimate stream itself. The determinate duration *remains, endures,* in that it itself is sustained as a moment within the retentional dimension of the self-constituting flux-unity. As a result of these analyses, it is no longer possible to think of the hyletic data as something foreign that, as hyletic data itself, comes into the stream from outside. Immanent objects—hyletic data—*come to be* in the originary temporalization. They do not have the ontological meaning of being signs or indications of yet other individuals that somehow exist "outside" of the stream itself. As an *identity*, understood as a temporal individual, the hyletic data "*belongs to the immanence of transcendental becoming itself.*"[75]

§ 4.3. The "Presence" of the Immanent Object

What of the meaning of 'presence' if presence is the presence of an object and the object, as the Same, has its being as a moment of the streaming life of the intentional functionary? "Being past" is the sinking-down of what nonetheless remains the "same fact." It is "the same" and not another precisely in that its duration is now fixed, thanks to its no longer being "now," no longer being new. Husserl says:

> Its position in time, and then, more precisely, its situationally determined duration, gives for each individual a determination that concerns its existence, its factuality as such. It is ordered according to its own system of

---

74. As Husserl puts it in *Experience and Judgment* (305/254–55): "*immanent time, in which lived experiences are constituted, is thereby at the same time the form of givenness of all the objects intended in them*; and, so far as it belongs originally to them, it is not something which we only add to them, as if there were an in-itself for them that was completely without relation to time. The necessary relation to time is always present."

75. Landgrebe, "The Problem of Passive Constitution," 63.

> pasts and is the identical element which, continually fading away, sinks ever further into the past. It remains *the same fact*, and because of this it is different from every other fact, each being differently determined in time. . . .
> (*EJ*, 466/385)

Therefore one must say the following: to be past does not mean to "go out of being"; it means to no longer be enlivened by the new. To be past is to be, though not be actual.

Thus, the "limit" of presence—"being"—is not the non-presence of past and future. Rather, the limit of presence is the limit of givenness. This difference between givenness and nongivenness cannot be identified with the difference between the Now and its horizons. Or, in other words, the temporal differences are not analogs for the ontological differences between being and non-being. Rather, the entire temporal field is itself a field coextensive with the showing of what is. As Husserl says: "*Complete submergence* is . . . only *a limit of what has receded*, as, on the other hand, the opposite limit is complete intuitiveness" (209/178–79).

What is does not simply intrude mysteriously, from the nothingness of the not yet and the no longer, into the now, where the now would be a plenitude of being marked on both sides by the sheer absence of past and future. As Husserl puts it, "intuitiveness does not really denote a breach" (209/179).

For this reason, the acts of re-consciousness are said by Husserl to "awaken," to "vivify" the identity brought to re-consciousness. Such acts do not constitute originarily what is awakened or vivified; rather, they call to mind what has receded from the Now but has its being regardless of any such re-consciousness as "what persists obscurely in the horizon of what is still actually intuitive" (209/178). The past, therefore, is not an emptiness, an otherness than being, but a "repository" of samenesses, which, as past, move toward a *limit* of absence.[76]

---

76. Husserl says: "nothing in consciousness that has once been given in experience, especially in intuition, is lost . . . everything remains efficacious" (*EJ*, 231/197). This is also the beginning of Husserl's account of habitualities. This "abiding in retention" is, properly speaking, a sedimentation. As sedimented, what abides in retention and is first a unity of the like and the similar, "a '*sensuous*' unity . . . already passively constituted in advance, a unity in 'subconsciousness,' which unites the different situations of actual and submerged intuitions" (210/179) and which is then awakened through the syntheses of association, acquires the status of what is either continually awakened through such syntheses or is continually drawn upon in the further course of experience and judgment.

Chapter Ten
Derrida and Non-Phenomenologically Reducible Transcendence

§ 1. Context for Discussion of Derrida

We established the methodological legitimacy of Husserl's inquiry into the problem of transcendence in our discussion of the transcendental reduction. We were then able to elaborate the results of Husserl's investigation: transcendence is transcendence-in-immanence, both in the case of the real intersubjective object and the primal immanent object, because (as the problem of the transcendent becomes the problem of identity) identity is always only the result of synthesis. Husserl can reach this conclusion because his investigation affirms that all transcendence that shows itself as such is susceptible, precisely in virtue of its showing of itself, to a transcendental phenomenological analysis of its constitution. The result of that analysis is the discovery of the dynamic of originary temporalization, the fundamental synthesizing activity of the transcendental functionary in which identity is first constituted. In view of that discovery Husserl affirms that transcendental phenomenology is transcendental idealism.

Yet it is precisely in terms of this affirmation of transcendental phenomenology as transcendental idealism that Derrida's *Speech and Phenomena*[1] poses a very real difficulty for Husserl. Derrida's interpretation of the originary temporalization has two results: first, it amounts to a denial of the possibility of the transcendental reduction, a methodological procedure that is intended to legitimate the phenomenological investigation of transcendence; second, it points to an alterity within, but not arising as a result of, the constitutional dynamic, and hence an alterity that cannot be phenomenologically clarified. If Derrida's criticism of Husserl is right,[2] then the entire Husserlian enterprise is in vain, for we would once again have to assert the original Husserlian problem, that is, the epistemologically problematic assertion of the being of transcendence or alterity, while conceding that Derrida has demonstrated the impossibility of clarify-

---

1. Page references in the body to this text in the present section are indicated by the abbreviation *SP*.
2. Derrida's argument really aims to show the impossibility of the reduction: "transcendence" is found to inhabit primally the originary temporalization and therefore cannot be *constituted* by it.

ing the ontological status of that problem. As a consequence, the problem—which is just as great for Derrida as for Husserl—would then read: If "otherness," "alterity," "transcendence," is already, to use Derrida's word, "irreducibly" implicated in the "act in which all origination lies," then "transcendence" is "manna fallen from heaven," something that is not constituted. Were this correct, then phenomenology would be unable to approach its most vital concern: the meaning of transcendence established through intentional analysis.

We shall first articulate the implications of Derrida's position and then advance a critique of it, in which we shall attempt to show that and how the integrity of the Husserlian enterprise is maintained against Derrida.

§ 2. Derrida's Position and its Implications for the Husserlian Enterprise

Derrida's criticism does not take place at the margins of Husserlian phenomenology. On the contrary, not only does it question Husserl's interpretation of the primacy of the intentional functionary, but it also places in doubt the very possibility of a transcendental phenomenology. Derrida says:

> If the punctuality of the instant is a myth, a spatial or mechanical metaphor, an inherited metaphysical concept, or all that at once, and if the present of self-presence is not *simple*, if it is constituted in a primordial and irreducible synthesis, then the whole of Husserl's argumentation is threatened in its very principle. (SP, 61)

And elsewhere:

> Despite this motif of the punctual Now as "primal form" (*Urform*) of consciousness (*Ideas I*), the body of the descriptions in *The Phenomenology of Internal Time-Consciousness* and elsewhere prohibits our speaking of a simple self-identity of the present. In this way . . . what could be called the metaphysical assurance par excellence [is] shaken. . . . (63–64)

Why is this? Because (and here the Derridean presupposition begins to assert itself):

> the presence of the perceived present can appear as such only inasmuch as it is *continuously compounded* with a nonpresence and nonperception, with primary memory and expectation (retention and protention). These nonperceptions are neither added to, nor do they *occasionally* accompany, the actually perceived Now; they are essentially and indispensably involved in its possibility. (64)

Derrida interprets those dimensions of the phenomenon of originary temporalization to which Husserl points through the terms 'retention' and 'protention' as the "presence"—the manifestation—of "the other," of "alterity":

> As soon as we admit this continuity of the Now and the not-Now, perception and nonperception, in the zone of primordiality common to primordial impression and primordial retention, we admit the other into the self-identity of the *Augenblick*; nonpresence and nonevidence are admitted into the

blink of an instant.... This alterity is in fact the condition for presence, presentation, and thus for *Vorstellung* in general; it precedes all the dissociations that could be produced in presence, in *Vorstellung*. (65)

Two conclusions follow from this: first, that no dimension of immanence—a dimension of being that is not already "excessive"—manifests itself. Excess, a "transcendence" (to use Husserl's word) is always complicit in presence and hence would not submit itself to a phenomenological clarification, there being no position not already governed by transcendence. The second conclusion, the threat of skepticism, emerges again from the first. For transcendence is the possibility of "being other" than as it is claimed to be. This means that any "possession" is always open to "displacement" by further showings of the transcendence in question. Because this "displacement" can always—in principle—be more than just a further qualification, can always be a *cancellation*, a "change of sign," then the epistemological appropriation of a transcendence or identity can never afford "metaphysical assurance" or sure possession of its term.

The crucial step in Derrida's argument is his rejection of Husserl's principial distinction between retention and recollection: "The difference between retention and reproduction, between primary and secondary memory, is not the radical difference Husserl wanted between perception and nonperception; it is rather a difference between two modifications of non-perception" (*SP*, 65). In this step Derrida borrows the dynamics of recollection and imposes them on the dynamics of retention. All that can be found in, and said of, the dynamic of recollection—the encounter with the recollected as a transcendence and the possibility inherent in this excess of "displacement"—Derrida now claims to be also true for the functioning of retention.

In particular, his position only follows if, in the dynamic of originary temporalization, the "transcendence" in question is given as an identity and its further showings are *also* given as yet further subidentities that may be gathered in an ongoing synthesis of identification.

It is true that the dynamic of originary temporalization exhibits a *displacement*—but we shall show that it is different in essential respects from that displayed in the dynamic of recollection and expectation because the displacement evident in originary temporalization is not of the kind to generate a change of sign, or cancellation. Rather, it is one of "no longer being now," the undergoing of temporal differentiation. But far from loss, this effects a retention. We shall argue that Husserl's position emerges with its essential integrity intact precisely because the temporal phases that make up the dynamic of originary temporalization are not identities. Thus there is displacement here in the sense of being temporally "shoved aside," but no loss. Displacement alone is not the sign of transcendence, and Husserl's investigation receives its legitimacy and sense because the temporalizing moments, which effect this temporalizing displacement, are not identities. As such, transcendence is not, *contra* Derrida, complicit in its own constitution.

To elaborate on the claims just made, we shall first examine the dynamics of recollection and expectation. We ask: What are the conditions under which a temporalizing dynamic yields a displacement that can motivate a loss or change of sign? The answer will be seen to be that the moments making up the dynamic must be given as identities.

§ 3. The Dynamic of Recollection and Expectation

The object that is presented in the act of recollection is in principle always open to the possibility of a revision of sense. What makes this possible is that the recollected object is always able to show itself differently—more attention may reveal a detail not immediately clear, and the specification of its own temporal horizons (which, as we saw, in placing the entity within its own temporal position within the stream, establishes the thing in its particularity) may itself require a great deal of attention and corroboration. Husserl therefore recognizes that the object of recollection sustains an excess beyond its givenness (the What it has shown itself to be, up to this point). Therefore the object of recollection is a genuine transcendence. Thanks to the ontological excess of the transcendent, it is always possible that the object may come to show itself as being other than it is at any point taken to be. As such, a displacement, in the form of a revision of the sense of the object, is always possible. In fact, *this* displacement is properly characterized not as a loss of the being of the displaced so much as a "change of sign" regarding it. It has this form: the being that was taken, in its being, to be truly characterized as "such and such" now shows more of itself, by virtue of which "such and such" is now recognized as a non-adequate determination of its being.

But two conditions must hold if "displacement" is to take the form of a change of sign—a revision or loss of possession, a loss of "certainty." First, the excess of the yet-to-come must be prescribed—must be identifiable—in some way. It must be held in such a way as to be able to enter into conflict with the actual and utterly unpredictable showing of this excess, as it comes to light in the process of temporalization. That is to say, it must be given in protentions as a specific identity-content. And that with which it comes into conflict—that is, what actually comes to pass as opposed to what was protentionally expected—must also be identifiable if a conflict is to arise. That is, displacement of the kind Derrida claims occurs here presupposes the putative specification of the excess in terms of identity.

But this is not enough. Second, this kind of displacement also presupposes a ground for conflict. Not only must the excess be given as identifiable; that excess, that protentional expectation of what is to come, must be further prescribed as a moment of the unity of the transcendence in question. This affirmation of a more fundamental unity is the ground for the conflict that results in displacement of one identity by another. In short, conflict is only possible on the ground of a fundamental unity by virtue of which two different claims to be true are incompatible. This fundamental unity is the transcendent object in question, its transcendence consisting in the fact that, due to this excess, it can come to show yet more of itself.

Because of this excess, the being-sense of the object is always subject to the provisionality of the yet-to-come. This "being in excess" is the condition for the possibility of a revision. But what is displaced is not the "being" of the "object." It is, rather, a putative determination of it, a grasp of the object displaced by a further revealing of the entity itself. It is, of course, true that the presence of the object is "continuously compounded with nonpresence and nonperception." But the "nonperceived," the "nonpresence," could only ever effect a revision, a loss, or pose a threat to possession if this "nonpresence" is nonetheless present as the excessiveness of the being of a present transcendence. And only because this transcendence, this excess, is putatively present in the form of an identifiable expectation through the rule of harmony, in which the identity of the transcendence is preserved, could any "to come" motivate loss or revision. There must be a phenomenon of "mis-fit" in order for a conflict to arise.

This is the structure of the dynamic to which Derrida commits himself in his claim that the displacement at the heart of the transcendental temporalization brings with it the threat of loss, the threat that possession can never be certain, may always "give voice" to "otherness," and in doing so show itself to be other than it was claimed to be. But is he justified in doing so?

§ 4. Critique of Derrida

Derrida sees just this structure at the heart of the originary temporalization. In saying that the "decisive frontier" passes not, as Husserl has it, between retention and recollection but between recollection and retention on the one hand and the Now on the other, Derrida's claim is that the mode of being present of the retentional content is identical to the mode of being present of the recollected content: "the possibility of re-petition in its most general form, that is, the constitution of a trace in the most universal sense—is a possibility which not only must inhabit the pure actuality of the Now but must constitute it" (*SP*, 67). That is, Derrida interprets the dynamic of displacement that occurs in originary temporalization as one of *repetition*. And what does this mean? As a re-petition, it is a re-consciousness. Thus for Derrida—and in direct conflict with Husserl—retention is the *repetitive* giving of what is *no longer perceived*. For Husserl retention is a "still holding" that is *constitutive* of identity. But for Derrida it is "nonperception" (64). It is a giving of something that has already been given; as a re-petition, it is a re-consciousness of something that has already been constituted *as a being that can offer itself for re-consciousness*, which is to say, as an identity. Derrida says: "the presence of the perceived present can appear as such only inasmuch as it is *continuously compounded* with a nonpresence and nonperception.... Thus, in retention, the presentation that enables us to see gives a nonpresent, a past and unreal present." It is Derrida's talk of retentional content as "nonpresence," of retention itself as "nonperception," that establishes his thesis of the subverted origin: for, on his reading, "presence" is a function of a prior repetition. According to Derrida, this means that certainty, even at the transcendental heart, is shaken because presence is a function of the very excess beyond what is "properly" present and that is supplied by temporalization as a movement of repetition.

However, in order for Derrida's conclusion regarding the "displacement of origin," etc., to be legitimately drawn from the phenomenon of originary temporalization, it must be established that the displacement in question is of an identical kind. Otherwise, the conclusion that originary temporalization is itself already a function of otherness, and hence subject to the threat of loss that is implicated in the unfolding of the hiddenness of an alterity, would not be justified. Can this be legitimated?

We base our critique of Derrida around an investigation of the following question: What is involved in his interpretation of the content of retention as "nonpresence," as "other," as "alterity" (*SP*, 64, 65)?

It makes no sense to speak of the retentional content as a transcendence in relation to, a being-in-excess-of, the so-called Now-consciousness, for the same reason it makes no sense to say that the retentional consciousness yields a "something" that has being in excess of what it "presents." For to understand the content of the retentional consciousness as an "otherness," an "alterity," which could subvert any claim to the possession of the so-called Now-content would again require that a conflict between the retentional content and the Now-content could establish itself. And this would require the retentional content, as well as the Now-content, to be presented as identities. And these identities would have to have the sense of being different presentings of the one unified object, whose being exceeded any particular presenting. But this is not possible.

Speaking of the constitutive phases, the experiencing, to which Husserl refers through the terms 'retention', 'primal impression', and 'protention', he insists that no phase that is *constitutive* of temporal endurance can itself be thought as an identity: "in principle, no phase of this flux is be broadened out to a continuous succession; therefore, the flux should not be thought to be so transformed that this phase is extended in identity with itself" (*Hua* X, 74/99). However, because retentional content does not present itself as an identity—that is, as a determinate temporal duration—there is no possibility of its content entering into conflict. Because no conflict can emerge, Husserl speaks of the "absolute right of retention" (*SP*, 66–67 n. 5). Husserl does not, as Derrida believes, simply express a metaphysical presupposition in this claim. Rather, it rests upon good phenomenological grounds: the absolute right of retention is not grounded in the presupposition of absolute self-identity—Husserl himself undoes this presupposition—but upon the ground that retention does not ever present a transcendence (an identity) because a transcendence must be an endurance if it is to be given as an identity, and only as an identity can it enter into conflict. On the contrary, it constitutes it. Retention is not repetition of an already constituted identity but rather a dynamic moment in yielding identity-in-constitution.

Husserl's account places more stress on the fluxing aspect of the originary temporalization than does Derrida's. Husserl denies that the difference between the phases can be given as one of mutual exclusion, of utter contrast, and in the attempt to think originary temporalization, Husserl goes to great lengths to find ways of speaking about it that are legitimate. Applying this to Derrida, we can say that it is not possible to think the difference named through the terms 'primal impression' and 'retention' as the *exclusive* distinction between presence and nonpresence, as a play of identifiably different signs, as the contrast—again exclusive—between trace and non-trace, for all such renderings presuppose that the phenomenon of originary temporalization gives difference as a line that would divide the terms that enter into these contrasts and thus would presuppose the phase moments as constituted—temporally differentiated—identities. Otherwise, the contrasts would contaminate each other, and their power to render difference would evaporate.

Husserl recognizes this difficulty. The phases cannot in any way be thought as "differences in kind." He speaks of the temporal differentiation manifested in the flux as a "continuous alteration" (*Hua* X, 74/99) rather than a differentiation of identities. "Consequently," he says, "any object that is altered is lacking here, and inasmuch as in every process 'something' proceeds, it is not a question here of a process. There is nothing here that is altered, and therefore it makes no sense to speak here of something that endures." For this reason, Husserl rules out the kind of rendering of the originary temporalization offered by Derrida, a rendering that characterizes the temporal difference in terms that exclude each other and that already find transcendence prior to presence. The constituting phases "are not individual objects, in other words, not individual processes, and terms that can be predicated of such processes cannot be meaningfully ascribed to them" (75/100). This gives rise to Husserl's caution regarding the meaning of the language in which the temporalizing differences are captured. He warns:

> We can only say that the flux is something that we name in conformity with what is constituted, but it is nothing temporally "objective." It is absolute subjectivity and has the absolute properties of something to be denoted metaphorically as "flux," as a point of actuality, primal source point, that from which springs the Now, and so on. In the experience of actuality, we have the primal source-point and a continuity of moments of reverberation. For all this, names are lacking.

This is not to deny that a displacement occurs in originary temporalization; for

Husserl, such a displacement is the very condition for the presence of any identity as the constitution of temporal differentiation and, through that, temporal distention, duration. But it is to refuse any interpretation of it that—implicitly or explicitly—presupposes the phases as identities. And insofar as it does this, it is a rejection of the interpretation of this displacement as a presentation of the threat of loss or revision of anything already "possessed." For, as Husserl points out, the Now-content, the experienced correlate of the primal impressional phase, is only ever an *ideal limit* (40/62); any rigid distinction between the "content" of such a phase and the retentional phase is only a function of an abstraction. No determined object-content corresponds to the primal impressional phase; such content is "just an ideal limit, something abstract which can be nothing for itself." *Contra* Derrida, who sees a radical discontinuity within the originary temporalization, who sees originary temporalization as sustaining a radical discontinuity between presence and nonpresence, between perception and nonperception, Husserl claims that the nonidentifiability of such moments means that it is "true that even this ideal Now is not something *toto coelo* different from the not-Now but continually accommodates itself thereto. The continual transition from perception to primary remembrance conforms to this accommodation." Nor is this to deny that the originary temporalization manifests an alteration—a displacement—of the Now into the no longer, and the not yet into the Now. But the "temporality" peculiar to this alteration is not the temporality of the identical. Thus, the "no longer" of the retention cannot be presumed to be identical to the "no longer" of the recollected. The "no longer" of the recollected, its being past, is a mode of transcendence; but the "no longer" of the retentional, displaced, "shoved aside," by the continually new Now, is only a moment in the *constitution of* transcendence.

Therefore, it is wrong of Derrida to equate Husserl's refusal to, in Derrida's words, "assimilate the necessity of retention and the necessity of signs" (*SP*, 66) with a metaphysical presupposition. Rather, it is grounded in the phenomenology of the matter, though this is often concealed. Husserl would not be able to understand the legitimacy of Derrida's rendering of the phenomenon of originary temporalization in terms of 'signs', 'traces', or 'repetitions'.

§ 5. Conclusion

While it is true that the retentional content is not "actual," it is illegitimate to consider it for that reason to be a transcendence—at least as phenomenology comes to understand that possibility. For the retentional moment does not display content that is *itself* given as an identity. The retentional content does not offer *itself* for re-identification in other acts. Rather, it co-constitutes a *duration* that, once determined, is so available—and hence a transcendence. And though the retentional content undergoes displacement (the sense of which we have elaborated), this is not capable of effecting a cancellation, a change of sign, regarding the sense of anything at all. Far from "assurance" being "shaken," the retention simply flows away as it does, still retained in this flowing. There is no transcendence, no alterity, already pregiven within the originary temporalization. Husserl's investigation emerges from Derrida's critique with its integrity intact.

Chapter Eleven
Immanence as Absolute Subjectivity

How are we to understand immanence in light of our attempt to clarify the original meaning of transcendence in Husserlian phenomenology? We recall that 'transcendence' names Husserl's problem, which is shown by the fact that he directs his epoché against "all transcendent affirmations." Of course, to pose transcendence as a problem is also to pose immanence as a problem as well; and it is to pose intentionality in its most fundamental determination as a problem. If one were to remain in the realm of naive inquiry, it would seem that the terms of the problem—'transcendence' and 'immanence'—offer at least a rough predetermination of the field to be investigated. Surely 'transcendence' names the realms of real and ideal objectivity, and 'immanence', the realm of consciousness and subjectivity that transcends itself in attaining such objects?

The phenomenological investigation of what appears in its appearing reveals the naiveté in this simple identification—one that Husserl himself begins with in *Ideas I*. In fact what it shows is that pre-phenomenological naiveté consists precisely in employing an unexamined notion of 'transcendence' and 'immanence'; the genuine meaning and significance of phenomenology consists in bringing this to light. For phenomenology investigates transcendence in terms of its constitution, and the radical overcoming of natural naiveté—a naiveté from which phenomenology is itself not always free—is displayed when Husserl sees reason to turn the apparatus employed in order to clarify the transcendent realm to the naively demarcated realm of immanence. The reason is the insight that "[t]he 'immanent' sphere also has its constitutional problems" (*FTL*, 237 n. 1). What is the justification for this application? It is this: Husserl's meditation upon constitution, upon how what shows itself does show itself, reveals "transcendence" within the sphere of "immanence." Furthermore, in considering the intentional functionary as an "ego pole," it itself emerges as an *identity*, which in turn raises questions about the peculiar synthesis that constitutes that unity.

This holds since the investigation comes to clarify the problem of transcendence as the problem of 'the same'. In fact every same is a transcendence, irrespective of its level. Why? Because a same is a unity; in showing itself as a sameness, it must abide. As a unity the same is something fixed. This fixity is revealed in the showing of itself as the same, a "being *one* and continuously the *same* through the continuous extension of consciousness in its duration" (*EJ*,

64/62). But because originary givenness—perceiving—is continually carried out in the face of the new, the actualizing of the yet-to-come, no fixity is ever had in the act of originary givenness. Such an act is, properly speaking, constituting. Fixity can only be had once constitution has already done its work, which is precisely to achieve fixity. This means that "the same," as the fixed, is always only had in an act of non-originary consciousness, an act of re-consciousness. Husserl derives the central notion of 'object' from this circumstance:

> It is what is identified in distinct acts that form a synthesis; in this synthesis we are aware of it as the same, as what can always be recognized, or also as what is freely repeatable in recollections or freely producible in perceptions (when we go there and take one more look). It is precisely this identity, as the correlate of an identification to be carried out in an open, boundless, and free repetition, which constitutes the *pregnant concept of an object*.

The act of re-consciousness attains an object whose temporality has already been established—which is the very condition for a re-consciousness. Such an object—a fixity—is then available for re-presentation in any number of acts of re-consciousness. It is "the same" for these distinct acts and thus sustains being in excess of its "presentness" in any one of those particular acts. This is reinforced by the fact that a revision of the sense of the re-identified object is always possible, upon yet other showings of itself.

This enables us to see how it is that Husserl is forced to recognize that the sphere of "consciousness" must also be investigated through a constitutional analysis. Insofar as the problem of "transcendence" transmutes into the problem of the identifiable, the immanent sphere is truly a sphere where objects are encountered. This shows that the naive demarcation is not originary at all, but one that employs an already constituted notion of 'inner' and 'outer', 'transcendent' and 'immanent'. For all the "objects" of the immanent sphere are such only as fixed durations; as such they themselves refer back to a more primordial synthesis of originary temporalization in which they are constituted.

Where does this leave the attempt to offer a determination of 'immanence', of intentionality understood as that against whose mode of being 'transcendence'—the same—is determined as "other"? How is the demarcation between 'immanence' and 'transcendence' to be established, now that "immanent objects" have been discovered within the sphere of immanence conceived of as the "stream of consciousness" and consciousness, as ego, is grasped as an identity?

An answer suggests itself in the attempt to distinguish between the absolute time-and-identity-constituting flow—which is not itself a temporal endurance—and all or any constituted identity. Brough brings this out in his discussion of the emergence of an absolute consciousness in Husserl's writings on time-consciousness.[1]

---

1. See Brough, "Absolute Consciousness."

Brough notes that Husserl develops this interpretation within the context of his rejection of an earlier account of the constitution of time-consciousness, in which he tried to explain temporalization by recourse to the old schema of apprehension/content of apprehension. Here a non-temporal "content" would be temporalized through its being apprehended by a temporalizing phase of consciousness. But this is unsatisfactory since it presupposes the apprehended content as a nontemporal "something." Husserl himself observes that such a schema is appropriate only at the level of static analysis: only to the extent that the contents undergoing apprehension are considered as simply given can it be appropriate, and its application, given this limitation, is only provisional. However, as soon as the question regarding the constitution of such contents is raised, a distinction is established between the "experiencing" or "sensing" of the immanent objects on the one hand and the objects so experienced or sensed on the other. Immanent objects then show themselves as constituted achievements. On this basis, and for the reasons already discussed, "Husserl . . . draws a sharp distinction *within consciousness itself* between two dimensions, one constituting in the ultimate sense, the other constituted but still immanent."[2] The constituted immanent object is an immanent unity that is, for that very reason, to be distinguished from the ultimately constituting flow. Not being itself an endurance, the constitutive temporalization is contrasted with its constituted endurances: "It is absolute subjectivity and has absolute properties of something to be denoted metaphorically as 'flux'" (*Hua* X, 75/100).

Brough points out that Husserl introduces a particular range of terminology in order to make this distinction between the peculiar mode of being of the constituted object and its temporality on the one hand and the being of the temporalizing phases that give effect to this temporal being on the other hand. Husserl employs two sets of terms here: to refer to the constituted object in its peculiar temporality, he uses 'now', 'past', and 'future'; to refer to the constituting phases, he uses 'primal impression', 'retention', and 'protention'. What is at stake here?

Any confusion between these two sets of terms reveals a failure to understand properly the distinction Husserl draws between the constituted (immanent) object and what he refers to as the "absolute time-constituting consciousness" (130/182). The sense of Husserl's point here goes back to the earlier elaboration regarding object-identity as the unity of a temporal duration; primal impression, retention and protention—as the time-constituting phases of the originary consciousness—are not themselves unities of temporal endurance, but they do achieve such endurances. This means that although the retentional manifests a "temporal" difference within the sphere of originary temporalization and although one is tempted to mark this difference as itself a

---

2. Ibid., 93.

temporal difference, it is certainly absurd to understand the temporal modification of the retentional phase vis-à-vis the primal impressional phase as being *past* in the sense in which the constituted object is past. For the pastness of the constituted object is its "being actual no longer." But if this were true of the retentional consciousness, there could be no consciousness, no presence as the presence of the object, whatsoever. In fact the retentional consciousness is a presence: it is the presence of the past. It is, as we saw, what can best be described as the "still-holding of the already flowing away" insofar as the already flowing away is already implicated in what it is for an object as temporal duration to be present. The same is true of the protentional dimension. As Brough says,

> according to Husserl, retention and protention are *not* past or future with respect to the Now; they are on a level dimensionally different from the Now and are co-actual with the primal impression which *intends* or experiences the Now moment.[3]

For the same reason, the Now is not in a continuum with the retentional and protentional phases of temporalizing intentionality:

> The Now should not be placed on the same level with retention and protention. The Now is rather the intentional *correlate* of primal impression and belongs properly with the past and future on the constituted immanent plane. The proper formulation would thus be: primal impression, retention, and protention, through which phases of the immanent object are experienced in the modes Now, past, and to come.[4]

It is thanks to this difference between the modes of the constituting flow and the constituted temporal unity that a temporal endurance is present as a temporal endurance, along with its own fundamental principle of individuation, its utterly unique temporal position within the stream. The requirement is this: the movement into the past must not be a movement into "nonbeing," a movement "out of consciousness," otherwise the object could not be *present* as a temporal endurance. Yet to be present as a temporal endurance requires that the temporal difference be maintained, for presence as temporal endurance is always only possible as the presence of temporal differences. It is due to the radical difference between the temporality of the constituted and the constituting that this is possible: "The just elapsed phase of the absolute flow . . . is no more lost to consciousness than the just elapsed phase of the immanent object. *It too is retained by the new actual phase of the absolute consciousness.*"[5] It is thanks to the fact that retention is not itself past but, on the contrary, "co-actual" that the just elapsed moment of the constituted object is not lost to consciousness.

---

3. Brough, "Absolute Consciousness," 93–94.
4. Ibid., 94.
5. Ibid., 96.

Thus Husserl introduces the notion of an absolute consciousness as a way of indicating and thinking about the dynamics of the originary temporalization, a dynamic that precludes any consideration of it in terms of prior or more simple identities. For any identity—as temporal endurance—is constituted. The constituting phases themselves "are not individuals in that sense," and thus the predicates of such cannot be meaningfully attributed to them. As Husserl says:

> We can only say that this flux is something that we name in conformity with what is constituted, but it is nothing temporally "objective". It is absolute subjectivity and has absolute properties of something to be metaphorically denoted as "flux." . . . For all this, names are lacking. (*Hua* X, 75/100)

What, then, can be said about the application of language that attains its legitimate sense in referring to constituted temporal identities, to the absolute and originarily constituting flux of temporalization? Certainly, to name it at all requires the use of such language. And given the qualifications that emerge through the phenomenological investigation, this use is legitimate. For insofar as the constituting site is given at all, Husserl recognizes that it, too, is qualified by a certain temporality. Were this not the case, no distinction could show itself between the constitutive phases of the originary flux itself, differences tentatively named 'primal impression', 'retention', and 'protention'. Thus Husserl uses a modified language to refer to the originary temporalization, attempting to preserve the sense of its peculiarity as what is originarily constituting. Husserl says:

> Accordingly, we believe that these retentions, constituted in the flux by means of the continuity of the retentional modifications and conditions, are continuous retentions of the continuously preceding ones; they are the unity of the flux itself as a one-dimensional, quasi-temporal order. (82/108)

The temporality of the self-constituting flux constitutes that flux as a singular stream, due to the functioning of the horizontal intentionality. However, because this particular form of temporalization tends toward but is never capable of attaining objectification in the sense of a fixed temporal endurance (which would no longer be "now" and would, in its temporal fixity, slip away into a past), the temporality of the self-constituting flux is only a "quasi-temporality," since the originarily constituting flux itself does not possess the properties of constituted temporal identities.

Here, in attempting to focus not upon the constituted immanent temporality but upon the dimension of the originary constituting itself, Husserl locates the truly immanent as the truly non-objective. As that which functions to achieve temporal endurance, it thereby functions to achieve identity. In this function, it constitutes the very possibility of transcendent being, establishing the conditions upon which excess of being, where this is the excess of the being of an object, an identity, can show itself. As the originary temporalizing, any identity is necessarily "other" than it, not only *de facto* (the possibility of *de facto* error, revision, deceit) but also in kind, in principle, ontologically. For it is no identity at all. Thus the most originary being of "intentionality," the most originary mode of intentional functioning, as the attaining or bringing into presence of otherness, is originary temporalization.

To complicate matters here, one must distinguish between the constituted stream of consciousness, in which all immanent objects are found occupying their particular position and the primal occurrence wherein this stream is established. That is, the ego itself, as the unified history of all originarily experienced Nows synthesized into the unity of this one stream, is itself constituted. Thus Husserl says: "The universal life of consciousness or ego of consciousness that, as a stream of consciousness, extends through a transcendental-immanent time is a founded intentional accomplishment."[6] What is founded is the dimension of being that is the unity of all that originarily presents itself as lived experience; it is the "stream," the ego in its full concreteness. This is the dimension of "absolute being" that Husserl considered in *Ideas I*. But it itself is constituted, is founded, as he says. And in *Ideas I* he recognizes this, in saying that this absolute has its ground in that which is "ultimately and truly absolute" (*Id. I*, 166). But what is this fundamental basis, and how is it to be thought? Landgrebe finds it in primordial temporalization. He quotes Husserl again:

> If we consider this transcendental life itself, this transcendental ego, or if I consider myself as I am to be posited prior to all my prejudgments and to all that which is for me precisely as the primal condition for their ontic sense, then I find myself as [the] streaming present.[7]

This "streaming present"—the originary temporalization—is that dimension to which Husserl refers in *Ideas I* as the 'truly absolute'; in Landgrebe's words: "This 'primeval, streaming, living present' is that fundamental level aimed at by the phenomenological reduction."[8]

If by 'ego' we mean something like 'utterly particular immanence', which is of course not at all personal, and in its primal passivity is utterly non-volitional, then one may grant Husserl the use of the term 'ego' in his reference to the dynamic of the primal temporalization. But how is the determination of it as "absolute" justified? *Only* on the ground that, as primal temporalization, it is the very possibility of any appearing as transcendence:

> This fundamental functioning ego is absolute inasmuch as it is the primal source for all constitutive accomplishments that are built upon it. It is the absolute ground for all transcendencies which it encounters because no intentional experience can be effected without it. In this sense it is the "primal

---

6. Husserl, MS. C 21, p. 11 (1931; cited from Landgrebe, "The Problem of Passive Constitution," 52).
7. Husserl, MS. C III, p. 10 (1931; cited from Landgrebe, op. cit., 52–53).
8. Landgrebe, "The Problem of Passive Constitution," 53.

phenomenon in which everything else that can be called phenomenon has its source. It is the standing-streaming self-present or the *absolute ego* present to itself as itself streaming in its standing-streaming life."[9]

What can be said about this primal phenomenon? In truth, it is neither active nor passive: it is not active in the sense that "the stream proceeds without the activity of the ego."[10] This is so because the ego itself, a unity of a peculiar kind, is itself constituted in this primal temporalization. Yet Husserl claims that "temporality is in every respect ego-accomplishment."[11] The temporalization is utterly immanent and particular, vis-à-vis the transcendencies that come to appearance in its functioning. However, Landgrebe warns: "It is clear that *one cannot speak of accomplishment in the sense of an active accomplishment* for 'activity' in general has, as such, its 'presuppositions,' 'its conditions of possibility,' that do not themselves arise through activity."[12]

What is the significance of this phenomenon, then? In the originary temporalization, which Landgrebe calls "pretemporalization,"[13] in the primal passive streaming, "an absolutely anonymous ontic sense that is not already [temporally] differentiated is temporalized."[14] It is only afterwards that it can be pointed to in a phenomenological reflection. This is both difficult and revealing. On the one hand, it is true that the ego is an identity of a peculiar sort: "What we have called the identity of the one who performs [these accomplishments] is something specifically unique."[15] Yet, on the other, as we saw, it is not an object-identity since, first, it does not itself become past in the way that the object that is no longer present does, and, second, it never becomes an identity proper in that it never becomes fixed for itself. Insofar as it *is* primal temporalization, it is always open and "not yet identifiable" as a determinate something. Insofar as it is primal originary temporalization, the site through which the actual becomes actual, its "identity" is always "bounded" on one side by the openness of the flux, an openness whose yet-to-come can in no way be thought.

---

9. Ibid.
10. Husserl, MS. C 17 IV, p. 1 (1930; cited from Landgrebe, op. cit., 53).
11. Husserl, MS. C 17 IV, p. 5 (1932; cited from Landgrebe, op. cit., 54).
12. Landgrebe, "The Problem of Passive Constitution," 54.
13. Ibid.
14. Husserl, MS. B III 4, p. 59 (1933; cited from Landgrebe, op. cit., 54).
15. Husserl, MS. C 10, p. 28 (cited from Landgrebe, op. cit., 55).

Conclusion

The investigation of transcendence in terms of the synthesis of appearing clearly shows why Husserl's final position is characterized as transcendental idealism. Given that the originary being of objectivity has its ultimate basis in the synthetic activity of the transcendental functionary—and that, principally, no other mode of self-presentation is conceivable in the case of such objects (CM, 96)—it becomes clear how phenomenology must finally understand itself as an "egology." If "transcendence" is, paradigmatically, the being of what is given in appearance and if the fullest extent of intentionality's self-transcending lies in its attaining of such transcendence, then intentionality does not go beyond and out of itself in attaining such a mode of being. For "transcendence" does not present itself as an in-itself, but as a peculiar play within a range of possible "immanencies" of functioning intentionality itself. To have an appearance—and hence to have encountered what appears—is not to have attained an In-itself, but to have encountered a particular order in the actualization of potentialities that are open to functioning intentionality. That order is one of "belonging together." An object is thereby constituted; but this gathering remains always and utterly within the domain of the qualitative modifications, the actual and possible undergoings, of the intentional functionary. Thus in his explicit self-understanding, Husserl closes intentionality in on itself. Its transcendencies are only ever transcendencies-in-immanence.

Is this, if not a contradiction, then at least a failure? Is it not implied in its own original self-dedication as the investigation of transcendence in its very being-transcendent that phenomenology must find its fundamental field "outside" the immanence of the intentional functionary? Is not "egology" a rather perverse description of phenomenology, which always intends to reclaim the intentional functionary in its very intentionality, its being directed beyond itself? For would not an egology find its fundamental field as the immanence bounded by that ego? Does not an egology forsake any field beyond the limits of the ego, the transcendental functionary?

To answer these questions satisfactorily, it is necessary to pose another: Is closure to be affirmed simply on the ground that objects—as identities—are constituted products, on the ground that, in knowing an object, consciousness does not essentially "go out of itself," but rather "stays within itself" by "gathering itself together"?

Husserl's analyses of constitution contain four different aspects which help both to qualify the sense of closure that his phenomenology entails and, at the same time, to establish transcendental phenomenology ultimately as a philosophy of openness. These are the facts that, first, the object in its idea is infinitely open; second, the transcendental constitutional abilities and powers are subject to development; third, protention does not command what actually comes to pass and enters into synthesis; and, finally, the identity of the ego is incomplete. We shall briefly discuss each of these in turn.

§ 1. Object as Infinite Idea

Because identity is not preexistent but rather is constituted in a synthesis that establishes identity by confirming harmony in the flux, and because harmony is not itself something preordained but rather established through the successful repetition of certain courses of coordinated experiences, any identity is always infinitely open: "an *actual* object belonging to a world or, all the more so, *a world itself, is an infinite idea*" (97). What establishes identity is not the coming to pass of a certain and particular range of experiences to which an omniscient knower could have actual access, but rather *the way* in which *whatever* may come to pass is gathered within the stream. The essential factor here is not the content of the flux but whether harmony can be exhibited between the flux contents. And harmony is a function of retrievability. Thus Husserl can say that the object "is never present to consciousness as a finished datum; it becomes 'clarified' only through explication of the given horizon and the new horizons continually awakened" (82-83). It is true that any one particular identity—if the harmony essential to its being an identity is to be maintained—will exclude the possibility of *certain* flux moments entering into a successful synthesis of identification. For example, the rule for harmony that is expressed in the sense 'pen' will exclude relations of harmony with those verifactory experiences referred to with the sense 'water'. Yet although certain flux moments will thus be ruled out on pain of loss of identity, it cannot be seen what new moments may come to be added by satisfying the principle of harmony.

Hence Husserl concludes that the object is only an "infinite regulative idea" (90) for the flux and does not provide an exhaustive specification of the totality of the flux moments that could be synthesized according to its regulation. Certainly, it is through the "object as rule" that any referring, any intending beyond, is possible. But, Husserl says, "the predetermination itself, to be sure, is at all times imperfect" (83). It does preempt the flow of actualization, but "never with more than a certain degree of adumbration," and is thus characterized by an essential "incompleteness."

This also explains why it is appropriate to characterize the identity itself as an "empty X": for although a thing becomes ever more richly determined in the progression of intuition and although one must recognize with regard to each type of identity "the 'idea' of determinate directions of infinity" that establish "typically determined predelineated directions" that intuition must follow if harmony is to be maintained among intuitions (see *Id. I*, 311–12), the process itself is endless, and new "directions" may be established and added to the type in question if the retrieval or "having again" of such new accompanying intuitions is to be successfully executed. Thus "no intuitive seizing upon the physical-thing essence can be so complete that a further perception cannot add something noematically novel to it" (312). Husserl elaborates this point elsewhere: "There are objects—and included here are all transcendent objects, all '*realities*' comprised by the title 'nature' or 'world'—that cannot be given in complete determinacy and in equally complete intuitiveness in a closed consciousness" (297). While it is clear that the maintenance of harmony among intuitions does require a particular order among flux-moments and that this order can be expressed in the form of a rule, the preemptive closure that such an account suggests must be qualified, because the idea of the object-identity is itself always becoming and so exceeds any preemptive closure that would claim to grasp it in advance. Husserl comes to this realization at the end of *Ideas II*:

> The question now is whether a physical thing, which remains *one* physical thing under all circumstances, is the identical something of properties and is actually in itself solid and fixed with respect to its real properties; that is, is a physical thing an identity, an identical subject of identical properties, whereas the changing element being only its states and circumstances? Would this not then mean that according to the various circumstances into which it can be brought, or into which it can be introduced, the physical thing has different actual states, but that in advance—a priori—how it can behave, and, further, how it will behave, is predelineated by its own essence? But does not each physical thing (or what is equivalent here: does any physical thing at all) *have such an essence of its own in the first place*? Or is the physical thing, as it were, always underway, not at all graspable therefore in pure objectivity, but rather, by virtue of its relation to subjectivity, is it principially only a relatively identical something that does not have its essence in advance or graspable once and for all, but instead has an open essence, one that can always take on new properties according to the constitutive circumstances of givenness? (*Id. II*, 298–99)

The conclusion that must be drawn from the analysis of the principle of harmonious synthesis is that identities are never finished; they are always only becoming in constitution. It follows that, although all objects are constituted in and by the transcendental intentional functionary, these constituted products always resist any conceptual totalization of their being. All particular identities, and the world that forms their horizon, are genuinely transcendent in the sense that the being of identity always exceeds adequate representation in a closed system. This is not due to any limitation accruing to closed systems, or the inherent finitude of subjectivity, but rather to the fact that identity is never completed.[1]

---

1. The main focus of this discussion has been the phenomenological constitution of the object rather than the eidos. A full clarification of the phenomenological status of the eidos

§ 2. The Development of Transcendental Constitutional Abilities and Powers

What is taken up in the synthesis and referred to by Husserl as 'protention' is in fact a dimension of the horizon. The horizon is a "fund" from which the synthesis selects its expectations for the future course of the flux. But this horizon is nothing other than "'predelineated' potentialities" (*CM*, 82). Husserl elaborates: "We can ask any horizon what 'lies in it,' we can explicate or unfold it, and 'uncover' the potentialities of conscious life at any time." This notion of potentiality underlies the Husserlian notion of possibility; thus the horizon is

---

would require a longer discussion than could be presented here. It is worthwhile to note, however, that the essential incompletion of the identity of any given object—and the corresponding provisionality with which any such object is "grasped"—is not necessarily overcome once we turn from object to eidos. To be sure, eidos is characterized by a determinateness not found in the real object: the real object is *essentially* manifest only in adumbrations, thanks to which the real object, in its very transcendence, remains concealed in its "yet more," whereas the being of the eidos is, in Derrida's words, "thoroughly transparent and exhausted by its phenomenality"; as such, it is "only what it appears to be" (Jacques Derrida, *Edmund Husserl's Origin of Geometry: An Introduction*, trans. John P. Leavey, Jr. [Lincoln: University of Nebraska, 1978], 27). Would it not be the case then that the eidos, "exhausted by its phenomenality," would conceal nothing of its being in its being given and therefore, qua given, would be given determinately? Would such givenness not justify the sense of the eidos's "not possibly being otherwise" and hence its authority as a rule, prescribing in advance the essential ontological and phenomenal structures of all particular instances that would fall as particulars under that ideal type? Certainly. Yet the status of the indubitability with which the eidos is given raises deep problems. After all, 'eidos' comes to function merely as a title for what an intentional eidetic analysis reveals as the conditions under which an object may be given through change and yet still maintain itself as a self-same identity. That is, the specification of an eidos is the specification of possibilities of givenness. Thus the eidos, as the objective Apriori, is nothing other than a rule specifying the limits of the alteration of givenness of identity through the changing flux of appearing. As such, the eidos is grounded in the subjective Apriori, the structure of experienceability that lies within the transcendental functionary. Nor are the limits of this power of experienceability themselves given in a fully determinate fashion to the phenomenologically reflecting subject. As Husserl observes in the *Cartesian Meditations* regarding the quality of the evidence with which the transcendental ego is given, "*adequacy and apodicticity* . . . need *not* go hand in hand. . . . In . . . experience the ego is originally accessible to itself. But at any particular time this experience offers only a core that is experienced 'with strict adequacy,' namely the ego's living present . . . ; while, beyond that, only an indeterminately general presumptive horizon extends, comprising what is strictly non-experienced but necessarily also meant. To it belongs not only the ego's past, most of which is completely obscure, but also his transcendental abilities and his peculiar habitualities at the time. External perception too is an experiencing of something itself, the physical thing itself: 'it itself is there.' But, in being there itself, the physical thing has for the experiencer an open, infinite, indeterminately general horizon, comprising what is itself not strictly perceived. . . . Something similar is true about the apodictic certainty characterizing the transcendental experience of my transcendental *I-am*, with the indeterminate generality of the latter as having an open horizon" (*CM*, 62). That is to say, structure and extent of the power of experiencing that comprises the lived experiences, abilities and dispositions of the concrete ego is, though horizonally predelineated, nonetheless infinitely open and indefinite. A corresponding indefiniteness is implicitly transferred to the eidos, as rule for the experienceability of an identity.

a fund of possibilities that belong to me, the intentional functionary. The possibilities that the synthesis takes up in protentional expectation, and in which the very possibility of endurance consists, therefore are not "pure" possibilities. They do not belong to a universe of things called 'possibilities' that exist in themselves, some of which the intentional functionary mysteriously encounters while remaining oblivious to others. Rather, possibility, as potentiality, is grounded in actuality. Husserl says: "every actuality involves its potentialities, which are not empty possibilities, but rather possibilities intentionally predelineated in respect of content—namely, in the actual subjective process itself—and, in addition, having the character of possibilities *actualizable* by the ego" (82).

This is the key to our claim. For the range of possibilities that lie at the disposal of the intentional functionary, through which it can act, is not fixed. These possibilities, which are gathered together under the title of the 'I can', Husserl understands as the transcendental abilities and capacities of the intentional functionary, and thus as subject to a profound development. As these abilities and capacities increase (or decrease) in power, mastery, and differentiation, the range of constitutional possibilities also increases (or decreases). The ability to discriminate within sense fields and kinetic functions also increases or decreases. The constitutional capacities available for an "adult" are richer than those available to an "infant" (to speak objectively, using a mundane analog), and consequently a richer world is able to come into being for the "adult" than for the "infant." With the exception of the syntheses of originary temporalization, all other syntheses—the kinaesthetic syntheses in particular—gather potentialities that themselves *emerge*; the horizon, one must say, expands with the acquisition of transcendental abilities, capacities, powers, the refinement of "drives," and the steady acquisition of habitualities.

Thus the structural openness that characterizes the subjective Apriori—that is, the a priori potentialities gathered together under the 'I can'—is of a unique kind: the intentional functionary is bound to go into action, that is, constitute identities, by the range of abilities, powers, and habitualities that are either actualizable or operational for it and that make up the horizon at any particular moment (though not a moment of real time, but rather a moment of the transcendental history of the becoming of the intentional functionary). Thus the constitutional synthesis is bound by the Apriori of the horizon, which is always a fund of possibilities. Yet this horizon is itself always only a becoming; the limits of this becoming—*its Apriori*, so to speak—which would determine the form of this becoming, can never be derived from an interrogation of the horizon itself. Thus the horizon is known to be open in terms of an indeterminate openness or, in Husserl's words, "without real boundaries and yet bounded and with variable boundaries."

These considerations open a wide range of questions in the theory of constitution, especially as they relate to the problems of history and transcendental intersubjectivity, with which Husserl concerned himself in the *Crisis*.

These cannot be dealt with here. It is worth pointing out, however, that the notion of the development of transcendental constitutional abilities bears upon the acquisition of habitualities and the role of such "abiding possessions" in still other constitutional activities, especially where higher order aesthetic, moral, cultural and scientific objects are concerned. The issue of the development of habitualities as constitutional functions is implicit in the discovery of the peculiar temporality to which each identity provides an intentional clue. As Husserl says:

> That a nature, a cultural world, a world of men with their social forms and so forth, exists for me signifies that the possibilities of corresponding experiences exist for me, as experiences I can at any time bring into play and continue in a certain synthetic style.... This involves a firmly developed habituality, acquired by a certain genesis in conformity with eidetic laws. (*CM*, 109-10)

The reason for this is that every synthesis has its "history":

> It is owing to an essentially necessary genesis that I, the ego, can experience a physical thing and do so at first glance.... In "early infancy,"... the field of perception that gives beforehand does not yet contain anything that, in that mere look, might be explicated as a physical thing. (112)

Habitualities thus play a particular role in the constitutional synthesis; due to the dynamic of retention, each act of constitution "sets up a habituality of my ego" (102). But because habitualities are acquired according to their own particular temporality and because new habitualities are continually being acquired (both subjectively and intersubjectively), it can never be seen in advance just what the constitutional possibilities offered by acquired habitualities will come to be. Thus the subjective Apriori is an open system.

§ 3. Protention and Actualization

The third factor to be considered when assessing the meaning of closure in Husserl's phenomenology is that protention, the pre-grasp of the future through anticipation of the yet-to-come, has no hold on or command over what actually comes to pass. Actuality is utterly gratuitous. The *actual being* of objects is in no way due to the synthetic activity of the intentional functionary, for although expectation is inseparable from that activity the satisfaction of that expectation does not in any way lie within the power of the intentional functionary. Protention is not the ground of its own satisfaction or disappointment. Thus although the term of the intentional act is nothing that has being in itself, "outside" and independent of the synthesizing functions of the intentional functionary and its horizons of potentiality, one is not justified in concluding that this intentionality itself is the sole ground of all that can be for it, precisely due to the contingency that characterizes the development of the intentional horizon and the contingency that characterizes the actual coming to presence. One is tempted to say that "being" comes from elsewhere than the intentional functionary. It is not its own ground, nor is it the final ground of the identities it constitutes.

§ 4. The Incompleteness of the Identity of the "Ego"

This final point is made against the interpretation of the Husserlian "ego" offered by critics such as Reiner Schürmann.[2] He sees that Husserl recognizes the temporality of the fully concrete transcendental ego, the "monad." But he criticizes Husserl, accusing him of expounding the usual naive metaphysics when speaking of the ego as the "identical substrate of habitualities." Schürmann writes: "The substrate . . . does not change . . . [it] is what remains stable. It is the I as the identical pole of given experiences. From the point of view of temporality . . . the substrate is thus assimilated to the world of facts. . . . It is as constantly present as the objects."[3] The substrate, Husserl recognizes, is an endurance: it is existent for itself, as he says, in "continuous evidence." But this is not to say that the ego is therefore "assimilated to the world of facts," unless by 'fact' one understands 'endurance' pure and simple. As such, Husserl himself recognizes that the transcendental ego, as that which abides, as that which constitutes itself as "the same" in all its "acts," is not truly "absolute." Insofar as the "ego grasps himself not only as a flowing life but also as I, who live this and that subjective process, who live through this and that cogito, *as the same I*," then Husserl recognizes that the being of this ego itself refers to a more originary achieving. Insofar as this ego is itself an endurance, "we encounter a second polarization . . . a *second kind of synthesis*, which embraces all the particular multiplicities of cogitations collectively and in its own manner, namely, as belonging to the identical ego, who, *as the active and affected subject of consciousness*, lives in all processes of consciousness and is related, *through* them, to all object pole" (*CM*, 100).

Though often obscured by Husserl's own language, there are two very important consequences of the discovery that the ego itself is an endurance. First, the ego itself is never present as a completed and fixed entity; it is always only present as a becoming. This would not necessarily be so if it were the case that the ego actually constituted itself only through its retention (though even this would not yield closure, for the limit of retention is not ever given), if it always only established in its "having been." But Husserl has shown that identity is not possible without the synthetic gathering of the protentions as well. The future-oriented protentions whereby the ego directs itself toward what is to be expected and experienced while knowing itself to be identical in this

---

2. Reiner Schürmann, *Heidegger on Being and Acting: From Principles to Anarchy*, trans. Christine-Marie Gros (Bloomington, Ind.: Indiana University, 1987).
3. Ibid., 67.

self-directedness, is as much a constituent of its identity in the "living present" as of what is retentionally present. It is precisely this protentional directedness toward "what is to come" that grounds the possibility of openness to new experiences. This open unfinishedness is the very possibility of the freedom for the ego. With this realization, the Cartesian intention to grasp the ego in an adequate evidence is shown to be incapable of achievement. The ego as substantial existent—or the principle that gives expression to such an ego—can no longer function as an absolute ground. This is why in the later Husserl talk of 'foundation' is progressively abandoned. He no longer seeks to offer a phenomenological clarification of what is in terms of the absolute ego, which would be in principle other than and apart from the entities, but seeks instead to grasp the "things themselves" in their originary self-manifesting.

Second, the focus on the ego as endurance leads Husserl to recast his thoughts regarding the meaning of 'foundation' or 'ground'. The word 'source' is much more appropriate. For the ego, insofar as it is present as an endurance, refers to a more originary synthesis which is its possibility. This is perhaps why Husserl remarks in passing in *Ideas I* that the transcendental ego, the only "absolute being," is not ultimately absolute but rather has its "primal source in what is ultimately and truly absolute" (*Id. I*, 163). That which is truly absolute is not any endurance or identity, but the originary temporalization. Thus the "ontological difference," as the difference between what comes to appearance and its coming to appearance, clearly emerges first in Husserl's phenomenological investigation.

§ 5. Beyond Metaphysics

We opened this study by observing that Husserl's original and enduring problem was the *being* of the "other" of subjectivity and the *possibility* of that otherness being claimed in its "being other" by subjectivity in its immanence, through its activity of representation. In the course of our analysis, we saw how Husserl was inclined to thematize the "other" of subjectivity, first as "transcendence" and then—based on his interpretation of the phenomenological method—as identity. That particular focus inclined Husserl to structure his subsequent descriptions of the constituting activities of consciousness around the *term* of that act and to consider alterity principally as a character of objects.

It is this inclination of Husserl's, and the way in which it influences the emphases and structurings of his descriptions, that has led many recent interpreters to label phenomenology 'metaphysics' and to locate Husserl within that way of Western thinking that is now widely regarded as "overcome," "closed," "deconstructed." Of course, these interpretations are justified to a greater or lesser degree; and in a sense, it has been one of the tasks of this study to show just how justified they are—after all, for Husserl transcendence is identity, and identity is constituted in the synthesizing activity of the transcendental functionary. However, our analysis has also brought to the fore reasons why those criticisms ought to be qualified and restricted, especially where they are intended as an adequate summary and assessment of the final meaning of Husserl's thought.

First, it must not be overlooked that, although transcendence is taken to be the transcendence of an identity that—qua evident showing of itself—is determined as presence for a subject, the *normative power* of presence is a function of its availability for *all possible* subjects, and not its being-possessed by *any particular* subject. The objectivity of the object consists in its *plenitude*—its "omni-temporality"—and not in the *surety* with which it is possessed. The authority with which any particular subject may exercise its judgment about what properly and truly exists depends upon the equal manifestation of that truth to other subjects. That plenitude and equality of manifestation places the authorizing power of the object beyond the assertive power of the particular subject.

Second, although it is true that Husserl tends to understand transcendence as identity and shows identity to be constituted in the synthesizing activity of the intentional functionary, no identity—not least that of the intentional functionary itself—is ever completed, nor given in a closed concept. Furthermore, the subjective Apriori—the horizon of potentiality, of possibility, the domain of transcendental constituting powers, processes and dispositions that make up the concrete transcendental functionary's experiential possibilities—is also always open. As Husserl says, "according to a law of 'transcendental generation,' with every act emanating from him and having a *new* objective sense, [the transcendental ego] acquires *a new abiding property*" (*CM*, 100). Thus the intentional functionary itself has an "open horizon" (62), thanks to which the constitutional powers are in continual development (or decline). Even as "presence," transcendence is therefore excessive, and the intentional functionary, in its open indeterminacy, is always "inadequate" to what might come to presence.

Third and most generally, Husserl's method expresses an anti-"metaphysical" intent insofar as it seeks—by means of the phenomenological principle of the return to what "shows itself"—to subjugate subjectivity in its spontaneity, egocentricity, and "willfulness" to its "other," that which comes to it from outside or beyond. Husserl organizes the phenomenological description of this difference around the dynamic of emptiness and fulfillment. It may be that this theoretical setting is insufficient to account for the excessiveness in question, the hiddenness of the actual too easily falling from phenomenological view in favor of the available prescriptivity of the protentions that order the yet-to-come—in favor, in short, of what the concept brings to presence in advance. However, Husserlian subjectivity is eternally confronted with the possibility of having to *abandon* its positings and position-takings, precisely because verifying syntheses are equally adapted to conflict as to confirmation and because nothing in the *activity* of verifying synthesis can guarantee its harmonious progression.

'Command' is therefore radically circumscribed in Husserl's transcendental idealism, and intentionality is not, first and foremost, a termination in objects—but is instead an openness. In the end, the transcendental functionary is revealed in its vulnerability: in its primal "waiting upon" what will come to pass, it is truly "subject."

Bibliography

Unless otherwise noted, all works cited are by Edmund Husserl. All abbreviations of his works employed thoughout this study are provided below alongside the relevant work. All translations are mine unless otherwise stated. Any translation cited has been modified whenever it was deemed necessary—primarily in the interest of maintaining consistent terminology and style. Wherever the original German pagination is provided in the margins of the English editions (noted below), solely the reference to the original pagination is provided. Whenever a text by Husserl is cited repeatedly within the text or notes, its abbreviation is provided only in the first instance. Likewise, page references are provided only in the first instance of quotation; subsequent passages that fall on the same page will accordingly remain under the scope of the preceding reference.

A. Works by Edmund Husserl

CM — *Cartesianische Meditationen und Pariser Vorträge.* Edited by S. Strasser. Husserliana I. The Hague: Martinus Nijhoff Publishers, 1950. English translation of the former text: *Cartesian Meditations: An Introduction to Phenomenology*, trans. Dorion Cairns (The Hague: Nijhoff, 1960). (Original German pagination in margins.)

Crisis — *Die Krisis der europäischen Wissenschaften und die transzendentale Phänomenologie.* Edited by Walter Biemel. Husserliana VI. The Hague: Martinus Nijhoff Publishers, 1954. English translation: *The Crisis of European Sciences and Transcendental Phenomenology*, trans. David Carr (Evanston, Ill.: Northwestern University Press, 1970).

EJ — *Erfahrung und Urteil. Untersuchungen zur Genealogie der Logik* (1938). Edited by Ludwig Landgrebe. Hamburg: Claassen & Goverts, 1948. English translation: *Experience and Judgment: Investigations in a Genealogy of Logic*, trans. James S. Churchhill and Karl Ameriks (Evanston, Ill.: Northwestern University Press, 1973).

FTL — *Formale und transzendentale Logik. Versuch einer Kritik der logischen Vernunft.* Edited by Paul Janssen. Husserliana XVII. The Hague: Martinus Nijhoff Publishers, 1974. English translation: *Formal and Transcendental Logic*, trans. Dorion Cairns (The Hague: Nijhoff, 1969). (Original German pagination in margins.)

Hua II — *Die Idee der Phänomenologie. Fünf Vorlesungen.* Edited by Walter Biemel. Husserliana II. The Hague: Martinus Nijhoff Publishers, 1950. English translation: *The Idea of Phenomenology*, trans. William P. Alston and George Nakhnikian (The Hague: Nijhoff, 1964). (Original German pagination in margins.)

Hua III/1-2   *Ideen zu einer reinen Phänomenologie und phänomenologischen Philosophie. Erstes Buch: Allgemeine Einführung in die reine Phänomenologie.* Edited by Karl Schuhmann. Husserliana III/1-2. The Hague: Martinus Nijhoff Publishers, 1976. English translation of *Hua* III/1: *Ideas Pertaining to a Pure Phenomenology and to a Phenomenological Philosophy. First Book: General Introduction to a Pure Phenomenology*, trans. F. Kersten (Dordrecht: Kluwer Academic Publishers, 1983).

Hua X   *Zur Phänomenologie des inneren Zeitbewußteins (1893-1917).* Edited by Rudolf Boehm. Husserliana X. The Hague: Martinus Nijhoff Publishers, 1966. English translation: *The Phenomenology of Internal Time Consciousness*, trans. James S. Churchill (Bloomington, Ind.: Indiana University Press, 1964).

Hua XI   *Analysen zur passiven Synthesis. Aus Vorlesungs- und Forschungsmanuskripten 1918-1926.* Edited by Margot Fleischer. Husserliana XI. The Hague: Martinus Nijhoff Publishers, 1966.

Hua XV   *Zur Phänomenologie der Intersubjektivität. Texte aus den Nachlaß. Dritter Teil: 1929-1935.* Edited by Iso Kern. Husserliana XV. The Hague: Martinus Nijhoff Publishers, 1973.

Hua XVI   *Ding und Raum. Vorlesungen 1907.* Edited by Ulrich Claeges. Husserliana XVI. The Hague: Martinus Nijhoff Publishers, 1973.

LI   *Logische Untersuchungen. Zweiter Band, Erster Teil. Untersuchungen zur Phänomenologie und Theorie der Erkenntnis* and *Zweiter Band, Zweiter Teil. Untersuchungen zur Phänomenologie und Theorie der Erkenntnis.* Edited by Ursula Panzer. Husserliana XIX/1-2. The Hague: Martinus Nijhoff Publishers, 1984. Includes A (1901) and B (1913) versions. English translation of the latter: *Logical Investigations*, trans. J. N. Findlay, 2 vols. (London: Routledge & Kegan Paul, 1970).

Id. I   *Ideen zu einer reinen Phänomenologie und phänomenologischen Philosophie. Erstes Buch: Allgemeine Einführung in die reine Phänomenologie.* In *Jahrbuch für Philosophie und phänomenologische Forschung* 1 (Halle/Saale: Max Niemeyer Verlag, 1913): 1-323. English translation: *Ideas Pertaining to a Pure Phenomenology and to a Phenomenological Philosophy. First Book: General Introduction to Pure Phenomenology*, trans. Marcus Brainard (Seattle: Noesis Press, Ltd., 2002). (Original German pagination in margins.)

Id. II   *Ideen zu einer reinen Phänomenologie und phänomenologischen Philosophie. Zweites Buch: Phänomenologische Untersuchungen zur Konstitution.* Edited by Marly Biemel. Husserliana IV. The Hague: Martinus Nijhoff Publishers, 1952. English translation: *Ideas Pertaining to a Pure Phenomenology and to a Phenomenological Philosophy. Second Book: Studies in the Phenomenology of Constitution*, trans. Richard Rojcewicz and André Schuwer (Dordrecht: Kluwer Academic Publishers, 1989).

Id. III   *Ideen zu einer reinen Phänomenologie und phänomenologischen Philosophie. Drittes Buch: Die Phänomenologie und die Fundamente der Wissenschaften.* Edited by Marly Biemel. Husserliana V. The Hague:

Martinus Nijhoff Publishers, 1952. English translation: *Ideas Pertaining to a Pure Phenomenology and to a Phenomenological Philosophy. Third Book: Phenomenology and the Foundations of the Sciences*, trans. Ted E. Klein and William E. Pohl (Dordrecht: Kluwer Academic Publishers, 1980).

Proleg   *Logische Untersuchungen. Erster Band: Prolegomena zur reinen Logik*. Edited by Elmar Holenstein. Husserliana XVIII. The Hague: Martinus Nijhoff Publishers, 1975. Includes A (1900) and B (1913) versions. English translation of the latter: *Logical Investigations*, trans. J. N. Findlay (London: Routledge & Kegan Paul, 1970), I: 41–247.

B. Works by Others

Aguirre, Antonio. *Genetische Phänomenologie und Reduktion. Zur Letztbegründung der Wissenschaft aus der radikalen Skepsis im Denken E. Husserls*. Phaenomenologica 38. The Hague: Martinus Nijhoff Publishers, 1970.

Bernet, Rudolf. "Perception as Teleological Process of Cognition," *Analecta Husserliana* 9 (1979): 119–32.

———, Iso Kern, and Eduard Marbach. *An Introduction to Husserlian Phenomenology*. Evanston, Ill.: Northwestern University Press, 1993.

Biemel, Walter. "Husserl's *Encyclopedia Britannica* Article and Heidegger's Remarks Thereon." In P. McCormick and F. A. Elliston, eds. *Husserl: Expositions and Appraisals*, 286–303. Notre Dame, Ind.: University of Notre Dame Press, 1977.

Brand, Gerd. "Intentionality, Reduction, and Intentional Analysis in Husserl's Later Manuscripts," 197–217. In J. Kockelmanns, ed. *Phenomenology: The Philosophy of Edmund Husserl*. Garden City, N.Y.: Anchor Books, 1967.

Brough, John. "The Emergence of an Absolute Consciousness in Husserl's Early Writings on Time-Consciousness." In P. McCormick and F. A. Elliston, eds. *Husserl: Expositions and Appraisals*, 83–100. Notre Dame, Ind.: University of Notre Dame Press, 1977.

Claesges, Ulrich. *Edmund Husserls Theorie der Raumkonstitution*. Phaenomenologica 19. The Hague: Martinus Nijhoff Publishers, 1964.

De Boer, Theodore. *The Development of Husserl's Thought*. Translated by Alvin Plantinga. Phaenomenologica 76. The Hague: Martinus Nijhoff Publishers, 1978.

Derrida, Jacques. *Edmund Husserl's Origin of Geometry: An Introduction*. Translated by John P. Leavey, Jr. Lincoln: University of Nebraska Press, 1978.

———. "'Genesis and Structure' and Phenomenology." In *Writing and Difference*, trans. Alan Bass (Chicago: University of Chicago Press, 1978), 154–68.

———. *Speech and Phenomena and Other Essays in Husserl's Theory of Signs*. Translated by David B. Allison. Evanston, Ill.: Northwestern University Press, 1973.

Fink, Eugen. "The Phenomenological Philosophy of Edmund Husserl and Contemporary Criticism." In R. O. Elveton, ed. and trans. *The Phenomenology of Husserl: Selected Critical Readings*, 70–139. Seattle: Noesis Press, 2d ed., 2000.

Føllesdal, Dagfinn. "Husserl's Notion of the Noema." *Journal of Philosophy* 66 (1969): 680–87.

Funke, Gerhard. "A Crucial Question in Transcendental Phenomenology: What is Appearance in its Appearing?" *Journal of the British Society for Phenomenology* 4 (1973): 47–60.

Landgrebe, Ludwig. "Husserl's Departure from Cartesianism." In R. O. Elveton, ed. and trans. *The Phenomenology of Husserl: Selected Critical Readings*, 243–87. Seattle: Noesis Press, 2d ed., 2000.

———. "The Problem of Passive Constitution." In *The Phenomenology of Edmund Husserl: Six Essays*, trans. and ed. Donn Welton, 50–65. Ithaca, N.Y.: Cornell University Press, 1981.

Levinas, Emmanuel. *Totality and Infinity*, translated by Alphonso Lingis. Pittsburgh: Duquesne University Press, 1969.

Lingis, Alphonso. "Hyletic Data." *Analecta Husserliana* 2 (1972): 96–101.

———. "Intentionality and Corporeality." *Analecta Husserliana* 1 (1971): 75–90.

Mensch, James R. *The Question of Being in Husserl's* Logical Investigations. Phaenomenologica 81. The Hague: Martinus Nijhoff Publishers, 1981.

———. *Intersubjectivity and Transcendental Idealism*. Albany, N.Y.: State University of New York Press, 1988.

Schürmann, Reiner. *Heidegger on Being and Acting: From Principles to Anarchy*, trans. Christine-Marie Gros. Bloomington, Ind.: Indiana University Press, 1987.

Steinbock, Anthony J. *Home and Beyond: Generative Phenomenology After Husserl*. Evanston, Ill.: Northwestern University Press, 1995.

Taminiaux, Jacques. *Dialectic and Difference*. Atlantic Highlands, N.J.: Humanities Press International, 1985.

Theunissen, Michael. *The Other*, translated by Christopher Macann. Cambridge, Mass.: MIT Press, 1984.

Twardowski, Kasimir. *On the Content and Object of Representations* (1894), translated by R. Grossman. The Hague: Martinus Nijhoff Publishers, 1977.

Welton, Donn. *The Origins of Meaning: A Critical Study of the Thresholds of Husserlian Phenomenology*. The Hague: Martinus Nijhoff Publishers 1983.

Index of Names

Aguirre, A. 164, 166

Bernet, R. 82, 132, 133, 146
Biemal, W. 63, 74, 76
Brand, G. 61, 64, 66, 69, 71
Brentano, F. 38, 136
Brough, J. 137, 138, 143, 182, 183, 184

Claesges, U. 154, 155, 156, 157, 158, 159, 160, 164

De Boer, T. 29, 35, 38, 39, 52
Derrida, J. xiv, 76, 119, 192, 171–79
Descartes, R. 4, 10, 61, 62, 66, 86, 91

Fink, E. 53, 54, 58, 60, 64, 66, 67, 68, 69, 73, 74, 101
Føllesdal, D. 34
Freud, S. 4
Funke, G. 71

Heidegger, M. 75

Kant, I. 104, 106
Kern, I. 132, 133, 146
Kersten, F. 63

Landgrebe, L. 82, 153, 155, 162, 164, 165, 166, 168, 186, 187
Levinas, E. 4, 76
Lingis, A. 154

Marbach, E. 132, 133, 146
Mensch, J. R. 42, 45, 46, 47, 104, 105, 108, 109, 121, 124, 126, 127, 128, 129, 130

Schürmann, R. 195
Sartre, J-P. 4
Steinbock, A. 128, 132

Theunissen, M. 70
Twardowski, K. 38

Welton, D. 142, 154, 155, 158, 161, 162, 163, 166, 167

Index of Subjects

Abiding being 112–14
Absolute
  and the living present 90
  as originary temporalization 186
  flux xiii, 128–30
Absolute being as founded 186
Absolute consciousness 182–83, 185
  and originary temporalization 185
  as truly grounding 129
Absolute subjectivity 181–88
Abstraction 10–11, 32
  as delimitation 50–51
  as procedure of exclusion 21–48
  as narrowing of focus 49–51
  methodological 35
  within mundane phenomenology 52–53
Act
  as interpretation 25
  intentional 25
Act-character
  as apperception 30
  as interpretive function 29
  as lived through 26
  as objectivating intention 25–26
  as really inherent component of act 26
  as self-transcending 25
  taking hyle as representative 28
Actual being as successful synthesis 108
Actuality
  as exceeding constitutional power of ego 121
  as founded mode of being 121
  as title for order of experience 120
Actualization and protention 194
Adequacy, adequation 11, 21, 43, 62
Adequate evidence 62

Adequate perception, not identical with inner perception 52
Adumbration 9
Alterity ix–xiv, 110, 118–19, 164–65, 168, 172, 176
Anticipation 123
Anticipatory capacity of constituting ego 123
Apperception, transcendent 8, 14–16
Appearance, ambiguity in meaning of 24
Appearing xi–xii
Association 146
Associative syntheses 158, 162–64
  as material syntheses 163

Being
  fixed, abiding 114
  of object 99–108
Being in itself 4, 5
Belonging xiii, 101, 118, 125
  character of 98

Capabilities of intentional functionary xiii
Certainty, as mark of immanence 52
Chaos 126
Closure ix–xiv, 101, 111, 167–68, 195
  via abstractive exclusion 24–48
Cognition x
  as enigma 6
Concept 108
Consciousness
  as absolute being 88
  as activity xiii
  as closed 48
  as immanence xii

Consciousness (cont'd)
  as intentionality xii
  as self-contained 9
  as stream of identity 25–26
Constitution xi–xii
  and unifiability of flux moments 107
  and temporal syntheses 142–53
  as function of act-character 29
  as governed by laws 107
  as sense bestowal 29
  as transcendental acceptance 76
  of endurance 144–46
  of identity 131–59, 134
  of individuation 146–49,
  of past and future 136
  of real object 93–131
  of stream 143
  passive 161
  preliminary notion of 28–30
Content
  of phenomenologically reduced ego 23
  really inherent 23–26
Contingency xiii
  of the course of experience 120
  of the being of the ego 122–28
Corporeality 154, 164

Defamiliarization
  as achievement of reduction xi
  as loss of naiveté 69
  of the epistemological problem 68–69
Definite duration as primal objectivity 149
Difference and sameness 135
Duration 151

Ego
  and absolute selfhood 127
  and incompleteness of identity 195–96
  as concrete 124, 127, 186
  as constituted 124, 128, 187
  as dependent 125, 127–30
  as field of immanence 23
  as founded 129
  as not truly absolute 125
  as one and the same 127
  as open 121, 124–30, 187
  as phenomenologically reduced 16
  as pure 127–28
  as result of synthesis xiv
  as unchanging 127
  as unified history 186
  as waiting upon contingent unfolding of empirical experience 15, 52, 121
  collapse of 130
  contingency of 122, 124–25, 127–28
  dissolution of 127
Egology 82, 110, 119
Endurance
  and constitution of transcendence 149–53
  and individuation 146–49
  and maintenance against loss 134
Epistemological problem
  defamiliarization of 68–69
  fullest form of 58
Epistemology x
  as science of cognition 8, 14
  scientific 32
Epoché
  and exclusion of transcendence 55
  proto- 30–32
  transcendental 60, 68
Error 4
Evidence, adequate and apodictic 61
Excess 12, 13, 22, 85–92, 173, 182, 185
  as condition for possibility of error 12
  as mark of transcendence 4
  of being over appearing 4, 5
  of the object 108
  ontological 30, 108
Exclusion 53
  by procedure of abstraction xi, 21–48, 49–56
  of objectivity 14, 18, 24
  of presupposition 11
  of real being x
  of transcendence 11
Expectation xiv
Experience, as horizontally structured 123

Facticity xiii, 44
and openness 110–11, 119–30
Fallibility of knowing 4, 108

Flux 101, 113, 131, 140, 183
  and identity 134
  and singular stream 185
  formal structure of 95-96
  of appearing xii 94-99
  order and disorder within 102-3
  temporality of 185
Foundation(s) xii, 61-62, 196
Fragmentation of the ego 126
Fulfillment, fullness xiii, 42-49
  and equation with knowledge 43
  as givenness of transcendent object 43
Functionary, transcendental xii-xiii,
Future 183
Futurity, originary givenness of 138-41

Genesis 161
Ground, transcendental 62

Habituality 123-26
  and individuation of the ego 125
  as abiding property of the ego 123
Harmony 101-2, 117, 118, 120
  principle of 98
Human, as ontological determination 59
Human being
  as thing-like being in the world 52
  as part of the order of nature 14, 31, 53
Horizon
  as fund of expectations 192
  external 122
  internal 122
  kinaesthetic 157
  of potentialities 96
  of prefamiliarity 58-61
  of retention and protention 95-96, 118
  open 122, 193
Horizon structure of world, noetic correlate of 122-23
Horizonal intentionality 149
Hyle, hyletic data xiii, 23-25, 131, 166
  as arising from subjectivity 164
  as belonging to transcendental immanence 168
  as check upon interpretation 45
  as constituted 166-68

  as really inherent component of act 28
  as representative 28
Hylomorphism 134, 153

'I can' xiii, 114-18, 156, 160, 193
  and kinaesthetic capabilities 159
Idealism 111
  transcendental ix 100
Identity
  and flux 96, 99-107
  and transcendence 94-99
  as achievement 107
  as constituted xiii
  as empty 190
  as function of harmony 107
  as function of temporality 91
  as function of unifiability 98
  as unfinished 191, 197
  consciousness of 25-26
  constitution of 131-59, 134
  incompleteness of 195-96
  of the ego 125
  of object as open 106
  originary constitution of 138
  not a fixed definitude 107
  problem of 94-99, 134
If-then xiii, 118-19, 126, 160
  and constitution of object 117
  and expectation 117
Immanence x-xiv, 13, 15, 21-48, 85-91
  as absolute subjectivity 181-88
  as domain of intentional act 9
  as purified domain 17-18, 27
  as self-transcending function 27
  ideal 107
Immanent object 131-59
  and alterity 164-65
  as arising from synthetic accomplishments 165
  as originary transcendence in immanence 166-67
  as result 165
  as transcendency 152
  presence of 165, 168-69
  status of 165-69
Index
  and determinate structure 102
  as normative 102

Index (cont'd)
  as rule governed 102
Individuation, constitution of 146–49
Indubitability
  and immanence 91
  principle of 85–91
Infinite idea 190–92
In-itself, being xi
Intention and fulfillment, dialectic of 42–49, 119–22
Intentional, as an ontological term 31
Intentional act or function 30
  as essentially referential 27
Intentional functionary 74
Intentional object xi, 30–32
  as actual object of act 38–39
  as ideally in consciousness 100
  as posited by consciousness 9
  as product of intentional act 30, 100
  as transcendence in immanence 31
  and distinction between real object 33
  intended as real 35
  no genuine transcendence 33
  not an abstract or ideal entity 34–36
  not an image or sign 36–37
  not a mediating term 37–39
Intentionality ix, 3–5, 11, 12, 123
  as human 52
  as ontologically predetermined as part of nature 54
  as open 198
  as originary temporalization 186
  as termination in object 33
  as transcendental 73–76
  as transcendental acceptor 72–76
  horizontal 185
  ontic determination of 59
  realist interpretation of 37
Interpretation 29
Intuitive act 43

Kinaesthesia 114–16
Kinaesthetic field 159
Kinaesthetic motivation and 'I can' 160
Kinaesthetic synthesis 154–62, 163
  and correlation with visual organs 157–58
  as constitutional synthesis 159, 161
Kinaesthetic system
  as apriori capacity for structuring 158
  as system of possibilities 156
  and perception 160
Knowing 4
  as consciousness of 4
  as intentionality 4
  as openness 4
  phenomenon of 3–6

Lived experience 10, 11, 32, 52, 96, 101
Lived through 22–23
  sense experience as 25
Living present xiv, 62, 91
  and absolute being 90
Loss 175

Memory, as re-presentation 136
Metaphysical assumption 45, 176
Metaphysics ix, xiv, 14, 15, 47, 110
  and phenomenology 196
Motivation 133

Natural attitude xi, 11, 14, 31, 44, 46–47
  as presupposition 42
  and ontology 57–62
  general thesis of 54
Nature
  as domain of objective being 14
Noema 10, 68
  and relation to object 69
Noesis 10
Noetic correlate, of horizon structure of world 122–23
Now 178, 183–84
  and newness 151
  as ideal limit 178
  as source-point 141
  primal impression 137

Object, objectivity xi–xii
  and alterity 93
  as being in itself 3

as exceeding the act 152
as excluded xii
as identity xii
as index 101
as infinite idea 190-91
as intentional 32
as meant 29
as open 100, 106
as pole of identity 103-7
as present within phenomenological sphere 31
as result 29
as rule 101-2
as rule for harmonious unification 103
as sustaining excess of being 4
as synthetic accomplishment 108
as that which appears 24, 94-99
as transcendent xii
as unity of sense 45-46
as 'X' 103-7
real 31
being of 99-107
immanent 21
of knowledge ix, 3-4
ontologically determined as part 50-51
presumptiveness of 107-8
Objectifying function or act 25, 48
Ontology of natural attitude 57-62, 68
Openness ix, xi, 42-48, 193
   and facticity 110-11, 119-30
   and subjective apriori 193
   as contingent dependency of ego 124-27
   of identity 187
   of the identity of object 106
   of subjectivity xii, xiii, 121-22
Originary temporalization 138-41, 149, 154, 165, 168, 172-73, 182, 185
   and displacement of origin 176-78
   as truly absolute streaming present 186, 196
Originary time consciousness 136
Origination, act of 149

Passivity, experiential character of 44
Passive synthesis 134, 144, 153, 161
Past 183
Pastness, originary givenness of 138-41

Perception 29
   adequate 22, 52
   and kinaesthesia 160
   inner 12, 52
   outer 12
Phenomenological method 7-19, 30
Phenomenology
   and metaphysics 196
   as egology 110
   as foundationalistic 61
   descriptive 46
   distinguished from psychology 15-16
   genetic xiii, 88, 131-42
   mundane 50, 52-53
   static xiii, 88, 131-42
   transcendental xii, 72
Phenomenon, as enrichment of being 72
Prefamiliarity, horizon of 58-60
Presumptiveness of the object 107-8
Presupposition xi, 14, 27, 33, 42
   and worldliness 61
   meaning of xi
   underlying abstraction 49-51
   underlying exclusion 51
Presence
   and distinction between sense 45
   and fulfilling moment 46
   and non-presence 177
   as acceptance 72
   as function of prior repetition 176
   as result of intentional achieving 72
   of the immanent object 168-69
   of the past 96
   of the future 96
   of transcendent object 43
Presuppositionlessness 32, 66
   as deactivation of general thesis of natural attitude 65
   as exclusion of objectivity transcendence 17-18
   as guiding principle for phenomenological method x, 7
   as impossible requirement 28
   as not achieved 50, 56
   as revocation of complicity in worldliness 81-83
Primal impression 183, 185

Principle
  of harmony 98
  of indubitability 85, 91
  of retrieval 114
  of synthesis 118–19
Protention xiv, 135, 176, 183, 185, 194
  and actualization 194
  distinction from expectation 137
  as fixed 151
  horizon of 95–96
Psyche xi, 10, 15, 46–47, 57
  as ontological signifier 54–55
Psychological reduction 67
Psychologism ix, 53
Psychology 5, 57, 68
  as branch of science of nature 15–16
  descriptive 10, 12
  phenomenological xi
Pure ego 128
Purity x, 10, 14
  as artificial 55
  within the natural attitude 52–53
Purified region 28–30

Real, meaning of 33
Real inherence 10, 23–26, 28
  and intentional act 26–28
  as domain of immanent being 87
Real object
  as function of harmony 106
  as transcendence-in-immanence 108–10
  constitution of 93–130
  phenomenological meaning of 108
Receptivity, experiential character of 44
Recollection, and expectation 174–75
Reduction 28
  and failure to establish presuppositionlessness 56
  as abstractive exclusion 16–17, 49–56
  as enclosure 39–41
  as exclusion of the real 41
  as leading back 70
  epistemological x, 7–19, 26, 49
  phenomenological x, 12, 49, 62
  transcendental xi, xii, 11, 57–77, 62
Repetition 138

Retention xiv, 112, 135, 176, 183, 185
  distinction from recollection 137, 173
  as perception 137
  as presence of the past 184
  double intentionality of 142
  horizon of 95–96, 118
  horizonal 143
  vertical 143
Retrieval 116
Rule xiii, 115
  object as 101

Sameness, and difference 135
Sensation
  and constituting function 114
  as basis of interpretation 25
  kinaesthetic 115–16
  motivating 116
Sign 43
Signitive act 4
Signitive intention, as empty 44
Skepticism, threat of 173
Spatial apriori 156
Spatiality, constitution of 155
Subject, cognizing ix
Subjective apriori 193
  as open system 194, 197
Subjectivity xi
  as acceptance-correlate 72
Synthesis xiii
  and constitution 159
  as achievement by consciousness 145
  of association xiii, 131, 158, 162–64
  as gathering of flux 97, 125
  kinaesthetic xiii, 131, 154–62
  law of 111–18
  of fulfillment 43
  of identification xii, xiii, 43, 97–98, 100–2, 114–15, 118
  passive 144–46
  temporal 131, 142–53

Temporal extension 136
Temporal synthesis 142–53
Temporalization, originary xiv, 131, 135
Thing-in-itself, transcendence of 32

Time consciousness xiii
Totalization xv
Trace 177
Transcendence ix–xii, 3–6, 15, 85–91, 164
   actual presence of 42–44
   as achieved meaning 71
   as being in-itself 59
   as constituted xiii, 42
   as identity 94–99
   as kind of excess 85–86
   as non-real inherence 28
   as possibility of being other 173
   as present within purified region 27–28
   as transcendental acceptance 72–76
   as within consciousness 42
   in immanence xiii, 9, 31, 108–10
   ontic determination of 59
   phenomenological clarification of 42, 108
Transcendental
   abilities and powers 192–94
   meaning of 73
Transcendental acceptance 76
Transcendental epoché
   as defamiliarization of ontic predeterminations 63–69
   as limited 65
   as negative moment of reduction 63–65
   and retention of transcendence 64–65
   meaning of 65–68
   not an abstraction 67
   not an exclusion 66
Transcendental idealism 110, 119
Transcendental reduction 57–77
   as loss of naiveté 69
   as revelation 69
   as revelation of supplement 70
   no loss of world 69
   not a procedure of exclusion 62
   positive moment 69
Transcendental subjectivity
   and mundane subjectivity 75
   as closed 119
   as concrete and actual 74–76

Verification, as constitutional function 113
Vulnerability 141

World, loss of 112
World annihilation experiment 75, 98, 101, 112, 125
Worldliness
   as fundamentally obscure 61
   as intentional achievement 60–62
   as intentional clue 73
   as ontological signifier 60–61
   as presupposition 61–62
   as unity of acceptance 70
Worldly ego
   as given through meanings 72
   not identical with constituting ego 72

'X'
   as point of unification 105
   as thesis of the ideality of object 106
   empty xiii, 108, 190
   never given in a closed concept 109

www.ingramcontent.com/pod-product-compliance
Lightning Source LLC
Chambersburg PA
CBHW080730230426
43665CB00020B/2693